TEACHING

TYPEWRITING

BY

GRACE McNICOL, B.A.

SECOND EDITION

Pitman

PITMAN PUBLISHING LIMITED
128 Long Acre, London WC2E 9AN

Associated Companies
Pitman Publishing Pty Ltd, Melbourne
Pitman Publishing New Zealand Ltd, Wellington

First published in Great Britain 1964
Second Edition 1968
Reprinted 1970, 1972, 1974, 1976, 1978, 1979, 1980, 1982, 1984

Printed in Great Britain at The Pitman Press, Bath

ISBN 0 273 40528 4

Preface to the Second Edition

IN this Second Edition of TEACHING SHORTHAND AND TYPEWRITING a new chapter on the teaching of audio-typing has been included.

As with the shorthand-typist, the audio-typist must be trained to a high level in the use of English, especially in spelling, punctuation and attention to the sense of the passage. In addition, the audio-typist needs constant training in the power of listening in order to avoid mishearings; therefore, lessons in audio-typing must cater for these skills as well as for speed in reproducing the subject matter which has been dictated.

A second point to remember is that teaching methods in audio-typing are not in any way standardized, mainly because so much experimentation has gone on, quite rightly in view of the fact that typewriting methods have been developing over a long period. The teaching of audio-typing must continue to be subject to development.

The best advice that one can give to teachers is the following—

1. The aims of the lesson must be clear to both students and teacher.

2. Ear training in each lesson is essential. It is more likely that mishearings may occur through slight defects in the dictating machines, through variations in tone and pitch of the dictator's voice and through variations in the capacity of the student to recognize words.

3. As with shorthand writers and typists, it is essential to recognize that students need a wide English vocabulary in order to become competent in this work; so regular attention must be given to English.

4. Speed and accuracy in typewriting must be developed in every lesson.

It is to be hoped that teachers in various Colleges will co-operate with each other in order to spread the development of new ideas.

My thanks are due to the Royal Society of Arts and the Scottish Council for Commercial, Administrative and Professional Education for permission to include examples of their examination papers, and to all who have by their comments assisted me in the production of this Second Edition.

PUBLISHERS' NOTE

The Publishers record, with deep regret, the death of the Author in 1967, before this edition was published.

Preface to the First Edition

THIS book has been written in answer to many requests for information and guidance on the teaching of shorthand and typewriting, and in deciding on its scope and content the author has kept in mind two important considerations. Firstly, the teaching and learning of any one subject involve the application of some principles common to all; secondly, modern developments in office procedures, with the consequent broadening of courses for shorthand-typists and secretaries, have made the need for an economic use of teaching time and of effective teaching methods more and more apparent.

Since the subjects of shorthand and typewriting are today taught to a greater variety of students in a greater variety of courses than they were a decade or more ago, teachers must have a wide range of methods and materials if the courses are to meet the students' needs and the students are not to be made to fit into ready-made courses. Just as no two sets of students are likely to be identical in their manner or rate of learning, or in the degree of their interest in the subject, so no two teachers are likely to use the same methods or materials with equal success. This book, therefore, is not intended to indicate how shorthand and typewriting *must* be taught, but only to bring together (perhaps for the first time in this country) some points of historical interest, an appreciation of what the teaching of each subject involves, some *suggestions* on methods and materials and, lastly, sources of information on researches and teaching aids.

My thanks are due to the Royal Society of Arts for permission to include examples of the papers in the examinations for a teacher's certificate in shorthand and typewriting, and to Mrs. W. Coxon, Miss M. Peachey and Miss O. Wareham for their helpful criticism and work in reading the manuscript and proofs. I would like also to express my appreciation to all those students with whom I have worked and from whom I have learned so much. It is indeed they who have made this book possible, for in seeing them at work learning the subjects or how to teach them, I have been stimulated to clarify my own thoughts, to assess my own methods and to maintain my own enthusiasm for the subjects and for teaching.

Contents

PAGE

Preface to the Second Edition iii

Preface to the First Edition iv

CHAPTER I

UNDERSTANDING THE TASK 1

Shorthand—Typewriting—Skill in Teaching

CHAPTER II

ANALYSIS OF THE SKILL OF SHORTHAND READING AND WRITING . 22

Shorthand Reading—Shorthand Writing

CHAPTER III

ANALYSIS OF THE SKILL OF TYPEWRITING 31

Specific Areas of Knowledge Necessary to Typewriting—Specific Sub-skills Making up the Total Skill

CHAPTER IV

ANALYSIS OF THE SKILL OF TRANSCRIPTION 39

The Seven Component Skills—Factors Likely to Affect Transcription Skill

CHAPTER V

GENERAL PRINCIPLES OF LEARNING 43

When Students are Likely to Learn—Student Activity—Individual Differences—Classroom Conditions—Ideal Learning Conditions—How Students Learn

CHAPTER VI

CLASS, GROUP AND INDIVIDUAL TEACHING 64

Class Teaching—Group Teaching—Individual Teaching—Repeated Cycles of Work—Course and Lesson Planning—Selection in Teaching—Testing and Teaching

CHAPTER VII

TEACHING SHORTHAND 79

The Classroom and Its Organization—Choice of Teaching Approach—Word Frequency—Standards of Attainment—The Shorthand Syllabus—Scheme of Work—Lesson Plans—Teaching Aids—

PAGE

Characteristics of Pitman Shorthand—Shorthand Problems and the Learner—The Teaching Unit—Writing for Speed and for Style—English and Shorthand—Use of Literary Material—Plateaux of Learning—Dictation—Testing and Marking

CHAPTER VIII

TEACHING TYPEWRITING 128

Typewriting Room Equipment—Classroom Organization—The Scope of the Typewriting Syllabus—Teaching Machine Manipulation—Typewriting Rhythm—Audio Aids—Practice Material—Teaching Display—Teaching Erasing—Teaching Duplicating—Correlation of Subjects—The Student's File and Folder—Project Work—Testing, Marking and Examinations

CHAPTER IX

TEACHING AUDIO-TYPING 174

Aims—Equipment—Standards of Attainment—Teaching Methods—Dictated Instructions

CHAPTER X

TEACHING TRANSCRIPTION 182

History and Research—Problems and Objectives of Transcription—Standards of Attainment—Teaching Material

CHAPTER XI

TEACHERS' EXAMINATIONS AND TEACHER-TRAINING FACILITIES . 207

Qualifications—Facilities for Training—Teachers' Certificates in Shorthand and Typewriting

Appendix 1: English-shorthand Word List Correlated with *Pitman Shorthand New Course* 212

Appendix 2: Some Audio and Visual Aids 220

The Use of the Lintograph or Felt Board—Demonstration Stand—List of Typewriting Films—Audio Aids

Appendix 3: Questions on Teaching Shorthand and Typewriting 224

Bibliography 227

Index 231

CHAPTER I

Understanding the Task

THE first requisite in any task if it is to be successfully accomplished is for the performer to have an understanding of what is involved—of the materials to be used, the methods or techniques which are likely to prove effective, the difficulties to be prevented or overcome, and the goal to be achieved. The shorthand and typewriting teacher has a task of some complexity, as indeed has the student who sets out to acquire these skills. The skills themselves are complex, teaching is anything but a simple, straightforward activity, and the learning process is one for which no one detailed specification can be drawn up.

Shorthand and typewriting teachers must have an understanding of skills in general, since all skills have common factors, and of their own skills in particular, if they are to be able to select and use effective methods of teaching. Expert performances of all skills show some common characteristics, and ability to recognize them and to estimate their significance in shorthand and typewriting is essential for selecting and devising drills and other practice material. Such ability also helps in deciding how far to break down the total skill for the development of what may be called the component techniques, or sub-skills.

To any observer the most obvious characteristics of a skilled performance are the *ease* and *absence of tension* with which the performer acts. There are the *speed* and *fluency* of action, with the different movements flowing into each other *smoothly* and *rhythmically*; there is also *economy of movement*, arising from good *positioning* and *posture* before any movement is made. The performer develops the "knack" or *habit* of starting a movement from a good position, of following it through in the right direction, with the right amount of effort and pressure up to the right moment of release. *Habit* and *automaticity* of action are the outcome of effective practice and are basic to, though not the only essentials for, the performance of any skill.

In Chapters II, III and IV the skills of shorthand, typewriting and transcription are analysed in detail, but the following special points are worth mentioning now.

In the performance of any complex skill the performer is, consciously or unconsciously, basing his movements on acquired knowledge. Without the appropriate basic knowledge one or more of the characteristics of a skilled performance will be lacking. For example, it is obvious that anyone who works with tools must have the knowledge which will enable him to choose the right tool for the particular job or part of the job in hand; the use of the wrong tool will result in awkward movements and probably an inferior product. The carpenter frequently changes his tool or his manner of using a tool according to the material on which he is working; the dressmaker changes her method of sewing according to the fabric; the shorthand-typist also works with a variety of tools and materials and the better her knowledge and experience of them, the more likely is she to be able to produce the typed documents with efficiency. Another requirement in the acquisition of a skill is that there should be an understanding of the component parts or sub-skills, so that suitable practice, time and effort may be given to each and an understanding gained of how the total skill is best perfected. Without such knowledge the teacher may fail to select the right kind of practice material and the student may fail to make progress to the maximum of her capacity.

There are three skills in which the shorthand-typist needs to become proficient, i.e. shorthand writing, typewriting and typewritten transcription. In shorthand writing the training of the ear and the mind is fundamental; in typewriting emphasis is needed on developing the ability to produce "mailable" documents at first attempt; in typewritten transcription recognition must be given to the fact that it demands responses different from and frequently calling for more judgement and alertness of mind than do the separate skills. A fourth skill, audio-typing, is now part of many secretarial courses.

The teacher must understand the subject, both as expert and learner, and have knowledge of, and competence in, the skill of teaching.

SHORTHAND

As a subject, shorthand has an interesting history, and certainly an international one. It is now common knowledge that "some kind of shorthand was . . . in existence, going back perhaps to the fourth century B.C. . . . Its invention has often been attributed to his (Cicero's) freedman Tiro, but it is difficult in the present state of our knowledge to decide whether he invented an entirely new system or whether the *notae Tironianae* are simply his own adaptation into Latin of a Greek system already in existence."[1]

Since that day shorthand has become a necessary tool in all civilized countries and, as Godfrey Dewey[2] has pointed out, "in the century since Pitman inaugurated the modern era of English language shorthand more than a thousand different systems of shorthand—not textbooks—*systems* have been published in English alone!" E. H. Butler has given us a most interesting account of British shorthand, which runs to nearly 250 pages, and W. J. Carlton, who was a verbatim reporter for a number of years at the International Labour Office, Geneva, had a unique shorthand library, now housed in the University of London Library, known as the Carlton Collection. It comprises about fifteen thousand pieces, including printed books, manuscripts, periodicals, etc., in sixty languages and dialects, as well as portraits of famous shorthand authors and writers, shorthand bookplates, professional cards, and even stamps with shorthand inscriptions.

Whilst the history of shorthand systems makes fascinating reading, the effects of their use have been revolutionary in the field of women's work. On 29th August, 1887, a Miss Reynolds read a paper entitled "Shorthand for Ladies" at the public conference held in the Mayor's Parlour at the Manchester Town Hall in connexion with the Celebration of the Jubilee of Phonography and of the Tercentenary of Modern Shorthand. In it she said—

> Until recently, this art [shorthand] has been almost exclusively confined to men and practised by them; women have passed it by unnoticed, as having no reference to themselves, and being *entirely unfeminine* [my italics]. . . . The first introduction of shorthand to the women of this country, and the first efforts for teaching stenography amongst them took place under the auspices of Miss Emily Faithfull, who in 1874–75 kindly offered the use of her dining room at Norfolk Square, Hyde Park, London, where a number of ladies, from a dozen upwards, assembled every week to receive instruction. Mr. Rundell was kind enough to render his services gratuitously, and the result of this experiment seems to have been highly satisfactory. Miss Faithfull had the pleasure of placing some of the learners in good business houses in London as soon as they became proficient, the first commencing with a salary of one guinea a week.

Miss Reynolds adds—

> It is very necessary to point out that in order to become a proficient

[1] Marrou, H. I., *A History of Education in Antiquity* (London, Sheed & Ward Ltd., 1956).
[2] "Teaching Shorthand," *Proceedings of* 1945 *Business Education Institute* (Teachers' College, University of Cincinnati).

phonographer, perseverance, close application and industry will be required; no desultory or superficial study will answer the end in view.

Miss Reynolds and Miss Faithfull would certainly be happy if they were alive today to learn from the reports of examining bodies that candidates for shorthand examinations are now counted in their thousands each year and yet represent but a fraction of the total number of young women who obtain employment as "phonographers." Even Sir Isaac Pitman, with his intentional popularizing of shorthand learning, through his cheap textbook *Stenographic Sound-hand* published in 1837, could not have imagined the economic revolution to which his invention would give rise.

As the use of shorthand writing has increased, so the scope of its use has changed and widened. In the centuries B.C. in Rome and in the later centuries in England and elsewhere, shorthand writing was used almost exclusively for verbatim reporting of speeches; today the majority of shorthand writers are employed on business correspondence and other forms of office communication. A longhand transcript is a thing of the past (except in examinations) and shorthand and typewriting are today sometimes called the "twin arts." Miss Reynolds's recommendation that women should learn shorthand as "a pleasant and profitable accomplishment, a refreshing intellectual recreation to be reserved for leisure moments" would be followed by few young ladies today. Shorthand is now regarded as a means to an end; there is indeed scope for verbatim writers, but all too few aspirants to such attainment. Teachers and students would do well to read the interesting accounts of reporting work given by practising high-speed writers in *High-speed Shorthand Round the World.*[1]

Another trend in the training of the shorthand-typist today is the broadening of courses to include a number of other subjects such as commerce, office practice, and elements of law, the emphasis being on training the office worker who will use the skills of shorthand and typewriting in the course of many other activities.

Since shorthand is usually but one of a number of subjects in a course, the time factor for teaching and learning it is of great importance to both teacher and student. Shorthand has been described as a "one hundred per cent subject"—one error in a document may make it useless; there is no place for doubts or time for frequent hesitation and consultation. In the classroom, therefore, every moment is

[1] Editor, Emily D. Smith (London, Sir Isaac Pitman & Sons Ltd., 1961).

precious and must be used to advantage. Good use of teaching time implies good understanding of what to do and how to do it. The skill of shorthand must be analysed to see what is involved. By shorthand writing we mean taking down the spoken word; the writer's hearing must therefore be trained so that there is no delay in recognizing what has been heard; when the sounds have been received the mind must comprehend and must recall the outlines without hesitation, so that they may be signalled to the hand; the hand then transmits them to paper, adding or omitting whatever will assist in securing a good note and a fluent transcript. Thus, capital letters or abbreviations are indicated, whilst minor punctuation signs are omitted.

In order to give a complete picture of shorthand writing skill more must be said about the English language, and it may be useful to draw an analogy between an interpreter and a shorthand writer. The former, no one will deny, needs to develop the skill of *rapid* transference of one set of words to another. The element of speed is as important in his case as it is to the shorthand writer. To carry the analogy a little further—the longhand writer may be likened to the translator; both work from a visual medium and both can set their own rate of writing. The interpreter and the shorthand writer, on the other hand, both work from a sound medium and have to subject themselves to the speed at which the sound is delivered. The interpreter does not work mechanically—if he did the result might be amusing, but disastrous. He does not have to work out the translation for every word or phrase consciously but he needs the skill of quickly grasping the meaning, of comprehending the ideas. The shorthand writer has also to recognize far more quickly than other people the general sense and the actual words of what he is hearing. In order to take a good note which can be transcribed fluently and accurately (the sole purpose of most shorthand writing) there must be control. The shorthand writer does not write automatically so many symbols a second or so many a minute; very simple and familiar words are recognized with such rapidity that the correct shorthand characters are "flashed" on to the page without thought, but immediately the mind registers unfamiliarity with a word, or lack of meaning in a passage, there is control, and writing is slowed down so that the necessary decision can be made. It is the speed at which the decision is made and carried out that shows the degree of expertness of both the interpreter and the shorthand writer. Writing shorthand entirely without thought leads to difficult and probably inaccurate transcription. English thus becomes a mental skill and the shorthand writer who has not developed it to a fair degree will be unaware of the possible dangers of mishearing, of the tendency to write the outline for the familiar in place of the unfamiliar word, of writing what one expects to hear instead of what one does hear, or of the need to "register" when a passage does not make sense. We shall return to this English skill when considering in detail the skill of transcription.

From this consideration of the areas of knowledge and sub-skills, which combine to make the total skill of shorthand writing, arises the question of the relative ease or difficulty which each presents to the learner. For instance, can we say that the mental skills are more difficult to acquire than the manual? Is it easier to learn to increase one's span of "retained words," and to keep behind the speaker, than it is to adapt one's listening powers to differences in accent or pace? How quickly can one acquire good penmanship as compared with the ability to recall an outline? Are all sections of the shorthand system equally easy or difficult to learn and to apply? All these are questions not only of academic interest but of practical importance in teaching because they affect the choice of material and methods of the teacher.

TYPEWRITING

By comparison with shorthand writing, typewriting is very young, but not so young as one might imagine for, as Commander Gould's interesting article *The Story of the Typewriter*[1] tells us, "the first typewriter of which there is any record was invented by an Englishman, who took out a patent for it (No. 395 of 1714) in the days of good Queen Anne," but "there was no general demand for such a machine, and, if there had been, this could not have been met. Only in the middle of the last century did the rapid improvement of transport and communication emphasize the necessity for some similar acceleration in business methods and office-work; while, at about the same period, the development of machine-tools and repetition-processes made it possible for the first time to produce piecemeal and to assemble in quantity complicated mechanisms. . . ."

By 1888 not only had the "typewriting machine" become a part of office equipment, but the "female type-writers" were being employed in place of men copyists in the Civil Service. The following extracts

Gould, Rupert T., "The Story of the Typewriter," *Office Control and Management* (1950).

are provided for us by Dr. O. G. Pickard from the Second Report of the Royal Commission on Civil Establishments (1888)[1]—

[Sir Algernon West] "Perhaps I ought here to say that we employ women, and that we employ very largely the type-writer. I am a very quick, and I am very sorry to say, a very illegible writer myself, but these type-writing women can beat me two to one in writing, that shows the amount of work we get from them. . . . Of course I do not want to discharge the copyists we have got, but in the future I should like never to see another man copyist employed in the public service. . . .

The copies they make are always tidy and regular and perfectly legible, and very quickly done. There is a new typewriter now which has capital letters. . . .

The type-writers have 17s. to 24s. a week. Then they must come to us qualified. That is skilled labour. . . ."

The School Board for London was one of the first providers of training for this new skill and in 1894 it had twenty-four machines on hire which by 1897 had increased to ninety-six. In 1904 the Board reported—

The increase in the use of typewriters in offices has increased the demand for a knowledge of the machine, consequently it has become necessary to increase the number of machines, and to adopt a scheme providing that as a rule the instruction should be given . . . only to those pupils who are able to write shorthand at the rate of forty words a minute, and to transcribe the same correctly.[2]

Today the order in which the two skills are learned is frequently reversed, many local authorities insisting on a degree of competence in typewriting before enrolment in a shorthand course is permitted. This question of shorthand before typewriting, typewriting before shorthand, or concurrent study of both obviously has no one answer and factors such as age and background of the students, the duration of the course, the vocational needs of the students, and the course curriculum have to be taken into account before mere expediency.

Side by side with the development of the typewriter—from the small portable machine to the Varityper, the accounting machine, and the teleprinter, we have a widening of the typewriting skill. If the "female type-writer" in 1888 were asked to produce more than one copy she would probably have had only two methods which she could use—the copying press or a re-typing for each additional copy. Today our "lady typists," in addition to the ability to use machines

[1] "Office Work and Education, 1848–1948," *The Vocational Aspect of Secondary and Further Education*, Vol. I, No. 3 (November, 1949).
[2] Pickard, O. G., op. cit.

differing in design and purpose, may be expected to be capable of preparing different "masters" for a number of different duplicating processes, of using audio-transcribing machines, and to produce a far greater variety of typewritten documents with stationery in a wealth of form and quality which their predecessors would certainly have found bewildering.

In contrast to the lack of research work in connexion with the skill of shorthand writing, a quite impressive list of experiments and studies can be established for typewriting. For those readers who would like to follow this line of interest further, a bibliography is given on p. 228.

One of the earliest (1925) studies of importance is that of William F. Book,[1] Professor of Psychology at Indiana University, U.S.A. Part I of this book of 450 pages is devoted to an exposition of skills in general, habit formation and habit improvement. Part II deals specifically with the acquisition of the skill of typewriting, speed development and factors which condition the development of the skill, whilst Part III is concerned with the role of the teacher in the selection and direction of learners of typewriting. Professor Book describes the task of learning to typewrite as—

> (1) Getting the material to be written from a printed or shorthand page; (2) typing this material on the machine without omissions or errors; (3) learning to handle and manipulate the machine as a mechanical device; (4) acquiring the proper finger dexterity and correct technique for striking and releasing the keys.

By "typing this material" Professor Book means "reading the copy accurately *while writing it on the machine.*" Professor Book's work is dedicated to "the winners of the international typewriting contests who have reached the highest levels of skill yet attained in typewriting . . ." and this dedication, together with the description of the task of learning to typewrite quoted above, indicates what must be regarded as a limitation to the value of the study for teachers today, namely, that the study does not go beyond the skill of straight copy from longhand. "Learning to transcribe from shorthand notes" says the Professor "involves a separate instance of learning which cannot be treated in this book." He makes no reference either to the great difference between "getting the material" from a printed, unamended script and getting it from the kind of media usually met with in the office—the badly amended manuscript, from more than one document,

[1] *Learning to Typewrite* (London, The Gregg Publishing Co., 1925).

or from a mixture of manuscript, printed and typed matter, etc. Nevertheless, Professor Book was able, from his research, to show that the basic principles of the acquisition of skill apply as much to typewriting as to other skills. One point in particular which he makes, and to which we shall have occasion to refer again, is that a skill must not be broken down too much. He writes "Our detailed analysis of how each task involved in typewriting was performed, checked up by accurate data showing everything that our learners did, showed conclusively that all typewriting habits make gains together, and that the best way to perfect letter habits is in and through their use in writing connected discourse." One must notice that he uses the verb "perfect," not "learn"; earlier he writes "letter habits must be developed *up to a certain point* [my italics] before the learner is able to react in a unified way to a group of letters composing a familiar word, and word habits must be *fairly well* [my italics] fixed before a learner can successfully react to a *series of words* taken as a group."

Professor Book also stresses that speed is built up on accuracy of details and he is definitely against allowing students to type faster than they can go with accuracy. However, he adds 'mere accuracy in details or in the work taken as a whole will not insure effective speed. The latter depends upon the acquisition and perfection of the highest order of habits used by the expert."

Although by the early 1930s, a considerable number of studies had been made of typewriting skill and its acquisition, there was apparently dissatisfaction in America with the methods of teaching. Through funds provided by the Carnegie Foundation for the Advancement of Teaching, the work of Dr. F. B. and Dr. Lilian M. Gilbreth was followed up by Professor Dvorak (better known for his "simplified" typewriter keyboard), a research assistant, a Professor of Education and a typewriting teacher. The results were published in 1936[1] and the editor, in his introduction, says—

> As at present taught, typewriting is about the most time-consuming subject in any educational programme on any level . . . between two and three full years—often more—are needed for the rather low degree of mastery required in this subject.

Bearing in mind the date of the work, the extracts given from it on the following page are particularly interesting.

[1] Dvorak, A., Merrick, N. L., Dealey, W. L. and Ford, G. C., *Typewriting Behaviour* (New York American Book Co., 1936).

Superior improvement accompanies practice of complete typing patterns as contrasted with piecemeal material. . . . The keyboard is a spatial pattern. Ability to handle spatial relations has little to do with mere finger dexterity.

The experimenters therefore recommend learning touch typewriting by *looking first* to get a visual impression of the direction and distance which the fingers must move, and then practising *without looking* on complete word and sentence patterns in order to develop the *habit* of correct finger movement.

A shoddy compromise with the visual check-up is tolerated in most typing classes. . . . This banishes the keyboard with its actual inclined plane and other spatial relations, but places a mere letter chart before the eyes of the typewriting initiates. . . . The chart tests tried out by Long[1] show little relation between knowing the keyboard by letter chart and actual success. . . . The only place for metal shields, aprons, and blank key caps . . . is the rubbish heap. The wonder grows that someone has not adapted horses' blinders . . . for typing students. . . . Fast, correct stroking is not mastered in slow practice. The correct motions of the expert, in fact, cannot be made slowly. The slow finding motions used to discover the keyboard are not typing motions. . . . The Gilbreths are fully justified in their stress on correct motions first, speed second, accuracy last. A high quality of work is possible without insisting on high accuracy constantly throughout the learning. Often insistence on other features of technique is better.

Today in American colleges the development of good technique is stressed and more material provided in typewriting textbooks for specific drills than is generally the case in Great Britain. Courses in American business colleges also provide more opportunities for transcription training and "production" work as opposed to "exercises" than do their counterparts here—although the value of "production" work is now being increasingly recognized in this country. Just as most shorthand teachers now recognize the value of the principle of "dictation from the beginning, theory to the end," so typewriting teachers might adopt the principle of "technique and speed from the beginning to the end." Certainly those who have already adopted it have found that it gives better results than insistence on "perfect copies" before any speed development.

From the many typewriting and work studies which have been carried out it is obvious that today the typewriting skill required by the office worker goes far beyond the ability to make automatic reflex responses of the fingers to the sight of "copy." L. J. West[2] says—

[1] Long, N. C., "An Experiment with the Relative Efficiency of Various Methods of Teaching the Typewriting Keyboard," Monograph No. 11, *Research Studies in Commercial Education* (University of Iowa, 1929).

[2] *Review of Research in Typewriting Learning with Recommendations for Training* (Texas U.S.A.F Personnel Training Research Center, 1957).

Strictly speaking, the problems involved in learning to apply basic typing skill to particular job-type activities such as the preparation of correspondence, reports, tables, etc., are not, psychologically, typing problems in the sense used here. They have to do, rather, with what may be called problem-solving behaviour; consequently they are not relevant here.

As with shorthand, there are areas of knowledge which are essential for success in the skill of typewriting as required in the office, i.e. knowledge of the machine and materials, business terminology, conventional display for various business documents, duplicating processes, and, of course, an especially good knowledge of English.

SKILL IN TEACHING

If students are to be helped and guided in their efforts to acquire these skills so that time is not wasted and so that there is opportunity for more than "instructing" or mere "training," the teacher will need to be knowledgeable and skilful in the application of his knowledge, not only of the subject, but of how he may best contribute to the student's learning. In a word, there is a skill in teaching as in any other occupation and it would be impossible within the compass of any one book to deal with it comprehensively. From the long lists of available books it is difficult to make any one selection which will suit the needs of all readers; the only justification for the list given on p. 227 is that each book is likely to make a useful contribution to one's knowledge and to stimulate one's thinking on topics concerned with a teacher's skill.

For the present chapter, seven topics are selected for brief discussion preparatory to a more detailed examination of desirable principles and methods in the teaching of shorthand, typewriting and transcription in the later chapters. The topics chosen are—

1. Personal qualities of the teacher.
2. Teaching techniques in general.
3. Knowing the student.
4. Classroom and class organization.
5. Course and lesson planning.
6. Work and mark records.
7. Teaching aids.

Personal Qualities of the Teacher

A list of all the desirable qualities of a teacher would read like an enumeration of virtues not likely to be encountered in any one human being—but if students were asked for one virtue only in a teacher it would undoubtedly be that they would like him to be "human," that is, understanding of their weaknesses and difficulties. Among the personal characteristics mentioned by A. Pinsent[1] are "a pleasant, kindly, dignified, humorous, and tolerant personality"; he also recommends teachers to "cultivate a pleasant voice with clear diction and avoid monotony in delivery; avoid unnecessary mannerisms and noisy movements; look at, and speak to the class as though personally interested in each pupil; avoid sarcasm, superior aloofness, and disdain." For the shorthand and typewriting teacher in particular the first qualities of a pleasant voice and clear diction are especially desirable. It is not always realized that one's voice does not sound the same to the audience as to oneself, and the manner of dictation to a class may even hinder instead of help the student note-taker. Every teacher should therefore listen to a recording of his voice and if the result is not pleasing he should seek help in voice production. J. H. Panton[2] thinks it unwise to be dogmatic about a teacher's personality, but he mentions the power of leadership which, he says, is "not a single trait but a composite quality involving a large number of characteristics." He adds that "as a rule good leaders are fairly assertive people, possessed of initiative, tact, and capacity for understanding those whom they lead." Panton also mentions carefulness, sociability, a sense of humour, and an "attractive, cheerful expression." One might add that many of these qualities arise naturally if one possesses a genuine interest in teaching and is sincere in one's dealings with the students. Most classes prefer a teacher who is firm and purposeful in manner and they respect and are inspired by teachers who know their subject and who always expect a good standard of work.

Teaching Techniques

These are usually classified as either formal or informal, the main difference consisting in the extent and form of student participation. Formal techniques include the lecture, debate, exposition by the teacher without participation of the students through questioning, and, in certain cases, film presentation. Informal techniques include talks punctuated by question and answer, discussion, team games, group

[1] *The Principles of Teaching-method* (London, George G. Harrap & Co. Ltd., 1952).
[2] *Modern Teaching Practice and Technique* (London, Longmans, Green & Co. Ltd., 1948).

tutorials, project work, problem solving, role playing, assignments, visits, and field studies, etc. Most teachers use many informal techniques because they involve the students in learning by doing which is invariably more effective than merely listening. It is generally true that the younger the student the less likely he is to benefit from formal teaching methods, but the current practice in management studies is also to reduce formal lecturing to a minimum and to create situations in which the students are actively engaged in finding out answers to problems for themselves, with experts in the background to give guidance when necessary and to discuss with the students their conclusions.

Informal methods require more skill on the part of the teacher and generally more detailed preparation, for the teacher is forced with these methods to look at the subject from the standpoint of the student approaching the problem for the first time. A formal lecture, on the other hand, does no more than offer knowledge; how it is to be received, or whether it is received at all, is not always considered either in the preparation or in the delivery. With informal techniques failure is often more obvious than with formal methods.

Knowing the Student

An essential for good teaching is the ability to look at the subject matter at the student's level; all students do not learn at the same rate or through the same kind of material; reactions to the learning situation are influenced by previous experience, temperament, motives, and other factors. Panton[1] reminds us that "The child-centred education . . . means that education must fit a child and be in accordance with his particular needs and individual capacities. The reverse process in which children are made to fit into an educational mould has no place in modern education." If we read "student" for "child" and also remember that any teaching situation is an opportunity for education, it will be apparent that knowledge of the subject matter to be taught and of a few teaching "techniques" will not be sufficient. The "learning process" has been and will continue to be a most fruitful field for research workers and in spite of the fact that every class is different and that all classes are composed of individuals, teachers can derive considerable help in the task of planning and presenting lessons from a knowledge of the results of such studies. This is

[1] Panton, J. H., op. cit.

particularly true for teachers of skill subjects, and although learning theories are certainly as yet anything but finally determined, there is a core of acceptable principles of which teachers should be aware. References are made in each chapter of the present volume to relevant research work, but just as students are individuals, so are teachers and it would be presumptuous for any writer on educational topics to say that this or that was the correct method. Every class is a social unit and creates its own code of behaviour and responses; the teacher today is not a person aloof and apart, but is one of the group—generally, of course, the leader and the guide. The students need to be active participants, not passive receivers, and it is with such thoughts in mind that courses and lessons are planned and take place.

Classroom and Class Organization

Some of the classroom organization may be outside the control of the teacher—the room may be in the charge of another member of staff; if an evening class is held in a day school or college, the members of the two staffs may never meet and no provision may be made for a satisfactory organization of the evening class materials. If in these circumstances conditions are unsatisfactory, some approach must be made through the head of the college or institute to his opposite number.

Supervision of individual work is essential in all classes and therefore seating should be so arranged that there are sufficient gangways to enable the teacher to move around without disturbing students unduly.

By class organization is meant the establishing of simple routines, understood by all members of the class, and designed to save the time of the teacher and the students in such matters as distribution of books, collection of work, cleaning the chalkboard, etc. The co-operation of the students is nearly always more easily secured if the teacher informs the class of his methods at the beginning of the course. One golden rule should be made and adhered to always, namely, that when the teacher or any student is speaking to the class, no other talking is allowed. Panton[1] has some good advice to give the new teacher on the use of the voice. He says—

> The cultivation of a habit of prompt decisive speech will aid materially in building up confidence. When giving orders or instructions he [the teacher] should express them simply and in a manner which suggests to the pupils that

[1] Panton, J. H., op. cit.

he expects them to be obeyed. A quiet, firm, tone of voice is all that is usually necessary. There is practically never any occasion for raising one's voice unduly when teaching. In fact, the more one does so, the more one may, because the pupils become accustomed to shouted orders and respond only to them. . . . The teacher should wait in silence for pupils who lag behind in their compliance rather than keep repeating the order. It is surprising how effective a silent pause can become in teaching, it often compels attention, and in a measure acts in itself as a reproach to the laggards.

If such silence, one may add, is accompanied by the teacher looking purposefully at all sections of the class, the effect is enhanced and students are soon ready to receive instruction.

Course and Lesson Planning

Any course of instruction must first be seen as a whole, planned as a whole and then broken down into workable units. The course syllabus will therefore be the starting point and will incorporate the examination syllabus, if any. An examination syllabus is rarely ideal or completely adequate for a course; in shorthand and typewriting, for example, it is obvious that some aspects of the work will not and probably could not be tested in a public examination and yet are essential in the training of an office worker. A teacher who confines his syllabus to examination requirements is doing his students a disservice.

Out of the course syllabus will be evolved the scheme of work; in some cases the individual teacher makes up his own syllabus and in this case it can serve as his scheme of work. The scheme of work also serves as the central thread which links all lesson plans and on which all lesson plans are based. New knowledge needs to be linked to existing knowledge; existing knowledge needs to be reiterated and reinforced by use. Lessons are not therefore individual items, separate from each other, but rather links in a continuous chain, and they connect with the future as well as the past. What happens in a current lesson is bound to affect the next or some future lesson. The following documents or records are therefore usually required for any course—

1. The course syllabus.
2. The examination syllabus.
3. The teacher's scheme of work.
4. The teacher's lesson plans (notes).
5. The teacher's record of work done (including mark records and homework set).

The Course Syllabus. This can include such items as the standard of attainment required on entry and at the end of the course, textbooks to be used, internal tests or examinations to be held, and any other general items connected with giving both to the teachers and to the students a fairly comprehensive picture of what will be required of them.

The Examination Syllabus. This usually gives in very general terms the intended subject coverage at the various levels of the particular examination. It may also give an outline of the form which the examination will take (time, number of sections and questions, etc.). It will *not* dictate the order in which the topics are to be studied, nor the degree of emphasis which each shall receive. It is intended as a general guide to those responsible for organizing courses to meet the requirements of the particular examining body.

The Scheme of Work. This is an expansion of the syllabus, giving an indication of the order in which the subject topics will be dealt with, the division of the coverage into weekly, monthly or terminal periods, the main methods of teaching to be used, the periods to be allocated to revision and formal tests, etc. It should be in sufficient detail to enable anyone having to act as a substitute for the regular teacher to pick up the threads of the course at any stage.

Lesson Plans. These plans are for the use of the individual teacher and the form in which they are written is an entirely personal matter. Some teachers write very full notes, others very brief ones, and yet others plan their lessons but do not use formal "lesson notes" in the classroom. Most teachers, however, find that notes are useful, for they can prevent lessons degenerating into a diffuse succession of activities which lack cohesion in themselves and with the course as a whole. The less experienced teachers find notes invaluable as a basis for new plans and schemes of work in succeeding years; and it has been known for new members of the profession to describe lesson notes as the life-lines which have saved them from collapse! Lesson notes which are prepared for use in the classroom generally include the following items—

(*a*) Designation of class (e.g. Secretarial A, Day Release C, etc.).
(*b*) Date, time, and duration of lesson.
(*c*) Aims of lesson.

(*d*) Approximate time allocation to each unit of work.

(*e*) Brief indication of subject matter to be taught—(fuller notes, if necessary, will be on separate sheets).

(*f*) Teaching methods to be used.

(*g*) Aids to be used.

(*h*) Matter to be put on chalkboard (some teachers prefer to show this information on a separate sheet).

Although the form in which lesson notes are prepared must be a personal matter, the author has so often been confronted as an examiner with lesson plans in essay form which gave no clear picture of the lesson development, in which there was no indication of the methods to be used, and which seemed to lack any attempt at selection, that a little guidance may not be amiss. The following sets of headings are commonly used, although others may occur to readers and may be preferred—

Outline A

Class.................. Time.................. Date..................

Aims: (Main) ....

(Subsidiary) ....

Approx. Time	*Subject Matter*	*Methods*	*Chalkboard*

Comments

....

....

Outline B

(*Headings as in Outline A above*)

Approx. Time	*Subject Matter*	*Teacher Activity*	*Student Activity*	*Aids*

In shorthand and typewriting the amount of material to be used is often considerable and can only be *indicated* in the lesson notes. It must also be remembered that in teaching skill subjects application is all-important and it is therefore beneficial to organize the lesson into fairly small units of work, that is to say, the sections of knowledge to be dealt with at a time will be small, followed immediately by student practice (application). The Herbartian steps—preparation, presentation, association, generalization and application—are not appropriate if applied in one sequence to a skill lesson as a whole. If, however, they are applied to each separate unit of work they can be helpful. Since there must be variety of matter and method, the question to be asked and answered constantly is "Why?"—"Why is this method suitable?" "Why choose this material?" "Why is this method not as good as that?"

The examples of lesson notes given in Chapters VII, VIII and X are shown in a form which is concise and clear and which makes for ease of use in the classroom. Lesson notes should never be so detailed and voluminous that they come between the teacher and the class—they are essentially *aides-mémoire* and should be planned and used as such; better no notes at all than a teacher who spends more time looking at teaching notes than at the class. Again, lesson notes should never dominate the pattern of a lesson so that no deviations are possible and spontaneity is lacking.

In addition to planning lessons, a good teacher will frequently record details about a lesson held, or about the students, which he thinks useful for the next or subsequent lessons. It may be a note of a topic which needs revision later, a comment on how a new form of exercise was received by the class, a point raised by the class which needs following up, or the performance of individual students which is worth noting.

Work and Mark Records

The function of work records (required by most authorities) is fourfold—

1. To enable the teacher to adjust the scheme of work and plan future lessons in accordance with the progress and needs of the particular class.

2. To provide the basis for any report which may be required by college or school authorities (e.g. heads of department, responsible teachers).

3. As a check that the requirements of the syllabus are being met.

4. In case of absence of the regular teacher, to enable a substitute to continue the course with the necessary knowledge of what has been covered.

The form in which the students' marks are recorded is also often an individual matter, although mark books or mark sheets are usually provided by the administrative authority. Marks are generally required for classwork, homework and any internal examinations. Classwork and homework marks are often combined to give one percentage mark. Where internal examinations are held, the marks awarded are also combined with the classwork and homework marks. In the final total the examination work is often allocated a maximum of sixty marks, and homework and classwork together, forty marks.

The function of mark records is, of course, self-evident, but it may nevertheless be helpful to summarize them—

(*a*) They provide the statistics for records of individual and class progress and attainment.

(*b*) They enable comparisons to be made between students and classes.

(*c*) They enable a rank order to be established for all parallel classes in a subject.

(*d*) They can give some indication of the likely achievement of students in public examinations.

(*e*) They may give an indication of whether a course or an examination is of appropriate standard for the type of student concerned.

For homework and classwork the particular form and number of tests, the subject matter to be tested and the marking scheme are all matters usually left to the individual teacher or group of teachers concerned with the subject. The result is that little if any standardization exists and it is often difficult for a teacher to get to know the type of marking scheme or standard of marking of other colleges or schools. Many try to base their schemes on their experience of the successes and failures of their students in public examinations. In the subjects of shorthand and typewriting (including transcription) a great service could be rendered towards the improvement of standards if some degree of standardization of marking could be achieved as between different colleges and schools. This could well be started on an area basis and, after experience, extended to a national coverage if that were felt to be desirable.

Teaching Aids

The author is indebted to her colleague L. S. Powell for permission to use the following extracts from his pamphlet.[1]

The Chalkboard.

It is difficult to generalize over so versatile an aid, but, as a rule, it should be planned in advance and cleaned when it is not in use. For emphasis it should be uncrowded, colour may be used sparingly, outstanding words can be printed in capital letters or boxed in, and key words can be spoken and written simultaneously.

Technical words, key words and definitions are given extra force if they are written on the board as they are used. This gives definiteness to the presentation and is an implied invitation to the students to write notes. Once such notes as these have served their immediate purpose they should be erased unless they form part of the summary. Similarly, problems and their solutions should remain on view for only as long as the students are using them: their transience gives emphasis to the dynamics of the learning and, if a summary is being developed, gives that the major prominence.

For shorthand teachers the chalkboard is the main teaching aid; no other aid enables the movement and fluency required in shorthand writing to be demonstrated as clearly as is possible with the teacher writing on the board while the students watch.

Felt Board, Plastigraph and Lintograph.

Surfaces on to which shapes, diagrams and captions can be fixed simply by placing them in position. . . . The fact of having prepared material reduces both the versatility of this group of aids, as compared with the chalkboard and also the intimacy of the presentation.

For the typewriting teacher a felt board is extremely useful, both because it saves a great deal of time and also because the presentation can be more vivid, more exact and more artistic. Its use in the typewriting room is dealt with in Appendix 2.

Photographs.

The chief value of a photograph derives from its air of authenticity. For the most part photographs should be studied individually and without haste, and learners should know precisely why they are studying them.

[1] *A Guide to the Use of Visual Aids* (London, B.A.C.I.E., 1961).

Posters, Charts, etc.

These fall into two main categories—those to be used as lesson illustrations which should be bold and clear, and those for wall display, which should be of sufficient interest to attract attention, and carry sufficient detail to warrant inspection and contemplation.

The typewriting teacher has a fairly wide choice of posters and charts, and discrimination is necessary both in their selection and in their use. Keyboard charts, for instance, serve very little purpose, if any, since there are better methods of achieving what is allegedly their main purpose.

Projected Pictures and Diagrams.

Film strips and films are the most useful forms of projected material for the shorthand and typewriting teacher. Most film strips have between twenty and forty frames and the material can be prepared by any teacher to suit the purpose of the lesson.

In the shorthand world there are very few films, but the typewriting teacher has a good range of them from which to select, mostly loaned free, a list of which is given in Appendix 2.

L. S. Powell[1] gives the following advice on the use of films—

Films differ from the other projected aids in that, whilst a film is showing, it takes over the teacher's role completely. Consequently it must be of sufficient merit to justify its solo performance, and this, in turn, means that it must be pre-viewed, pre-set if possible, and carefully introduced. Except when it is used either to consolidate what has already been learned, or to orientate attitudes, it should generally be shown twice. The first showing, which gives an idea of its content and sequence, should be followed by a discussion, or teaching, during which the students become clearly informed of what they can learn from the film. When they are ready for it and know precisely what they want from it, they should see it again.

The more specialized teaching aids for typewriting, such as shields, records, etc., are discussed in Chapter VIII.

[1] Powell, L. S., op. cit.

CHAPTER II

Analysis of the Skill of Shorthand Reading and Writing

THE skill of shorthand writing is sometimes referred to as though it consisted of nothing more than a mechanical movement of the hand in response to sounds through the ear—a reflex action achieved after sufficient practice and no more complicated than writing one's own name. But skills are of different degrees of complexity and depend on different areas of knowledge. Reference to Dr. Skeat's etymological dictionary reminds us that the origin of the word "skill" is the Scandinavian *skil*, meaning "discernment," "tact," often in the sense of "reason." Other dictionaries refer to "knowledge." No one would deny that a sound knowledge of the shorthand system itself is essential to successful note-taking, but evidence that this is not the only field of knowledge required is not far to seek. The best shorthand writers have always been people with a very good knowledge of English, a wide general knowledge and (since shorthand is mainly used in business) a good knowledge of business matters and business terminology. On the point of terminology, or vocabulary, there is an interesting feature about the knowledge of words required by a shorthand writer. Shorthand is a linguistic skill and we all know that there is a difference—generally considerable—between the number of words which we can recognize in our reading or listening (known technically as our "recognition" or "passive" vocabulary) and the number of words which we use in our own speech or writing (known as our "active" vocabulary). The extent of our passive vocabulary is that we understand the general meaning of the words in the context in which they are used; we could probably not spell them all or transfer them correctly to matter of our own composition. Words of our active vocabulary, however, we use without hesitation, generally correctly, though not always with accuracy of spelling. The shorthand writer, both at the stage of taking notes, and more particularly at the stage of transcription, needs a wide vocabulary which is more than passive, yet not necessarily active. That is to say, he has to recognize the sound and sense of innumerable words which he never uses in his own speech; he has also to reproduce these words correctly in conventional spelling—a feat which the ordinary listener or reader is not generally called upon to perform. If a listener does not quite catch a word, his general understanding of what has been said may not be affected—he may not even become aware that he has missed anything. If the shorthand writer fails to recognize and write the symbol for any word, however, the transcript becomes less than perfect and its usefulness decreases as the number of such failures increases.

As well as the size of the vocabulary and the need for correct reproduction, there is the further element of speed to contend with. Longhand writers on copying work, or if not held up by thought when composing, may write as slowly as 15 or as fast as 50 words per minute. Some adults can copy simple matter, for two or three minutes, at as much as 80 words per minute. The shorthand writer needs to write at a minimum of 80 words per minute, often for long periods, and dictation at 140 words per minute and upwards is not unusual. Transcription rates vary from 20 to 50 or 60 words per minute according to the type of matter involved and the skill of the transcriber. This increased speed compared with the longhand writer means greater mental skill and, as every high-speed writer knows, it is not so much the writing of the outlines which holds one back, as the time lag between hearing, mentally registering the words and recalling the outlines for them.

We find, then, that for efficient shorthand reading and writing there must be a more than average knowledge of English in addition to the knowledge of the shorthand system. The author believes that English, shorthand and typewriting activities constitute a skill; it is certainly true that shorthand writers and typists frequently possess a facility with words greater than other people of similar educational background. One is, of course, speaking here of competent shorthand writers and typists.

SHORTHAND READING

There are two main purposes of reading shorthand in the classroom, and each calls for a somewhat different technique. Firstly we want students to read shorthand in order to show that they understand the symbols and the principles of the system; secondly we want students to be able to read and at the same time mentally supply the necessary spelling, punctuation and display so that the typewritten transcript may be a "mailable" document at the first attempt. Transcription habits are formed, often unconsciously, in the course of the shorthand class.

The degree of difficulty in reading shorthand depends on a number of factors, but fundamental to the development of any degree of skill is the need to increase the shorthand and English recognition vocabularies. The fluent and intelligent reading necessary for transcription requires more than simply an automatic recognition of the shorthand symbols. There is, further, the question of the different stimuli presented to the reader by the different forms of the shorthand notes to be read; the printed textbook shorthand, the chalkboard shorthand, the more cursive style shorthand written by an expert and duplicated, the "fair copy" shorthand of the student, and lastly, the student's notes taken from dictation. In "unseen" shorthand copy the style of writing may also affect the reading; if the shorthand is small and cramped, or large and spread out, the fluency of the reading is often reduced until the students have had sufficient practice to be familiar with the style. Apart from the style of writing there are the differences in phrasing and contraction as between one writer and another; in Pitman shorthand there is also the question of the insertion or omission of vowel signs.

As our students are for the most part learning shorthand in order to use it in business, taking down and transcribing their own notes into typewritten form, it may be asked why it is necessary to present them with so many different forms of shorthand reading matter during training. The answer is that most teachers find such training a definite help in developing good transcription ability, as well as a quicker method than relying on the shorthand notes taken by the students. Passages can be chosen for reading which are too difficult for note-taking but which serve to enlarge the students' vocabulary and to prepare them for important points in transcription other than the shorthand symbol reading. Just as in typewriting the finger movement must be automatic so that the mind is free to deal with those parts of the total skill of typewriting which require decision or judgement, so the symbol recognition in shorthand reading needs to be automatic leaving the mind free to comprehend, to whatever degree is necessary, the thought content of the passage and to give the appropriate messages to the hands operating the typewriter. In the shorthand class, therefore, it is useful to establish a reading skill at the "shorthand recognition" level as a preliminary to the "transcription" level.

There are, of course, other sound reasons, connected with general principles of teaching and learning, for presenting shorthand reading matter in a variety of forms and these are dealt with in Chapter X on the teaching of transcription.

SHORTHAND WRITING

There does not seem to have been any scientific study of the skill of shorthand writing and the analysis offered below has been made as a result of the author's own experience as a high-speed writer on a wide variety of work, and of her study in the classroom of shorthand students of different backgrounds and at different stages of learning. Empirically, then, there seem to emerge three main groups of skill, these being aural, mental and manual.

Aural Skills

Ability to deal with—

1. Variation of intonation.
2. Variation of accent.
3. Variation of pitch and volume of voice.
4. Variation of pace of speech.
5. Irrelevant noises (e.g. other people speaking, traffic, door shutting, etc.).
6. Unfamiliar words.

Mental Skills

Ability to—

1. Recall shorthand outlines, or to form new ones.
2. Recognize words.
3. Retain rapidly spoken words until the hand is ready to write them (the span of retained words may vary from five to twenty-five).
4. Give some attention to, and comprehend the general meaning of, what is being said.

Manual Skills

1. Skilful holding of pen or pencil.
2. Skilful handling of notebook (left hand preparing for and turning page).

3. Ability to anticipate transcript by indicating display or points for transcript (e.g. writing name and address separately from body of notes of a letter without being instructed, indicating capitals, abbreviations, etc.).

4. Dexterity in writing shorthand outlines.

"The whole is greater than the sum of its parts" is a well-known axiom and it is true in shorthand writing no less than in other spheres. Having broken down the total skill into its parts of aural, mental and manual activities, we are left with the important factor of co-ordination of ear, mind and hand. The longhand writer is never called upon to respond in writing to the spoken word at the same rate, and over such periods of time, as is the shorthand writer. If a longhand writer cannot spell a word he may stop to look it up, or he may write "something" and leave it to the typist to put it right. The notes which are made in longhand are fragmentary, not verbatim, and the hand (or even the ear and the mind) can take a rest at intervals; the object is merely to note the main points. The previous experience of such note-taking is of little help (it may even be a hindrance) to the shorthand student in acquiring the new skill. The experience of shorthand teachers with different types of students is, however, instructive. The graduate, who has developed the technique of taking rapid and fairly full notes at lectures, is sometimes much nearer to the mental skill needed in shorthand note-taking than is the secondary-modern school student who has had little such experience. It is frequently found that the latter type of student cannot attain the requisite speed in shorthand writing, not because she does not know the outlines, but because she cannot co-ordinate ear, mind and hand with the necessary rapidity. Speed is a characteristic, to a greater or lesser degree, in all skills, but in the skill of shorthand writing it ought to be developed to the maximum of the performer's capacity, consistent with accuracy.

Variation of Intonation, Accent, Pitch and Volume. In all shorthand note-taking there is need for alertness, ability to "take in" what has to be "taken down." Charles L. Swem,[1] an American Court reporter, speaking of the need to train the ear and the mind, says—

The smaller, more common words, mostly of one or two syllables, would be the hardest of all to hear, because of the unconscious manner in which they are slurred in all speech, were it not for the fact that they are so common. A word

The Technique of Shorthand Reporting (New York. The Gregg Publishing Co., 1941).

that is familiar to us is, by reason of its familiarity, usually readily grasped even though part of it may become lost in transmission. . . . This is especially true if we are not engrossed in the mechanics of shorthand but are following the context and the thought of the subject. . . . The word may be slurred, it may be amputated at the front or at the rear—it may be completely lost sometimes—but, because we have met it so often before in just such context, we recognize it instantly as familiar—even to supplying it when it is gone and only the ghost of its presence remains. It is when we meet the unusual word, or the familiar word in a new dress—in some unusual combination, or masquerading under a strange pronunciation—that our ears are put to the test. Even if the word is distinctly articulated, if we are not alert, very frequently we miss it.

Although Mr. Swem is talking as a verbatim reporter, shorthand writers in business offices and elsewhere encounter similar difficulties of non-registration of sounds through unfamiliar intonation, accent, pitch or volume of voice. It is for this reason that, whether one's maximum speed is 80 or 180 words per minute, it is necessary to develop the skill of writing beyond the stage of "being engrossed in the mechanics of shorthand" if an accurate transcript is to result.

Variation of Pace of Speech. Probably because of the tradition of shorthand reporting and the high speeds necessary for such work and because of qualification by examination at so many words per minute, dictation in the classroom at irregular speeds or, as it is termed "office style" dictation, is of comparatively recent development. This is surprising when one reflects that the students to whom we give "regular" dictation in the classroom are going to spend most of their shorthand-writing time in the office taking dictation under entirely different conditions. It is not difficult to imagine that a writer trained on steady, timed dictation will need a period of adjustment to be successful with untimed material, for we must constantly remind ourselves that habit formation is the basis of skills. If, as has been known to be the case in the past, the student encounters this variation of pace in dictation for the first time when being tested for a post, the teacher will have done her a great disservice.

Ignoring Irrelevant Noises. It is fairly certain that all shorthand students will at some time or another be in the situation of having to write from dictation against incidental noises; if, therefore, students are not trained to develop the necessary power of attending to one stimulus and excluding others, they will be less than competent and probably find difficulty in their early office days. Shorthand teachers are sometimes over-careful throughout the whole of their teaching to make it as easy as possible for the students to hear what is being dictated.

Ability to "Register" Sounds of Unfamiliar Words. This topic is connected with the choice of vocabulary for teaching and testing in shorthand classes. As with foreign language work, it is wise to teach theory in a controlled vocabulary in order to reduce the learning load of the student in the early stages. We also know that a large percentage of everyday matter consists of common words (some authorities put it as high as 80 per cent) and it therefore seems logical that those words should be emphasized in any training programme. If, however, we come back to the elements of speed and automaticity in shorthand writing, we see that it would be wrong to neglect the other 20 per cent of the normal vocabulary. With many students it is even necessary to give a good deal of attention to the minority of more difficult words. Indeed, some would argue that since the common words occur so frequently anyway, there is no need to concentrate on them. No matter which argument one favours, it is essential for speed development that any hindrance to "receiving" the spoken word should be eliminated if it is possible to do so.

The Mental Skills of Recall of Outlines, Formation of New Outlines and Recognition of Words. These skills are all connected with a basic knowledge of the shorthand system and of English; the better such knowledge is, the more likely is the shorthand writer to be successful.

Ability to Keep Behind the Speaker. This means keeping the spoken word in mind until the hand is ready to write. It can be assisted through training in shorthand phrasing, but is also an attitude of mind. Students are fearful of falling behind, they panic if they are not right up with the speaker and confidence in their word retention powers and the consequent relaxation of "fear tension" must be shown to be possible and help given in developing it.

Ability to Give some Attention to and Comprehend the General Meaning of What is Being Said. This is again a matter of knowledge—shorthand knowledge, general knowledge, vocabulary knowledge. It is also a matter of habit formation; students may be trained, quite unconsciously through the teaching methods used, to write without paying any attention to the content, even though their writing skill is sufficiently automatic to leave the mind free to do so. Interest, motivation, conditioning, may all play a part in the training; certain it is that in the first place it is more a matter for the teacher than for the student.

It is interesting to note that over the last two or three decades there has been a definite change in shorthand teaching methods from emphasis on the manual skills to recognition of the importance of ancillary knowledge and mental and aural skills. The manual skills of handling the tools and of assisting fluent transcription by arrangement of notes are not difficult to acquire.

Dexterity in Writing Shorthand Outlines. Skill in writing shorthand outlines needs more attention and on this topic there have been, and probably still are, different points of view, brought about by changing teaching methods. When shorthand was learnt as an academic subject more than as a skill, that is, when the theory was acquired by learning the rules and transcribing longhand into shorthand from the visual stimulus of the printed word, the style to be adopted was that of the printed shorthand examples: the emphasis was on theoretical knowledge, not on movement. With the adoption of the skill approach to teaching more freedom and variation of writing style were allowed, until today some teachers will go so far as to say that style is not important as long as the notes can be read. Reference to general principles of learning will enable us to see that there are sound reasons for taking a middle road. Firstly, our student comes to us with a skill already developed in writing; if it is good, on the basis of transfer of training, we can let well alone and only seek to utilize it in the shorthand writing skill; with another student there may be need for some modification but we should never seek to impose an unnatural style. Just as there is no one writing posture suitable for every student, neither is there one style of writing. Secondly, the principle of individual differences makes it impossible for a number of shorthand writers to produce identical styles even if a great deal of time and effort were given to such an unnecessary task. Thirdly, we know that no two skill performances, even by the same person, are identical; according to the speed of dictation in relation to the writer's ability, according to his mood, according to the conditions under which the writing is done, there will be slight or even major changes in style. There are many good styles of shorthand writing, as can be seen from any set of examples of notes by experts; it is for the teacher to watch each student, to praise and encourage good movements and to correct only those which he can from experience recognize as likely to hinder speed or a good style.

Penmanship is, of course, at the basis of all good writing and if one is to be dogmatic about anything it will be about the need to avoid grasping the pen or pencil so tightly that the muscles of the hand and arm are not sufficiently relaxed to allow speedy movements.

CHAPTER III

Analysis of the Skill of Typewriting

UNLIKE the skill of shorthand writing, which has remained essentially the same since the earliest of modern writers, the skill of typewriting has changed in essential techniques from the two-, four-, six- and eight-finger methods to the ten-finger method, and from "sight" typewriting to "touch" typewriting. If we could have a visual comparison of the typist of, say, the 1880s, when most typists were two-finger sight typists, and the present-day ten-finger touch typist, the contrast would surely be most interesting. We should also like to know what the speed of a good average typist was in those early days.

Although the claim of *The First Typewriter Catalogue* (1875) "that hour's [*sic*] practice, daily will soon enable you to write from 50 to 100 words per minute, upon the machine" may have proved wishful thinking (or just salesmanship—96·5 words per minute was achieved by a F. McGurrin in a typewriting contest held in 1888). A report of the International Labour Office in 1924 on motion study in typewriting by a French research worker, J. M. Lahy,[1] contains reference to one of the subjects in the experiments as "a well-known champion typist, who uses only one finger of each hand." At this time a championship speed was in the region of 130 net words a minute on a one hour's typewriting from printed copy. Albert Tangora achieved this speed in the championship tests in the United States in 1924 and 1925. Mr. Lahy's report also contains the following interesting passage—

> It is a curious fact that . . . the ten-finger method . . . is based on erroneous observations, and yet enjoys the greatest popularity and is the most frequently taught in typewriting schools. The error involved is the analogy drawn between typewriting and piano playing. . . . It has often been noticed, though hitherto insufficiently emphasized, that typists taught by the ten-finger method nearly always end by abandoning it. . . . Teachers had to admit that after laborious training each pupil adopted his own method. . . . The adoption of one or other method for teaching typewriting should depend on many factors. One of these is the anatomical structure of the hands and fingers (the ten-finger method presumably requires a large hand); the functional independence of the muscle groups which determine the agility of the fingers is also an important factor.

[1] "Motion Study in Typewriting," *I.L.O. Studies and Reports, Series J.* (*Educational*), No. 3 (1924).

It would seem that Lahy did not connect this last point of independence of muscle groups with piano playing.

Our present-day champions reach speeds of 110 words a minute and more—they are, of course, all ten-finger touch typists!

Whether they would do even better if the typewriting keyboard were different is still a matter for investigation. As long ago as 1925, August Dvorak, an Associate Professor of Education in the University of Washington, discovered the following facts when analysing the typewriting skill—

1. The weaker left hand does 57 per cent of the work and the more skilful right hand only 43 per cent.

2. Too little typewriting (only 32 per cent) is done on the home row and too much (68 per cent) on the upper (52 per cent) and lower (16 per cent) rows.

3. The weaker left hand alone has to type 3,300 different words while the right hand idles, e.g. "extra," "exaggerate," "address," "was," "were"; over 500 words must be typed by the right hand alone while the left hand idles.

Dvorak therefore devised this "simplified" keyboard—

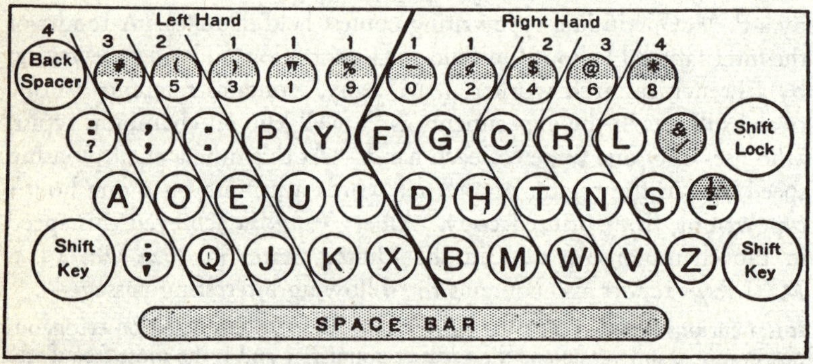

The following are the characteristics of the simplified keyboard—

1. The right hand does more work than the left—56 per cent and 44 per cent respectively.

2. The work assigned to the different fingers is more proportionate to their strength and skill.

3. Seventy per cent of the typing is done on the home row, only 22 per cent on the third, and 8 per cent on the bottom row.

4. Finger motion has been reduced by more than 90 per cent. A 100-word-per-minute typist's finger tips, in an eight-hour day travel only a little over a mile in motions from row to row as compared with 12 to 20 miles a day on the

standard keyboard. There are only two two-letter hurdles, the infrequent *xp* and *rv* on the simplified keyboard.

5. More than 3,000 different words (35 per cent of all the words used in ordinary copy) are typed exclusively on the home row.

6. Only 61 different and infrequently used monosyllables are typed exclusively by one hand, whereas on the standard keyboard over 3,800 different words are typed by one hand.[1]

Although the simplified keyboard seems to have been used in America and in international typewriting contests (1933–1941) it does not appear to have gained any general use; in this country one or two trials have been made but the difficulties inherent in a change-over on a large scale are enormous.

At present we are not concerned with other methods than the ten-finger, touch method on the standard keyboard, but we are concerned with more than "keyboard mastery." The typist in the office generally spends only a small part of her typing time copying correct and perfectly legible matter. Whether a task in typewriting is easy or difficult depends as much on the medium in which it is presented, on its language content and on the degree to which the display of the "copy" corresponds to what is required as the final form, as it does on the skill of the typist (see Chapter VIII).

Keyboard mastery alone is not sufficient. The following is offered as a useful analysis for the typewriting teacher of what the typist must know and do when typewriting is interpreted as the skill required for producing mailable documents from the normal variety of media—

SPECIFIC AREAS OF KNOWLEDGE NECESSARY TO TYPEWRITING

1. The machine.
2. Typewriting theory (conventional display).
3. Materials (paper, carbons, etc.).
4. English.
5. General knowledge.
6. Business knowledge.
7. Duplicating methods.

It is unnecessary to amplify this section except in the matter of materials. It does seem that much more should be done in typewriting courses to make students knowledgeable about qualities and types of

[1] United Business Education Association Forum, No. 4 (New York, 1946).

paper, and their appropriate uses; to give students the ability to name the small labour-saving devices, and even important parts of the machine instead of referring to everything as "the gadget"; and, above all, to acquaint them with the current cost of stationery if only in an endeavour to make them more waste conscious.

SPECIFIC SUB-SKILLS MAKING UP THE TOTAL SKILL

1. Manual (machine manipulation, handling materials, erasing).
2. Mental (recall, comprehension, English, judgement in display, retaining instructions until job is complete).
3. Visual reading span (manuscript reading, proof-reading own work, spatial perception).
4. Aural (for audio-typing).

There would, however, seem to be no one skill which one can call the typewriting skill; rather are there different combinations and integrations of the various sub-skills and areas of knowledge to form different complex skills. Four of these are sufficiently different to be classified separately—

1. Copying skill, without need to make alterations (e.g., from good typescript).
2. Producing good typescript copy from different media (manuscript, corrected typescript or print, or shorthand, with perhaps matter to be taken from different sources).
3. Audio-typing.
4. Typewriting in office conditions (work interruption, external noises, answering telephone, etc.).

Manual Skills

The manual skills have been mentioned first since in typewriting, as opposed to shorthand, they have more significance and need more preparation. The skill of handling the materials used is one which is often neglected, but teachers are not always to blame as training in economy of movement and avoidance of waste in handling paper, for example, requires adequate space, and typewriting classrooms are so often equipped with tables only just large enough to hold the typewriter and a book. The method of handing out one sheet of paper at a time to each student has its advantages in elementary courses, but when students reach the stage of production work a more realistic method should be adopted.

Emphasis on keyboard mastery is beginning to give way to a more all-round training in machine manipulation to include drills on using the margin-release key, adjusting margins, using the tabulator key, etc.

One account of research work[1] states that—

there is considerable variation in the time required to strike the various letters of the alphabet; but if the time taken for striking an average letter of the alphabet be taken as one, then the time required to strike the space bar is 0·8, to make a capital about 2·9 and to return the carriage 7·0.

Relating this latter figure to the use of records which give 8 seconds for the return of the carriage and to the general principle of learning that no movement or habit should be allowed at the elementary level which is not required at the expert level, we see that we need to be very cautious on the amount of practice which we give to students with such records. In a small experiment carried out several times at Garnett College it was found that novices at typewriting who had little aptitude for the skill were able to acquire a carriage-return skill of about 2 seconds after only two hours' tuition. It is also interesting to know that champion operators of a manual typewriter can beat the normal electric typewriter on carriage return. If the latter are used in championship contests they are sometimes specially adjusted to give a quicker return.

Reading for Typewriting. D. C. Fuller[2] studied the reading habits of typewriting experts and found that—

the eyes normally keep about one second ahead of the hand to supply copy as it is needed; more rapid reading is likely to cause errors.

He then adds—

since most mechanical errors in typewriting seem to involve the central letters of words and since in ordinary reading the most common word errors are likewise in the centre of words, is it not safe to assume that teachers err in telling their typewriting students to read faster, to read by word-wholes, and to read for meaning when seeking to improve or test their maximum typing speed?

A study reported in *Education and Commerce*,[3] (the journal of the

[1] Blackstone, E. G., "Summary of Research in Typewriting," *The National Business Education Quarterly* (Washington, D.C., Spring, 1940).

[2] "How to Read for Typewriting," *The National Business Education Quarterly* (Washington, D.C., December, 1943).

[3] Davison, P. S. and Tilley, K. W., "The Reading Span of Typists," *Education and Commerce* No. 28 (July, 1959).

National Association for Business Education, formerly the National Association for Education for Commerce) found that "the great majority of typists read by whole words and not by syllables or letters," and "the more able subjects and the good spellers tended to read further ahead than the poor subjects," although they found that "only low correlations exist between reading span and typing speed. . . ."

These two studies may, at first sight, seem to contradict each other, but the final phrase in Mr. Fuller's statement must not be overlooked, i.e. ". . . when seeking to improve or test their maximum typing speed." In drill work, in forcing speed and in testing speed only, reading for meaning is not essential—that is the requirement when the typist is performing the more complex task of making a fair copy from imperfect copy, such as amended manuscript, or taking matter from several sources, etc. If we train students *never* to read for meaning, how are they going to perform when they are faced with these problem situations?

An important point for the development of quick finger action in typewriting is brought out in all the studies on speed work, namely, that words requiring alternate hand operation can be typed faster than other words; more use could be made of this fact in the earlier drills and exercises.

Mental Skills

Most employers would wish their typists to work intelligently, with initiative and interest; certainly it should be the aim of all teachers to help each of their students to develop these qualities. Suitable exercises and practical work must therefore be provided as it is only by "doing" that students can show what they are capable of. Straightforward copy and timed tests are amongst the easiest and less challenging forms of typewriting and it is generally found that students will respond to the other forms with greater interest and effort. Suggestions for such work are given in Chapter VIII.

One factor in the typewriting skill which is often regarded as an area of knowledge, but which needs to be developed as a skill, is that of word division at line ends. The modern tendency is to avoid this as much as possible, but there are still many occasions when it is necessary and just knowing the rules is not sufficient to prevent the speed and rhythm of the typing being broken; there must be the skill of rapid decision and action on the hyphen key.

Visual Skill

Very little has been written on the question of the appropriate kind of reading for typewriting. In speed development the important factor is control and whilst most words will be read "by wholes" because they are familiar, or because they have been typed before, when the eyes meet an unusual or unpractised word pattern the right reaction is to type at the letter level, in the same way that proof readers will work at the letter level for unfamiliar foreign words. Some teachers spend longer than others on the letter stage before proceeding to words, phrases, sentences and finally to continuous matter. The modern trend is to teach in the word pattern first, as being more meaningful and therefore easier to learn than single letter associations. The writer has taught by both methods and found the word and sentence method far superior. The students found the exercises more real, they were actually producing something which had a relation to their ultimate goal and they felt a sense of satisfaction from that fact. This method also interferes less with the normal reading habits than the letter reading method. Two interesting researches into the teaching and learning of typewriting have been reported in issues of *Education and Commerce*. The aim of the first[1] was to ascertain "some of the important factors contributing towards typing ability in training." One of the conclusions given was—

> The decrease in speed performance noted when difficult words were presented suggests the existence of a reading problem in typing for both touch and non-touch typists experienced this difficulty.

It may be suggested that this difficulty could be due to both manual and reading problems, for the fingers will tend to slow down if the mental response is slower, and also if the movements involved in the letter combination are less familiar kinaesthetically.

The second research[2] sought an analysis of typing speeds and recorded speeds of students on five different kinds of copy, ranging from a random arrangement of consonants, without grammatical structure, to a meaningful sentence. This report concludes thus—

> It would appear that the most important factor which gives an even typing speed is the development of an "ocuo-manual" gap, i.e. the ability to read the

[1] Mattock, G. and Tilley, K. W., "Factors Involved in the Teaching of Typewriting," *Education and Commerce*, No. 16 (July, 1956).

[2] Genest, M., "An Analysis of Typing Speed," translated from the French by M. A. Le Cudenee and reported in *Education and Commerce*, No. 27(April, 1959).

test well ahead of the stage being typed; this gives a sort of cushioning effect between the act of reading and typing. The reading need not necessarily be at an even speed; familiar words and sentences are read quickly and the more unusual ones slowly, but the typing speed remains constant and is set at an average speed of reading. . . . The matter read is, so to speak, stored for a few seconds in advance of the act of typing. In fact, the act of striking the keys becomes less important than the mental preparations required to "store" what is read and this mental preparation is the most important item to be mastered when learning to type.

CHAPTER IV

Analysis of the Skill of Transcription

Of the three skills which we are considering, the typewritten-transcription skill is the most complex, for it is a combination of seven sub-skills.

THE SEVEN COMPONENT SKILLS

1. Fluent reading of shorthand symbols.
2. Spontaneous mental recognition of the sense of what is being read.
3. Mental punctuation—commas, hyphens, apostrophes are not usually inserted in shorthand notes.
4. Mental vision of longhand version of shorthand.
5. Correct striking of keys.
6. Automatic division of words at line-ends where necessary.
7. Quick decision on display and consequent operation of machine (line-spacing, paragraph, display of insets, etc.).

It must be emphasized that these are *skills*, in which the degree of speed and accuracy needs to be very high; they are, of course, based on knowledge—knowledge of the shorthand system, English vocabulary, punctuation rules, word-division, and principles of display in typewriting. But possessing the knowledge is not sufficient for the competent typist—she must be able to apply it rapidly, with confidence and with intelligence. If she cannot do so her output will be low, there will be waste of time and stationery in second and third efforts, and poor transcription habits will be formed. Of course, a number of the above-mentioned skills are the same as for the separate skills of shorthand and typewriting, but the transcription skill consists in a fusion of the two already complex but discrete skills into a third skill involving some modifications of both. The greatest of these modifications is the change in the visual stimulus of the copy. In typewriting both the original and the final copy are in similar symbols—longhand letters and figures; in transcription the brain has to comprehend a different symbol and transmit it to the fingers in the symbols of the typewriter—longhand. How easy it is for the typist, striking the typewriter keys at even the modest speed of one hundred strokes (twenty words) a minute, to see  and, if not alert, to type "weigh" instead of "way" (or vice versa); such examples can be multiplied a hundredfold. It therefore needs much training and practice to become a fluent typist from shorthand notes.

In addition, of course, there is the choice and handling of stationery and other materials necessary for the production of documents. In one large organization the members of the central stenographic service may work for any of a dozen different departments, each with its own variation of the general letter heading or other stationery.

A competent shorthand-typist can transcribe continuous prose which does not call for display at 40 to 50 words per minute. The average performance is only about half this rate and it is not surprising that employers often report this as a common weakness. It is a pity that typewriting speeds are "awarded" on a form of test which represents only one aspect of the typist's skill—the ability to type from straightforward, unamended copy for a period of ten minutes. Now that teachers and students are becoming interested in transcription speeds it is important that false comparisons should not be made. It is not uncommon for a student to quote a copying speed of 40 words per minute and a transcription speed of only 18 words per minute, but while the copying test would undoubtedly have been on continuous prose, calling for no display, the transcription test would probably have been on a business letter requiring a number of adjustments of the machine for the appropriate display; the comparison is not of "like with like." Some standardization of what are desirable and achievable levels of attainment for students following different types of courses should be regarded by administrators and teachers as an urgent need.

FACTORS LIKELY TO AFFECT TRANSCRIPTION SKILL

There are several variables which may affect the total transcription skill even though the basic knowledge in the fields quoted above may be of an acceptable standard. The most important of these are—

1. The speed of the dictation relative to the writer's capacity. If the notes are taken at the writer's maximum speed, they will be more difficult to read.

2. The language level of the dictated matter, especially in relation to the transcriber's knowledge. Even technical matter, if familiar to the

typist, can be transcribed speedily and fluently; unusual language style will slow down shorthand transcription speed more than copying speed on similar material.

3. The period of time which elapses between the dictation and the transcription. The power of "immediate memory" is not always appreciated; many students pass tests on an immediate transcription but would fail if they had to transcribe at a later date. Practice in transcribing from "cold" notes is an excellent form of exercise.

4. The time allowed for the transcription. If the work has to be produced under pressure, the more inexperienced students are likely to perform less well.

5. The length and nature of the dictated matter. A series of short passages or letters is easier to transcribe than a long, continuous passage, even though the continuous passage may call for less typewriting display.

6. If the shorthand notes are written in pencil and transcribed under artificial light, the transcription rate may be reduced. Typists are not sufficiently often made aware of the greater clarity of ink notes and of the reduced strain of transcribing during even moderately long transcription periods.

7. The form in which the transcript is required, i.e. single copy, several carbon copies, a stencil, or some other form of master used for duplicating.

8. The reading habit of the transcriber. A typist who is a poor reader with frequent eye fixations will be less likely to grasp the sense of the passage than the good reader; hence a less fluent transcribing skill will result. Fluency, or unbroken rhythm, is a characteristic of all expert typewriting; even the expert statistical typist develops it.

9. The need to estimate the space which the transcript will require. Apart from the initial choice of paper size, line-spacing and margins, there are the instances where a change of display has to be made. It is always rather more difficult to make this assessment from shorthand notes than from typescript, or even manuscript. Shorthand symbols are deceptive—many brief outlines represent quite long words or phrases and although the previous experience with copy work may help, the transfer cannot be completely successful without some special training.

10. The "form" of the operator at the time the work is carried out. Health, mood, environmental conditions, are all liable to affect this.

The more complex the skill, the more likely it is that variations of performance will occur from day to day. It is important therefore that sufficient practice should be given so that the effect of such variations may be minimized. In other words "over-learning" will ensure control and a more stable level of performance.

From the above analysis it is quite obvious that it is wrong to assume that if a student can type and write shorthand competently he can therefore, *ipso facto*, produce mailable documents from shorthand notes in a competent manner. In America far more attention has been paid to the teaching of transcription than has been the case in this country. Even today cases may be found here where students have been faced with the task of typing from their notes for the first time when being tested for their first post: in 1950, from an inquiry carried out by the author,[1] it was found that no less than 18 per cent of 146 shorthand-typists had had no opportunity to type from shorthand notes during their college course, 24 per cent had never used a carbon, and 41 per cent had never taken "office style" dictation. Of the 45 employers reporting on employees' weaknesses, 50 per cent said that they frequently found the junior shorthand-typists slow in transcription, while 74 per cent reported frequent weakness in punctuation.

A comparison of the number of entries for the single subject examination of the Royal Society of Arts is also of interest in this connexion. In 1961 at Stage II there were 33,293 candidates for typewriting and 34,648 candidates for shorthand (80 and 100 words per minute) whereas for the shorthand-typist's examination there were only 5,010 candidates; this means that five-sixths of the students were either not trained or did not feel competent to try for a qualification in that aspect of their studies which would form the major part of the work for which they were preparing. The position in the 1965–66 examinations showed little improvement in this position. Whereas the entries for the single subject of typewriting jumped, compared with 1961, from 33,293 to 57,419 entries, and for shorthand from 34,648 to 52,654, the entries for the shorthand-typist's examination rose by only 1,147—from 5,010 to 6,157. Teachers could do a great deal to remedy this situation. Transcription is probably the most interesting skill to teach; it certainly offers the widest scope at present for experiment, co-operation (with other teachers and with employers) and for research.

[1] McNicol, Grace, "The Training and Work of Junior Shorthand-typists," *The Vocational Aspect of Secondary and Further Education*, Vol. III, No. 7 (November, 1951).

CHAPTER V

General Principles of Learning

The previous chapters have had as their main theme the first task of anyone preparing to teach shorthand and typewriting, namely, to understand what the student must master in the way of knowledge and sub-skills in order to acquire competence in the total skill. Such analysis is, of course, only part of a teacher's preparation. A teacher is effective only if the students learn more and learn with greater ease and permanence than they would without his help. To know how to teach, it is necessary to know something of how students learn. Fortunately for any would-be teacher "the learning process," as it is termed, has been the subject of much study and research. The purpose of this chapter is to outline some general ideas on learning which have come from such studies and which the author has found to be of particular significance to the teacher of shorthand and typewriting.

WHEN STUDENTS ARE LIKELY TO LEARN

It would seem that human beings have a natural desire for practical activities and for movement, and the Spanish writer Salvador de Madariaga thinks that this is a particularly strong characteristic of Englishmen. In his fascinating book *Englishmen, Frenchmen and Spaniards*[1] he classifies the Englishman as the "man of action" because he has found that he prefers to work out his problems at the moment of action rather than, as the Frenchman is more likely to do, as an intellectual exercise. It is certainly true that practical activities are generally popular with students of almost any age. Psychologists also confirm this "skill hunger" as it has been called and the fact of such a favourable "set" towards a subject leads to a consideration of the essential first condition for learning, namely, *willingness.*

Interest, Motivation and Mental Set

These are all terms used to describe the mental attitude of the student towards the learning situation at any given time.

[1] de Madariaga, Salvador, *Englishmen, Frenchmen and Spaniards* (London, Oxford University Press, 1928).

Interest. This attitude (often put forward by teachers in training as the panacea for all teaching difficulties) can be at different levels. We are interested when being entertained or amused; at the other end of the scale we are interested when we are engrossed in solving a problem. In the latter situation the degree of self-involvement and concentration is likely to be considerably greater than in the former. The initial interest in a subject may originate with the learner, through some form of self-motivation, or it may be stimulated by the teacher. In either case it can vary in strength and duration, and a knowledge of the events or situations which may affect it is valuable to any teacher.

Motivation. Evening-class teachers soon discover that what has brought their students to the class, or motivated them to attend, is often not a desire to learn the particular subject, but rather the wish to spend the evening with friends who have decided (probably for quite different reasons) to enrol. Attendance may, on the other hand, result from compulsion on the part of employer or parent, or from ambition, the urge to "get on," or to become qualified. It may even be the result of some interest established by earlier study, or the urge to emulate someone who is admired. All these things lead to some degree of interest. The American psychologist John Dewey[1] points out that the "significance of interest is in *what it leads to*; the new experience it makes possible, the new powers it tends to form. . . ." He distinguishes between "making things interesting" (stirring up pleasure in things not of themselves interesting to the student) and "utilizing interest." He adds that the "teacher who always utilizes interest will never merely indulge it. Interest in its reality is a moving thing, a thing of growth, of richer experience, and fuller power. Just how to use interest to secure growth in knowledge and in efficiency is what defines the master teacher."

Interest and Making Things Interesting. These are not the simple answers to teaching and learning problems which they might at first seem to be. However, sustained interest is essential for successful learning and a teacher must know what methods to try if interest flags too often or for too long. One of the most important conditions for the continuance of interest and effort is satisfaction resulting from awareness of progress and achievement. We are prepared to continue

[1] "Interest as Related to Will," Second Supplement to *The Herbart Yearbook* (1903).

making an effort if we have had the pleasure of success in our earlier efforts. "Nothing succeeds like success"; if progress is too slow to give this satisfaction, frustration sets in and the willingness to learn may cease.

Sustaining Interest. Apart from methods of sustaining or renewing interest, it is well known that teacher personality and teacher-student relationship are important factors in maintaining interest. If a student cannot get on with a teacher, then he often does not get on with the subject. Many a student's interest and progress in a subject have been destroyed in this way. Conversely, students have reached unexpected levels of attainment in one field of study mainly as a result of the favourable emotional setting (the social atmosphere) in which the learning took place, and this social atmosphere is to a very large extent the result of what the teacher *is* rather than what he *does*.

Routine and Variety

Well-planned lessons will obviously contain both routine and variety, for the following reasons. Routine prevents waste of teaching and learning time. There should be a simple routine (understood by all students and supervised by the teacher until the habit is established) for starting and finishing work. Routine in the form of a test is often desirable as it gives the students a feeling of security by knowing what to do. Systematic guidance in the study of the class textbook and on good private-study habits is also a worth-while routine from which the students will gain a sense of progress. Homework should, of course, be assessed and returned regularly, but it should also be a routine that both student and teacher follow up this work. It is a waste of both student's and teacher's efforts if work is returned corrected and simply filed (or even thrown away).

Routine does not, however, mean that every lesson must follow the same plan. Variety is essential in order to arouse or maintain the interest of students. It will also give opportunity for catering for individual differences. Students differ in ways and pace of learning, in ability to associate ideas, and in their background knowledge, capacity and motivation. Variety can be through a change of teaching material, of teaching method, or of teaching aids. Variety can help to heighten the impression made on the student; it can help to keep students mentally alert; it can help to bring back the focus of attention. Variety, however, should not be thought of as something to be used "as much as possible." There should always be a definite purpose in its use. It is often found that students will be quite happy to work for a considerable part of a lesson on what seems to be routine work—and will benefit from it. Conversely, routine work should not be used just for the sake of "keeping the students busy."

Incentives

Incentives form the next most potent factor in the continuance of interest and many experiments have been undertaken to discover the degree of effect which incentives have on learning, to find out the type of incentives most likely to influence progress, and to assess the degree of improvement resulting from the incentives used.

One authority[1] reports the following well-known experiment—

> Over a period of five days a group of students were given work on addition problems of six three-place numbers. All the students of the experiment were first tested and, on the basis of their scores divided into four groups, a control, a praised, a reproved and an ignored group. The control group was placed in a separate room but the other groups were given the tests in the same room and praised, reproved or ignored in the presence of the others.

TABLE 13. Average scores made on Arithmetic Tests by Groups Working under different Incentives for a period of five days.

Groups	First day	Second day	Third day	Fourth day	Fifth day
Control	11·8	12·3	11·6	10·5	11·4
Praised	11·8	16·6	18·8	18·8	20·2
Reproved	11·8	16·6	14·3	13·3	14·2
Ignored	11·8	14·2	13·3	12·9	12·4

> The results showed that praise is most effective, and reproof next. Being ignored in the presence of praise and reproof results in a little better achievement than when pupils work by themselves with no particular stimulation of any kind. Further analysis indicated that praise influences poor students most and that reproof has an unfavourable effect on them. Reproof, on the other hand, may have a desirable effect on some of the brighter children, though on the whole praise is better.

Competition is another familiar form of incentive and here Sorenson reports an experiment set up—

[1] Sorenson, Herbert, *Psychology in Education* (New York, McGraw-Hill Publishing Co. Inc., 1948).

to discover the comparative results when an individual works for his own record in competition with others and when his score is combined with that of his group and compared with the score of another.

> The children taking part were tested under four conditions (1) unmotivated, (2) working for self, (3) working for the group, (4) choice of working for self or the group.
>
> When the student was motivated by the desire to win the prize for himself, he did best; the amount accomplished in working for the group was greater than in working without motivation but not so great as in working for self. Consistent with this result is the tendency of pupils to work for their individual score rather than the group score when they have an opportunity to choose whether they wish to continue to work for themselves or for the group.

The most common form of incentive is the awarding of marks and this has proved a popular field of research, the results invariably showing that with both young and older students knowledge of achievement or of the marks awarded had a favourable effect on progress. Some teachers, however, feel that the constant awarding of marks leads to a poor attitude to work and hinders the development of a sense of responsibility. They argue that the student who will not give of his best unless he is to be rewarded, is hardly likely to be a reliable worker when not supervised or paid by results. The wise teacher will get to know the students and encourage and help them to keep the awarding of marks in perspective; it is never a question of "always give marks" or "never give marks" but of trying to achieve the aims of developing a responsible attitude to any task no matter how small and of giving sufficient incentives to sustain interest and effort.

STUDENT ACTIVITY

In the analysis of the three skills of shorthand, typewriting and transcription, we saw that in addition to—and, indeed as a basis of—the manual skills there is knowledge to be learned and mental and aural skills to be developed. Student activity, therefore, in these subjects as in any other skill, means much more than learning theory, writing shorthand outlines or striking the typewriter keys. In most books on educational psychology and theories of learning reference is made to the favourable results generally obtained in experiments designed to assess the amount and quality of learning achieved when students are given the opportunity of working things out for themselves, of being actively involved in solving problems, in discovering for themselves basic principles and in deciding what action they should take in certain circumstances.

The following are typical comments from secondary commercial school students in answer to an inquiry as to their own opinion of the most useful course which they had taken—

"benefited by any work done as an individual and not as a class"

"I benefited most by the more responsible jobs which we were given."

But long before the day of modern technique of questionnaires and scientific research, there were educationists, both theorists and practitioners, who stressed the greater value of "doing" and "discovering" by the student over the "telling" and "rote learning" method. The educational philosophies of the naturalists and pragmatists were based on the conviction that children would learn more effectively and develop better as people through first-hand experience than through knowledge received second hand. From Rousseau in France, Pestalozzi in Switzerland, Herbart and Froebel in Germany, Montessori in Italy, Helen Parkhurst in Dalton, U.S.A., A. S. Neill in England and Dr. Kurt Hahn, pioneer of the Outward Bound schools, we have evidence of the importance of student activity and of providing opportunities for the use of initiative.

Applied to the curriculum of a school, the "activity method" can mean that there is no formal, rigid time-table under which the students spend definite periods on the respective subjects, with formal teaching, testing and examinations. Under the activity programme subjects may be studied in relation to one another as and when they are needed, probably in the carrying out of an integrated study known as a "project." The projects are often chosen by the students themselves and are supervised by the teachers who give lessons on specific topics when required and are always available for advice and help. The emphasis is on learning in a natural situation, on having a purpose in learning and on the development of good work habits and attitudes. One secretarial student said of an economics project in which each student selected her own special topic—

> The economics thesis was a very good idea and I should be very sorry if I had missed it. The project at the beginning seemed a tremendous task, and would never have been attempted by any of us off our own bat. But it showed us what we could do.[1]

[1] Pickard, O. G., "Education for Office Work," *The Vocational Aspect of Secondary and Further Education*, Vol. 1. No. 2 (May, 1949).

In the narrower field of learning particular sections of a subject in the more formal setting of fixed time-table periods, the main difference in the teaching approach lies in the way in which the teacher presents knowledge, i.e. by "revealing" through student discovery, instead of by "telling" for student learning. This does not mean that the teacher is freed of all responsibility in this learning situation; obviously the student must be guided so that time is not wasted in fruitless effort over an unnecessarily long period. The project method has been found especially valuable in the teaching of typewriting and will be discussed in more detail in Chapter VIII.

INDIVIDUAL DIFFERENCES

Both the project plan, which can be group or individual work, and its close associate the assignment plan, which is usually individual, have the advantage of taking into account other important facts which we know about learning. Although a number of students are brought together and known as a "class," and although much of the teaching may have to be class teaching, every teacher is well aware that he is really teaching twenty or so individuals and that their progress will differ because of their individual differences in background, interest, aptitude, age, etc. Some students will be slow starters; some will need repetition of facts and instructions, while others will not; some will learn more easily through seeing than through hearing only; some will respond to challenge, others will need to be taken along one step at a time. Projects and assignments allow students the opportunity to work at their own pace, to ask for help in their own individual difficulties and, above all, to measure present achievement against their own previous attainment and not suffer discouragement by comparison with the greater achievement of others. In the acquisition of skills it is especially important to allow for individual differences, for no two performers of a skill are identical and in certain skills, as we shall see later, physical differences may play an important part. An interesting and enlightening piece of work for any teacher to carry out is to keep a "learning curve graph" for each student on a selected section of a subject. To those who have been only a short time in teaching it is often surprising, and perhaps disappointing, to find that a wide variation of attainment can develop in a class even though all students have followed the same course, have attended regularly, and have completed all the work set. This variation may be particularly noticeable in a class learning a skill subject and it is therefore important that teachers of shorthand and typewriting should be aware of the possible causes.

The two factors of intelligence and interest can account more frequently than any others for varying rates of progress in a class. Any consideration of intelligence naturally leads to the work of psychologists in measuring physical and mental qualities of human beings. Such studies provide abundant evidence that learning is affected by nurture as well as nature; a student may be very intelligent and yet fail to make the grade in a particular subject, while a less naturally gifted student achieves a very creditable standard. Indeed this "lower than expected" attainment of the bright student and the "better than expected" attainment of the duller student is a phenomenon not infrequently met with and one psychologist[1] has explained it by the fact that the "school system puts more pressure on pupils below the average and permits the brighter students to get by on less than they are capable of doing." In other words, the duller student is stimulated to his maximum performance, but the brighter student is not and, realizing that he does not need to make an effort, he performs at a level which is little, if any, better than that of the duller student.

A. Pinsent[2] classifies the possible differences between individual pupils as follows—

> *Differences in general intelligence*, which determine the rate of a pupil's progress, and the degree of difficulty of the tasks he can master.
>
> *Differences in specific abilities.* These will determine a pupil's interests and the kind of work at which he is most likely to succeed.
>
> *Differences in health and temperament.*
>
> *Differences in degree of maturity.* The younger pupils are incompletely developed. A pupil eleven years old cannot do work which he will be able to accomplish with ease at the age of sixteen or eighteen years.
>
> *Differences in local environment and opportunity.* Local conditions affect a pupil's interests and his previous education. Conditions of the pupil's home life, such as nutrition, opportunities for exercise and play, access to books, means to travel, etc., all affect his educational progress. . . .

In evaluating students' progress by the generally accepted methods of testing and allocating marks, it is desirable that the teacher should understand the significance of the distribution of the marks throughout

[1] Ellis, Robert S., *Educational Psychology* (Princeton, D. Van Nostrand Co. Inc., 1951).
[2] *The Principles of Teaching-method* (London, George G. Harrap & Co. Ltd., 1952).

the class or classes and know what is meant by the term "the curve of normal distribution." The following extract from *Psychology and its Bearing on Education*[1] is quoted for the benefit of those readers who have not met this term before.

The Curve of Normal Distribution. The student will sometimes come across a statement that the results of some test gave a "normal curve of distribution"; or a "slightly skewed curve." If we measure the heights of say, 10,000 men taken at random, and plot a curve showing the frequencies of the various heights, we get a curve like Figure 11 (see below).

This regular type of curve, with a high centre peak, and tapering gradually at each end, is also the kind of curve we may get by pure chance; for example, in tossing ten coins thousands of times and noting the number of times we get: (1) no heads and ten tails; (2) one head and nine tails; and so on. It is found that if sufficiently large numbers are taken, the results of very varied human measurements (height, weight, general intelligence, and specific abilities) give roughly similar curves to that in Figure 11. . . .

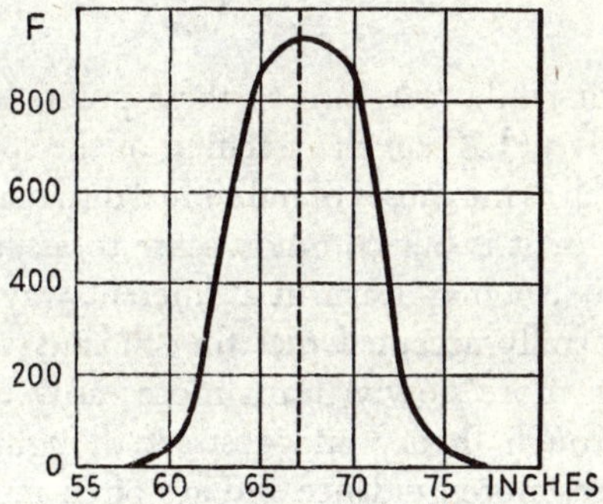

FIG. 11

Curve of Normal Distribution

A Skewed Curve. Suppose, when our measurements of the height of 10,000 men were just begun, a war broke out and the Government conscripted first the fittest men, ages twenty to twenty-five, who were over, say, 5 ft 5 in., and suppose we could not include these in our measurements. In a sample still taken at random, this would reduce the number of men over 5 ft 5 in. The peak in the curve would now be about 65 in., instead of about 67 in., as in the curve above, with a marked drop after 65 in. The curve would now be said to be "skewed"; it would not be symmetrical. Similar results are obtained if we test thousands of children of twelve years in schools from which many of the more intelligent children have been removed to Grammar Schools at the age of eleven.

[1] Valentine, C W., *Psychology and its Bearing on Education* (London, Methuen & Co. Ltd. 1960 ed.).

Thus the shape of a curve of results may be a warning of some selection or other error; but of course skewness, and indeed great irregularity, is likely to occur in any curve unless it is based on very large numbers.

In most classes for shorthand and typewriting there has been a certain degree of selection, e.g. by age, educational background, interest, or testing, but since no satisfactory diagnostic tests for these skills exist, it is unlikely that there will be a high degree of selectivity. In addition to size of group and degree of selection there are other factors which can affect the distribution of marks scored in any particular test. These are—

1. The test may be too easy or too difficult for the majority (the so-called "average" of the group(s)).
2. The conditions (physical or social) under which the work was done may be unfavourable.
3. The marking may be too lenient or too severe.
4. The subject matter coverage of the test may be too limited or too diffuse.

It will be worth while to return to these points in the succeeding Chapters (VII, VIII and X) on the teaching of the specific skills.

The effects as well as the causes of individual differences are of importance to teachers for it is but common sense to assume, for instance, that the bright student may learn in a different way from the duller student. It is generally accepted that the students who are less able intellectually learn more slowly, learn more easily through practical activities than through theory and abstract thought, that they also need more practice, more guidance and are often more willing to do repetitive work than are their brighter companions.

The latter are, in contrast, better able to reason, take greater pleasure in problem solving and can organize their studies and work on their own more effectively. It is obvious, then, that if both types of student are to be helped to develop to the best of their ability, different teaching methods and material will be necessary. Account has also to be taken of the fact that there are degrees of brightness and degrees of dullness. Even though members of a class may have been selected by some form of test, there will still be variations of intelligence and aptitude. This is also one of the reasons why teaching is not, as some people seem to think, "doing the same thing year after year." The challenge of a new class, with the need to discover the range of potential ability, to select the appropriate material and method, is indeed a new job every time and not the repetition of an old one, even though the general pattern of the aims remains the same.

Transfer of Training

Apart from the generally accepted elements of intelligence—verbal, spatial and number, each of which may be possessed to a differing degree by any one person—other abilities may affect a student's capacity to learn a particular subject. One very important ability for the acquisition of skills is known as the "motor, mechanical or concrete ability"—the aptitude for successful learning in situations involving objects, or things, or movement. The good athlete will have a high degree of motor skill. The degree of abstract intelligence has been shown by some researches to be low when the motor or mechanical aptitude is high.[1] But although this may be true of some, yet the teacher has always to remember that the majority of people are average and will therefore have an average endowment of both abstract and concrete aptitudes. Students may also have well-developed abilities in subjects likely to assist (or hinder) them in the learning of another subject. This may occur through the similarity (or dissimilarity) of either subject content or learning method and is known as "transfer of training." Transfer can also occur within a subject, from one situation to another in which knowledge and skill previously acquired are needed.

Transfer, as indicated above, may be either positive (assisting the new learning), or negative (hindering the new learning). The general conclusions from researches into transfer may be summarized as follows—

Positive Transfer

1. For such transfer to take place there must be common elements usable in the two subjects or situations.
2. Students must be aware of the common elements.
3. Students must have the opportunity to use these elements in the new situation.
4. There is generally more positive transfer with bright students than with less bright students (effect of ability to generalize and see relationships).
5. There is generally more positive transfer if the teacher makes an effort to secure it through appropriate teaching methods and material.

[1] Sorenson, Herbert, op. cit.

Negative Transfer

1. This takes place when the two subjects or situations have elements which vary only slightly, or in some, but not all aspects (e.g. influence of knowledge of Italian on learning Spanish, or vice versa).

2. Negative transfer takes place in motor activities when either the stimulus or response (but not both) is changed from one situation to another so that a correct habit in the one is incorrect in the other (e.g. transfer of ability on one make of typewriter to another).[1]

Social Atmosphere

A third kind of ability is sometimes called "social ability" or "characteristics of temperament." The social atmosphere in a class can affect the learning of the students favourably or unfavourably. Individuals may be helped or hindered in their learning through their ability (or inability) to fit in with the group, to feel secure, to gain confidence. If the teacher is not aware of such variations the shy student may drop behind because he is not given sufficient opportunity to consolidate his knowledge, and the more aggressive type of student may make the teacher, quite unconsciously, set the level or pace of the work at too high a standard for the average students.

Differences in health may not seem at first sight to be of much importance to the teacher of shorthand and typewriting, especially the evening teacher. There are two aspects to be considered: first the age of the students being taught and secondly the conditions in the classroom. Many shorthand and typewriting students are at the adolescent age, a time of rapid physical development when, all authorities agree, there may be temporary falling off in the rate of mental progress. Most books on educational psychology or teaching method deal fully with this topic since it is of interest to all teachers.

CLASSROOM CONDITIONS

The teacher needs also to take some responsibility for conditions in the classroom; good lighting, ventilation and temperature all contribute to good learning. Seating and posture are of special importance to the shorthand or typewriting student; a choice of tables and chairs

[1] For further study on this subject, see pp. 137–38 of *Philosophy and Psychology of Teaching Typewriting*, A. R. Russon and S. J. Wanous.

may not be possible, but an understanding of what is desirable will enable a teacher to make the best use of what is available and perhaps to obtain something better when opportunity occurs. To know what is desirable and the reasons for it being so is the first step to improvement. Apart from affecting progress, poor conditions in evening classes will certainly affect attendance. For a fuller treatment of classroom conditions likely to affect learning the reader is recommended to study Chapter IV of *The Principles of Teaching-method* by A. Pinsent.

The fact that in any group of learners there are differences of intelligence, temperament and experience, means that there are also different stages and areas of development. Aptitudes will develop into abilities or remain latent; according to the opportunities afforded, and to the different interests and attitudes, will be the need to find out the capacity of each student in language, in aural acuity, and in co-ordination of hearing, comprehension and hand movement.

IDEAL LEARNING CONDITIONS

We see, then, that the conditions for effective learning are mental, physical and social. To give even a brief account of the work and theories of educationists and psychologists in this field would need a separate volume, and therefore a short bibliography on the subject of teaching and learning has been given on p. 227.

The points which have been made in the preceding pages may be briefly summarized as follows.

Students are likely to learn when—

1. They are willing (have the right mental set towards the subject or the learning situation).
2. They are curious (are stimulated by interest).
3. They are inspired by a desire to emulate.
4. They have a definite purpose in learning, a goal to achieve (motivation).
5. They derive satisfaction from learning (awareness of progress, sense of achievement).
6. They have the capacity to learn (when the work is suited to their standard of attainment and account is taken of their individual differences).
7. They are actively involved (have an opportunity to "do" and to "discover" for themselves).

8. The social atmosphere is favourable (when students feel secure and "accepted"; when there is a feeling of group loyalty which includes the teacher).

9. Classroom conditions are satisfactory.

HOW STUDENTS LEARN

The American psychologist E. R. Guthrie stated in 1945 that "a scientific theory of learning has yet to be agreed upon by psychologists," and we can agree with B. R. Bugelski, who in 1956 added that the statement was "even a bit truer today." Nevertheless there are a few guiding principles which have emerged from most of the studies of the learning process and which are likely to be of value to teachers of skill subjects. One of the most important points for such teachers to bear in mind is that most skills are complex and require the rapid application of knowledge as well as the co-ordination of muscular movements. If the requisite knowledge cannot be immediately recalled, then the co-ordination of movement breaks down. Therefore, in acquiring a skill, the learner must be given adequate opportunities to recall *rapidly* the items of knowledge as well as to acquire automaticity in competent technique.

Learning by Imitation

The opportunities which everyday life offers for recognition of this way of learning as universal are too obvious and numerous to need much amplification. One example will suffice. Watch any group of children playing for a short while and you will see one or more of them quite deliberately imitating the activities of another or of a group; the younger children often have difficulty in performing and are probably soon told that they are "spoiling the game," but provided that the ages and capacities are fairly well matched, the members of the group learn from each other simply through imitation. In most fields of adult learning demonstration is accepted as an essential teaching technique because we expect our students to be able to learn by imitation. Yet it has not been unknown for shorthand and typewriting classes to be given little or no opportunity to imitate a good performance by the teacher. A demonstration stand which enables the teacher to give a demonstration of typewriting effectively with economy of time and effort, is still not found in every typewriting room. A sketch of an appropriate type of stand is given on p. 222 in Appendix 2.

In providing opportunities for imitation, however, the teacher needs to take account of four important elements in the learning situation thus created.

1. However perfect the demonstration, an identical set of movements should not be expected from all students because the general principle of individual differences comes into play. It is part of the expertness of a teacher of skills to be able to recognize the potentially good movements, the movements which will develop and help towards a skilful performance, and which are therefore to be praised, and those which may develop into awkward, ineffective sub-skills which will render the total skill less acceptable, and which must therefore be corrected.

2. Imitation on the part of the learner is rarely discriminating; bad points as well as good points of a demonstration or performance may be copied. The teacher needs therefore to make certain that the demonstration is good in every aspect of the skill which is being shown.

3. As a corollary to the last point, imitation may be conscious or unconscious; the learner may try consciously to imitate what the teacher is aiming to teach, but may also unconsciously pick up movements or knowledge associated with the demonstration which the teacher had no intention of putting over. For instance, in demonstrating stencil duplicating, the teacher may omit to arrange paper, stencils and other accessories in a way which will ensure economy of movement and methodical working. What is uppermost in the teacher's mind is showing how the machine works, but the students will almost certainly—and quite unconsciously—respond in the same way in all aspects of the task when they come to perform it.

4. It is not possible for a learner to imitate immediately a complicated pattern of movements. Dancing steps need to be shown individually before they are put together; demonstrations must therefore be appropriate in content to the students' capacities and attainments and must convey quickly and clearly the essentials of such content. It is on this last count particularly that one recognizes the difference between films which interest and films which teach. In shorthand there are a few interest films but as yet no teaching films; in typewriting, filing and duplicating, films of both types exist, though the former are more numerous.

Learning by Doing

Imitation naturally presupposes practice and this is, in the acquisition of a skill, the most important essential. But just as imitation is affected by certain factors inherent in the situation and established by the teacher, so practice is subject to certain principles of learning and teaching. Learning by doing consists of a process often referred to as "trial and error" or "trial and success." There is a goal to be achieved, an attempt is made which is not wholly successful, so in the successive attempts or trials whatever is felt to be a hindrance to success is dropped, i.e. the errors. Looked at from the point of view of success, because a performer tends to gain satisfaction from successful movements or trials, these movements are repeated and "stamped in"; therefore learning is through "trial and success."

The effects of practice on learning and the conditions of practice (to secure "trial and success") are fairly easy of control and measurement and have therefore been investigated frequently. The results can be studied in the many books on experimental and educational psychology which are available in most public libraries. (See bibliography, p. 227.)

The three aspects of practice which will affect learning are its organization, the material on which the practice is to be carried out, and the methods to be used.

Organization. The aim of the practice work should always be clearly understood by the student and opportunity provided for self-assessment as opposed to teacher-assessment as this is likely to help sustained effort. In *The Principles of Teaching-method*[1] A. Pinsent makes the following point—

> Drill ceases to be drudgery when its useful purpose is clear to the pupil. If it is impossible to make a pupil of a given age realize the purpose of drill, the drill should either be discarded as unnecessary or postponed to a later more mature phase of development.

This comment assumes, of course, that there *is* a useful purpose in the drill: unhappily, this is not always, it would seem, the case with some of the drills given in shorthand and typewriting classes.

The frequency and duration of practice periods affects their value, as can the time of day or the previous activity of the students. To illustrate the point of the students' previous activity, it is a common

[1] Pinsent, A., op. cit.

experience of teachers that a class coming from a lesson of considerable physical activity such as a games period in physical education, takes longer to settle down and focus their attention on the next activity, especially if it calls for mental effort. Regular, frequent periods with short intervals are usually to be preferred to longer periods and long intervals. But the age and stage of attainment of the students are factors to be taken into account here. Younger students and less experienced students benefit most from shorter, more frequent practice periods. Older students and those with some degree of competence are capable of more sustained effort and are likely to regress less during intervals. The author knew a French champion typist who, during the two weeks immediately before a contest, spent half an hour each morning on nothing else but carriage returns in order to improve her movement and bring her action to contest level. Such concentration and refinement of a sub-skill is, of course, valuable at that level of attainment but would certainly create boredom, frustration or fatigue for elementary students.

If the student is to know as soon as possible the results of his efforts, then obviously the teacher must supervise the practice work not by ust being in the room and (as is sometimes the case in typewriting lessons) sitting at her desk so that the students bring their work to her to mark and then return to their typewriters to carry on with the next exercise or repeat the first, according to her instructions. In any skill the manner of performance is at least as important as the final product; indeed, it often determines the quality of the product. Moreover, we have already seen that satisfaction and confidence are important contributors to progress and sustained effort; therefore it is the duty of the teacher to be able to give such help for it is during the early stages of practice that the future expert is given a healthy start, or stifled.

Lack of ventilation, a temperature too high or too low for comfortable working, poor lighting and unsuitable seating arrangements all inhibit effective practice by causing fatigue and a feeling of discomfort.

Practice Material. Practice material should be within the capacity of the student, but not so easy that it engenders boredom.

Practice material should have meaning for the student, either through its content or its purpose. Material which can be understood by the student is learned more easily than nonsense and can often be the means of incidental acquisition of collateral knowledge in addition to achieving its primary aim.

In addition to being meaningful, practice material can be purposeful. By this is meant that a situation is provided in which the knowledge or skills to be acquired form a natural part of an integrated task. Human beings of all ages often set themselves the task of learning one thing not because they have a direct interest in it, but because it is needed in the pursuit of another activity. A stamp collector, for instance, would probably take the trouble to practise small, neat printing or writing in order that his stamp album might have a neat appearance; his real interest is not in the printing but in the stamps. In some cases, as for example a typewriting class, it is common practice for work to be given which is to be used perhaps by another member of staff. In all experiments undertaken to assess the value of such work it has been found that the students have worked better and produced more accurate work than when similar material was given as an exercise. Against this method there is the argument that it engenders fortuitous learning and that sound, logical progression through a planned scheme of work is rendered difficult. Once again it is not a question of "either . . . or," but of careful planning to include both types of work according to the capacities and needs of the students.

Summary of Principles for Effective Practice

1. The aim of the practice must be precise.
2. The student must understand the aim of the practice.
3. The aim must be appropriate to the needs and capabilities of the student.
4. The practice period should be sufficiently long for the students to gain benefit from it, but not longer than is necessary to achieve the aim.
5. If signs of fatigue, boredom or frustration are noticed, the practice should be stopped.
6. Periods devoted to drills should always be of short duration, but should be regular and frequent.
7. The physical conditions in the room (accessibility of materials, lighting, temperature, ventilation) should be as good as possible.
8. The same goal or the same practice material (especially drills)

will not always be appropriate for a whole class or group. Material and goals should be selected to help individual students.

9. During practice the teacher should observe the technique and work habits of the students.

10. Praise for improved technique (however slight) is more important than correction. It helps to build up the confidence of the learner—an important feature in skill acquisition. Praise is especially important with the less successful students.

11. Students learn more effectively if the material on which they practise is meaningful to them.

12. Purposeful material (material which will be used) is often more valuable than mere exercises, but it must be appropriate to the stage of attainment of the student and must never be out of step with the planned course.

Whole or Part Learning

The main object of practice is the consolidation of knowledge or movements to the degree that forgetting does not take place. Practice must therefore be continued, as Pinsent puts it, "well beyond the critical point at which the material learned can just be recalled, or the task just accomplished with effort."

Practice material should ensure forward progression in the knowledge or skill. In this way confidence will be built up and, particularly in skill acquisition, confidence is an essential requisite for performance.

Size of Learning or Practice Unit. In learning a skill it is almost always necessary to analyse the total skill, choose the appropriate sub-skills and practise them separately before attempting any series of them together. However, it is just as necessary to avoid over-analysis as it is to avoid over-complex units. If the skill is broken down too far the resulting units of practice may hold little meaning for the learner or may engender habits which prevent the ultimate fusion of the parts. B. R. Bugelski[1] gives this warning on analysis and separate learning—

> . . . when parts are learned separately but where a number of parts must be strung together in the final test, . . . there is some danger that the associations will not be set up between the end of one section and the beginning of the

[1] *The Psychology of Learning* (New York, Henry Holt & Co. Inc.; London, Methuen & Co. Ltd., 1956).

next. The student would be well advised to practise the connexions or transitions even though he believes he knows them, and in a sense finds that there is nothing to practise. It is not unusual, however, to find the classroom orator or even the amateur actor caught in a rut of repetition or waiting for a cue. Once the cue is given, a lengthy speech may follow.

Typewriting teachers would do well to bear these points in mind when selecting practice material for their students.

Knowledge of Results. One of the features of the modern teaching machines (with which a good deal of work has already been done in America and which are now being given a trial in this country) is that they give the learner the result of his effort *immediately*. If the learner makes a move on a keyboard training machine or gives information to a question on a machine teaching a non-skill subject, the machine immediately accepts or rejects the answer and in the latter case the learner must try again or be presented with the same information in a different form. This procedure can, of course, be followed in a classroom, but not for every student for the whole of the learning time. All previous studies of the learning process confirm that ignorance of results reduces learning effort and hinders progress. But knowledge of results alone is not sufficient; students need to be given guidance on what to do to improve and also the right kind of remedial material on which to work.

Speed and Accuracy. It is not only in the field of learning to typewrite that the question arises of whether the aim should be to develop accuracy first because speed will improve automatically, or whether this method prevents the learner from acquiring the speed of which he would otherwise be capable if he were allowed to concentrate on speed as a separate aim. Supporters of the speed aim claim that many errors which the learner makes will drop out as experience is gained and that insistence on accuracy to the exclusion of speed sets up a barrier of "fear of making a mistake." As in many other things in life the truth lies in between the two extremes. The author has become convinced that, in learning to type, training for speed and training for accuracy need to be given separately, especially in the early stages, but this topic is discussed more fully in Chapter VIII.

The thoughts presented in the present chapter can perhaps best be summed up by quoting the following comments of Pinsent[1] in answer to his question "Why Teach?"—

> Teaching is not co-extensive with learning. . . . The good teacher knows what subject matter is most valuable, and he is the custodian of good methods of working. While it is desirable that pupils should learn as far as possible by their own personal activity, the teacher is necessary *to facilitate the learning process*. . . . The skilled teacher can adapt the teaching-processes to varying conditions and aims.

[1] Pinsent, A., op. cit.

CHAPTER VI

Class, Group and Individual Teaching

THE majority of teachers are concerned with students of different aptitudes and abilities who are brought together in one class to learn.

CLASS TEACHING

The classes vary in size and it is often no easy matter to organize the lesson periods and to select teaching material and methods which will meet the needs of all the students. To depend on class teaching in such circumstances, that is, to give the whole class the same work at the same time and for the same period of time is likely to aggravate the difficulties for the students and to lead to the need for much correction, remedial work and revision for the teacher. Since the general tendency with a class of mixed ability is for the work to be aimed at the level of the majority, i.e. the average, it follows that the more capable students may become bored and not achieve the higher standard of which they are capable (and to which they are entitled to be guided), while the weaker students may lose interest through frustration.

GROUP TEACHING

One alternative is to split the class into groups and teach each group separately for a portion of each lesson, leaving them to practise while another group is being taught. Two obvious advantages of this method are that different levels of students are catered for in both teaching and practice work and that there can be closer teacher-student contact. This latter point is particularly valuable in the lower ability groups since their members are often reluctant to ask questions of an elementary nature before the other brighter students, yet the knowledge thus missed may be essential to their progress. Group work is also economical of the teacher's time in the classroom compared with individual teaching, but makes greater demands on it in the matter of preparation than does class teaching.

Two serious disadvantages are that (*a*) the class may not acquire a corporate spirit, and (*b*) not all the members of the group will make the necessary effort or work at a reasonable pace during the practice periods.

INDIVIDUAL TEACHING

Individual teaching for the whole of the lesson period in a class of normal size is unsatisfactory from several points of view. The strongest argument against it is that the students lose the benefit of stimulation through exchange of ideas, of class questioning and of learning from one another; it also means that each student can receive the attention of the teacher for only a few minutes in each period and this leads to a slower pace of work by all. There is, too, the fact that a student may be held up by some difficulty yet the teacher will be occupied with other students and so time is wasted or incorrect work done. All these conditions can lead to indiscipline with some students and to resentment at lack of progress with others.

REPEATED CYCLES OF WORK

The solution is a combination of class teaching, group work and individual work. A good plan is a "cycle of work," i.e. to select from the range of work to be covered the main topics which must be thoroughly known by everyone and arrange to give a short exposition of each (not more than ten minutes) on several (say, three) occasions during the session to a whole class. Let us assume that there are three groups in the class—1, the more advanced group; 2, the intermediate group; and 3, the more elementary group. On the first exposition, Group 1 will receive the new knowledge and follow it up with practice, while the other two groups receive it as background knowledge only; on the second occasion, Group 2 will be able to apply it, Group 1 will receive it as revision and be able to answer questions on it, while for Group 3 it will still be background knowledge; on the third occasion, Group 3 will be the group to apply the knowledge and the other two groups will listen and take part in the exposition as a revision exercise and follow up with more difficult applications than Group 3. This system is repeated for the other topics. It has the advantage of giving the maximum amount of student activity and of providing opportunity for revision and consolidation in a systematic and logical manner.

There should, of course, be some individual work in every class and some individual consultation with the teacher. The combination of class, group and individual tuition avoids the necessity of the teacher having to try to do the impossible, namely, to give adequate time to each student individually at every class meeting.

COURSE AND LESSON PLANNING

The first principle which comes to mind when thinking of course and lesson planning is the fact that the role of the teacher cannot be limited to the imparting of knowledge. The subject matter or the skill to be taught is, of course, of primary importance but, as we have already seen, unconscious or unwitting teaching (and learning) is liable to take place in any lesson. The aim of any teacher should be twofold, for all human beings need more than training for economic independence. Every teaching situation, no matter what the subject or what the age or background of the students, presents opportunities for helping those involved (both students and teacher) to widen their horizons, perhaps to develop a much-needed self-confidence, to make contact with other minds; in short, to develop as people.

A second principle on which a teacher must plan and which also has some bearing on the first is that no subject can be taught well without reference to others. This is a fairly obvious statement in respect of shorthand and typewriting, and English, since the two skills are linguistic in their content, but the concept is true of all subjects considered in their entirety, though not necessarily in all their parts. It is probably possible, for instance, to teach and learn some sections of grammatical knowledge in a language, or some routines of double-entry book-keeping, without reference to any other fields of knowledge. In general, however, the opportunities are countless, but they need to be seized. It has become almost a commonplace to say that true education depends not so much on *what* is taught, but on *how* it is taught. The point may perhaps be strengthened by an analogy between the possible effects of teaching in the sense of educating and the effects of wide reading as described by T. S. Eliot in an essay entitled "The Experience of Literature." There he says—

> Wide reading is not valuable as a kind of hoarding, an accumulation of knowledge, or what sometimes is meant by the term "a well-stocked mind." It is valuable because in the process of being affected by one powerful personality after another, we cease to be dominated by any one, or by any small number. The very different views of life, cohabiting in our minds, affect each other, and our own personality asserts itself and gives each a place in some arrangement peculiar to ourself.

All teachers may not be "powerful personalities" in the generally accepted meaning of the words, but in planning courses and lessons they are powerful to the extent that it is they who determine whether the subject or section of the subject shall be taught with or without vision, whether the students shall be merely "instructed" or whether a conscious effort will be made to enrich their background. Professor A. N. Whitehead[1] expresses the same idea in his oft-quoted passage—

> The antithesis between a technical education and a liberal education is fallacious. There can be no adequate technical education which is not liberal, and no liberal education which is not technical; that is, no education which does not impart both technique and intellectual vision.

It is through the approach to the subject, through taking the opportunities to link one field of knowledge with another, through the conviction that "training" is not the only function of the teacher, that the ways and means of teaching with vision, and of giving the "adequate education" will be found.

Lessons should not be planned as discrete items. Learning is a continuous process but what is learned can also be forgotten. The term "law of use and disuse" found in psychological studies reminds us of the universality of this fact. Lessons are also but the elements of a course and the course generally aims to present a unified body of knowledge. The wise teacher will seek ways of linking new knowledge to old, not only for ease of comprehension of the new, but also to help retention of the old. In this connexion there is sometimes a misapprehension on the part of inexperienced teachers; they assume that, in order to ensure retention of what has been taught, every lesson must begin with recapitulation of the previous lesson. This method, though useful on occasions, will not guarantee the lively interest of the students during the recapitulation period, even though different methods may be used, and if interest is not present, the object of the method is defeated.

Recapitulation and Revision

The terms "recapitulation" and "revision" tend to be somewhat loosely used and for the benefit of those who have found them to be rather confusing the following useful definitions by A. Pinsent[2] are quoted—

> The primary purpose of recapitulation is to facilitate a clear, accurate grasp, by the learner, of the material to be learned, as a whole; to give a conspectus. Recapitulation should aid understanding rather than memorizing as such. In

[1] *The Aims of Education* (London, Ernest Benn Ltd., 1959 ed.).
[2] *The Principles of Teaching-method* (London, George G. Harrap & Co. Ltd., 1952).

so far as it aids understanding it also aids recall, but the latter is not its main purpose.

The recapitulation of a lesson or lecture should bring clearly to the notice of the learner, and emphasize, the *significant* elements to be learned. In recapitulation these significant items are recalled or re-presented if necessary, (*a*) to test whether apprehension and understanding are adequate, and (*b*) to enable the learner to correct errors and fill in gaps in the previous learning. . . .

Revision, on the other hand, should aim at *memorizing* the selected material after its interrelations have been grasped. Revision plays the same part in ideational learning as practice plays in the acquisition of skill. It off-sets the loss due to lapse of time, secures long retention, and facilitates accurate speedy recall on subsequent occasions.

If we accept this distinction it may be said that recapitulation is teacher-stimulated, while revision is student-activated. In the former the teacher works with the students, amplifying, correcting and guiding; in the latter, for which definite periods of time should be allocated, the students will repeat and apply the knowledge selected for revision.

SELECTION IN TEACHING

All teaching involves selection. Because of the need to present knowledge in more than one way, to link old knowledge with new, to recapitulate, and to give students an opportunity to apply immediately what they have been taught, it is obvious that the amount of knowledge which it is practicable or desirable to present in any one lesson period must be relatively small. It is a common failing of new teachers in their first few lessons to try to put over far too much material and have no time to "get it home" with the result that little learning is achieved and therefore the teaching can be said to have failed.

Teaching methods as well as subject matter and teaching material have to be selected, for a method appropriate to one kind of material will not be suitable for another. Finally, a selection must be made of the aids (if any) to be used.

Choice of Lesson Plan

Remembering that the human mind is not so constituted that it can pay attention at a constant level of concentration and effort for more than a few minutes at a time (ten minutes has been given as the maximum, but it is dangerous to generalize) the teacher will vary the methods of presenting the knowledge and of securing response from the students. It is a good policy to select two or three items which are to be thoroughly learned in the lesson and to recapitulate and revise on these with determination. It is also wise to vary the pace of the lesson, for no student can work at "concert" pitch all through a lesson, nor should the lesson pass without requiring one or two "peaks of effort." There is an old saying that if students are not sometimes asked to do the impossible, they will not achieve the standard of which they are capable. The psychologists and teachers who have studied reactions in different learning situations provide evidence that people respond to challenge by greater effort and concentration. Such short periods of peak effort should be followed by activities designed to relax the tension and consolidate rather than demand new learning. It is often very satisfying to students if the lesson can finish on a peak, either of interest or of effort. If there is a tendency for all lessons to finish in a slack manner, students acquire a habit of reducing effort automatically at a certain time because the rhythm of the lesson engenders the feeling that the rest of the lesson will not be important or interesting.

A teacher will naturally wish to know whether a lesson has been successful, that is, whether the students have learned what he set out to teach. To find this out time must be given, within the lesson, for some form of testing. This does not mean that there must be a formal test, handed in so that marks may be awarded. The most effective kind of testing is that which gives the student *immediate* knowledge of whether he is right or wrong and an opportunity to have doubtful points clarified. A lecture to an unknown audience given on one specific occasion is not *teaching*, nor is a lesson in which there is no two-way traffic in ideas.

It is perhaps unnecessary to conclude this section by saying that however excellent the lesson plan, it should never be given "in spite of" the class; lesson plans should be servants, not masters, and can and should be departed from partly, or even wholly, if the needs or reaction of the students warrant it. Sensitivity to the mood and needs of the class is invariably found to be one quality of a good teacher and it is this sensitivity which will determine what use is to be made of the lesson plan.

Summarizing, we can say that the points on p. 70 are some of the important principles to be borne in mind when planning a subject course or drawing up plans of lessons.

1. Every course or lesson is an opportunity for the teacher to offer something towards the development of the students as people.

2. All subjects have some interrelation and cannot therefore be well taught in isolation.

3. Each lesson plan should take account of the fact that previous knowledge is lost if not used.

4. Lesson planning means selection of subject matter and method. It is better to ensure satisfactory learning of a little knowledge than to risk confusion through the presentation of much.

5. Human attention oscillates. It is therefore wise to vary the kinds and the pace of activities within a lesson period.

6. Human beings usually respond to challenge. It is the teacher's duty to "cause to learn" by stimulating students to make the best effort of which they are capable. Challenging them from time to time with a goal which seems impossible of attainment can bring success and positive gains in learning.

7. It is more important for the teacher to know what the students have *not* grasped than what they have. The students benefit from immediate knowledge of success or failure. Opportunities for students to show the extent of their understanding are therefore necessary in every lesson.

Choice of Teaching Material and Methods

The main considerations which will determine the choice of material and methods arise from some of the principles of learning which have already been discussed in Chapter V and which we know have been confirmed by practising teachers as well as by the experimental work of psychologists in this field.

The Aims of the Lesson. If the aims are definite and appropriate to the class the students are likely to be stimulated to take an interest, or be motivated to make an effort, and finally, to derive satisfaction.

The Capacity of the Students Generally and their Attainment in the Subject being taught. In this case the material and methods will be graded in difficulty according to the standards of the students and when this is done individual differences will be taken into account and this in turn will lead to success more often than to failure.

The Teacher's and the Students' Interests. The use of the teacher's interests when choosing teaching material, especially in shorthand and typewriting, can lead to inspiration for the students and enrichment of their learning. Linking the material through which a certain subject is taught to the interests of the students is likely to create the right mental set towards the subject, to help understanding through the opportunity afforded to the students to make their own association of ideas, and to good relationship (social atmosphere) between teacher and taught because the students feel that the teacher is not just putting over subject matter in an impersonal way.

The Opportunities which Material and Methods offer for Enriching the Learning of the Students. Learning is more likely to be stimulating and permanent if the unity of the knowledge being taught can be seen by the students. The comment in the McNair Report that "the good technical teacher is no mere technician; he is also an interpreter of the world," is no less true of any teacher, and within the limits of any subject possibilities exist for the teacher to choose material which will be in accord with this principle.

In the matter of interest and enrichment of the learning situation, however, the teacher needs to keep things in perspective; over-enthusiasm for interest and enrichment may lead to a neglect of the main purpose, namely, to teach a particular section of the subject matter or to develop a certain skill. Again, the conditions for transfer should be kept in mind; as Bugelski[1] has pointed out "the transfer of content and methods or techniques is not a random affair but depends on the relationships between the materials in question." In an experiment by L. Postman and J. L. Senders (1946) which Bugelski reports, results "showed that while the subjects did better on features which they have been instructed to observe [during the reading of a short story] they also answered questions based on the other instructions." The degree of such incidental learning can obviously vary, but it is likely to be greater if the students' attention is drawn to the "incidental" knowledge which it is desired to convey.

TESTING AND TEACHING

Testing is often thought of only in terms of finding out what the students *have learnt* and on grading them according to their degree of success on a "qualifying" standard set for the class as a whole. Such a

[1] *The Psychology of Learning* (New York, Henry Holt & Co. Inc.; London, Methuen & Co. Ltd., 1956).

standard may take little or no account of the progress or weaknesses of the individual students. It is natural that both teacher and students should be anxious to know what learning has been achieved, but there is a difference between testing for grading and testing for learning. In the former case it is generally necessary for the test to be of a formal nature, for everybody to be given the same questions and for marks to be awarded; in the latter, the aim of the teacher will be to find out where individual students need help in understanding ideas, in the ability to recall information, or in the performance of a particular skill. Methods of testing will vary, and the content will also vary with the needs of the students, either in groups or individually. If the student is to be able to build up knowledge and skill it is more important for the teacher to know what he has not learnt than what he has. If we go back to our general principles of learning and remind ourselves that only a small proportion of what we read or hear is retained unless there is reiteration, application and repetition, we see that testing in the sense of constantly finding out what is not being comprehended and absorbed is far more important than testing for grading. Robert S. Ellis[1] of California classifies the function of tests as follows—

1. [Tests given] at the end of a course for the purpose of measuring achievement and, more specifically, for determining what students had passed and what students had failed.

2. Tests . . . have a very important influence on the methods of study used by students. If a teacher announces that an essay test or a true-false test will be given over a given assignment, the class will tend to make the kind of preparation best suited for the particular test. (In general it may be said that the tests will be more valid and reliable if the teacher does announce in advance the nature of the test.)

3. Tests provide an opportunity for student expression. Reaction is an important part of the complete learning process. Without tests, learning would tend to be too much a process of absorption. If we are to use knowledge, we must usually be able to recall it. Frequently a student thinks he knows a topic, but when he tries to recall it he realizes that his knowledge is inadequate. Knowledge is not satisfactory until expression in proper form is possible.

4. Tests given after teaching and during the course of the term are a most important basis for the location of errors resulting from learning. No teacher and no student is perfect. For this reason it becomes important to locate errors that still persist and make an attempt to correct them. Tests should be analysed for this purpose.

5. Tests furnish a basis for marks and reports of progress.

6. Tests . . . supply an additional motive for studying. . . . Students make

[1] *Educational Psychology* (Princeton, D. Van Nostrand Co. Inc., 1951).

better progress in learning when they have a knowledge of the progress they are making.

Ways of Testing

These may be briefly summarized thus—

1. Oral question and answer.
2. Written question papers—
   (*a*) for essay-type answers;
   (*b*) in "objective test" form.
3. Practical application of knowledge or skill (e.g. in the carrying out of a set task, or in solving a problem).

Oral Question and Answer. This method is useful when immediate checking of knowledge is required or when the teacher feels that opportunities to recall will help thorough learning. In asking questions orally the teacher can modify the question or give "clues" if answers are not readily forthcoming so that students are helped towards a correct answer. In such cases the teacher is using a form of testing for teaching purposes. Answers given orally may also help to stimulate interest, or questions from the class. Some less confident students may even be encouraged to give answers when they realize that other, allegedly brighter, students do not have all the answers. Questions should also be modified to suit individual students and so give all a chance of success.

Oral questioning has, however, its disadvantages; it is rarely possible to question every student in a class during one class period. Secondly, there is a tendency for certain students to be so ready with answers that other students become discouraged and give up active participation, not bothering even to think out an answer. Thirdly, testing by oral questioning is not a convenient technique for the awarding of marks, although this is not a serious disadvantage since other forms of testing can provide ample opportunities for mark records.

If questioning of every member of a class is not possible in one period, an obvious technique to ensure that no one is omitted for too long a period is for the teacher to use a list on which she ticks the names of those who have been questioned. Another useful method, especially if the teacher wishes to question at random, is to have a small card for each student placed in random order for the first period of questioning and, as each student is named, to turn the card over and to place this face downwards at the bottom of the pack. The teacher then knows that those students whose cards are facing upwards have not yet been questioned and can start the questioning with them in the next lesson.

It is recommended that a question should be asked of the whole class first, so that everyone has a chance to think about it, and then one student named to give the answer. Although a good deal of questioning in the classroom is bound to be spontaneous, some questions should be planned for every lesson. This is important not only to ensure that students are tested on the core of the lesson, but also in order to ensure satisfactory wording of the questions. The wording should enable the students to comprehend quickly what is being asked for and it should generally be such that it calls for more than a "yes" or "no" answer. If it is desired to test what might be called "items of knowledge," such as dates, technical terms, statistical information, etc., the objective form of test is most useful. J. H. Panton[1] summarizes the features of good oral questions thus—"They should be so worded that they are free from ambiguity, pertinent, challenging and stimulating."

When the oral questions come from a member of the class there is sometimes a tendency for the teacher to direct his whole attention to the questioner, even to moving towards the student's desk, with the result that what amounts to a conversation between them ensues which excludes the rest of the class. Sometimes, too, the question is not easily heard by the other students. Needless to say, if these things happen the interest of the other students is likely to wane and, at worst, the discipline of the class will suffer. It is important, therefore, that questions to or from the class should be clear and audible and that the answers should be directed to the whole class. A student's questions can with advantage often be thrown to the class and the answer drawn from them.

Essay-type Test. In such a test students are required not only to have the knowledge which is being sought, but also to be able to write continuous prose with a greater or lesser degree of interpretation and judgement according to the subject and the stage of its study. The student is expected to organize his material and present it logically and in correct English; errors in spelling and grammar are usually penalized and the total mark is thus reduced even though the information is correct. Students naturally resent this, especially as during tests they have almost always to work at speed. In order to overcome this many

[1] *Modern Teaching Practice and Technique*, Chapter VIII (D), (London, Longmans, Green & Co. Ltd., 1948).

teachers mark class tests and homework with two marks, one for "content" and one for "form," that is, from the latter mark deductions are made for English errors and the student thus knows his exact mark for subject knowledge.

As with oral questions, written questions should be graded in difficulty so that the weakest student may be successful at something and also that the brightest may have an opportunity to give of his best. Some teachers prefer to start with the easiest questions and finish with the most difficult; others prefer a random arrangement in the belief that the weaker members may without realizing it, tackle a rather more difficult question and be successful. If questions are of varying grades of difficulty there is the problem of the number of marks to be allocated to each. In a paper in which all questions are of equal difficulty the same mark can be allocated to each; but this is not always satisfactory with graded questions. It should be a matter for consultation between members of the staff so that a recognizable standard may be set up for all classes. One of the greatest needs in secretarial courses today throughout the country is the establishment of more uniformity in marking schemes.

In connexion with the procedure for marking written answer papers, most authorities recommend that each question should be marked in turn throughout the batch of scripts as in this way it is possible to maintain a more even standard of marking different answers on the same topic. Another recommendation is that after every fifteen to twenty answers have been marked a comparison should be made of the papers scoring similar ratings—if the possible total is twenty marks, those scoring fifteen should be looked at together, then the fourteen's and so on. This procedure is especially valuable where there are a large number of scripts and marking has to be spread over several sessions. Although many teachers prefer to mark numerically, others prefer a literal grading from A down to E, i.e. A = excellent, B = very good, C = satisfactory, D = weak and E = failure. Plus and minus signs may be added to each, thus A, A−, B+, B, B−, C+, C, C−, D+, D, E, in this case securing eleven grades. The pass mark for a particular test depends on the aim and form of the examination or test, the stage and the subject.

The Objective, or Short-answer Test. This form of test consists of various types of items (small units of information rather than topics for discussion) to which the answers are expressed by means of single words, underlining, or ticks and crosses for "right" and "wrong." Examples of some of the forms such tests can take—"true-false," "multiple choice," "matching" and "completion"—are given below.

1. *True-false Test.* Directions: in the following statements, indicate those which are true by putting *o* in the parentheses—

( ) Downward *r* initially is never written before *m*.

( ) After simple *t*, *d*, the *-shun* hook is always written on the right-hand side.

The following items are false, and this fact is indicated by the zeros in parentheses. Replace the word(s) in italics by a word or words which will make the statement true—

(*o*) To type on lined paper one should use the *paper release lever*.

(*o*) *Bank paper* is generally used for stencil duplicating.

2. *Multiple Choice Test.* (Generally five items are given, from which the correct one is to be underlined.) Directions: underline the correct word(s) in the following sentences—

(*a*) The instruction to change letters from capitals to small letters is given by the term "transpose," "run on," "lower case," "caret," "italics."

(*b*) "Record," "bichrome," "stencil," "carbon," "platen" is the name for a red/black ribbon.

3. *Matching Test.* Directions: in the parentheses at the right, place the number of the word from the left-hand column opposite the one in the right-hand column that it most accurately describes—

1. stapling press	in typewriting made by using small *c* and comma	( )
2. paper table	gives 12 letters to 1 in.	( )
3. elite type	made by using solidus	( )
4. sloping fraction	small handpress for fastening papers together	( )
5. cedilla	part of typewriter at back of cylinder	( )

4. *Completion Test.* Directions: in each sentence, fill in the blank with the word(s) necessary to complete the sentence—

(*a*) Paper measuring 10 in. wide by 16 in. long is called ......

(*b*) The method of typing a name and address with each line beginning at the same point on the scale is called ......

(*c*) The method of allowing a wider top margin on the first page of typed matter is called a ......

Disadvantages of the Objective Test.[1]

Generally, it is limited to the more factual elements of the course. It stresses the meanings of terms, definitions, opinions, and quantitative materials.

In order to keep the test as objective as possible, questions or items are omitted for which no one incontrovertible answer exists. Therefore, some of the best material in literature, history, sociology and other subjects must be excluded because it is speculative and hypothetical.

The usual objective examination does not provide an opportunity for the student to do independent and original thinking. The feature of this form of examination that keeps the student from bluffing also prevents the good student from speculating and expressing whatever original points of view he might have.

The objective examination causes the student to study in a manner that is not conducive to high scholarship.

Desirable Features of the Objective Examination.[1]

The objective examination handicaps the bluffer, for he is called upon to give precise and definite answers.

The items can be accurately scored. The score has a definite meaning in terms of the score of other students in the class. The instructor can feel more confident of the fairness of his marking standards.

One of the features that has made the objective type of examination popular is the ease with which it can be scored.

The objective test can cover the material of an area or field more completely than the subjective test can. It can sample the course materials more thoroughly. Because of the many items in the objective test no large section of subject matter is omitted.

This chapter has introduced in a very general and necessarily brief manner topics which are of importance to all teachers and to teachers of shorthand and typewriting in particular. Since shorthand and typewriting are linguistic skills, the opportunities for broadening the students' English and general knowledge through the selection of dictation and copying material occur in practically every lesson. This topic is taken up in greater detail in Chapters VII, VIII and X. Again, the pace of the lessons in shorthand and typewriting is of extreme importance, for these skills are not acquired without the stimulus of pace and drive. Finally, the knowledge on which the skills are based is cumulative, especially in shorthand. If gaps are left, bad habits may

[1] Sorenson, Herbert, *Psychology in Education*, New York, McGraw-Hill Publishing Co. Inc. 1948).

develop or failure result. Therefore revision and testing must be based on sound principles of teaching and learning. In the succeeding chapters the general teaching principles are taken up again and linked with the specific tasks involved in preparing and presenting lessons in the respective skills of shorthand, typewriting and transcription.

CHAPTER VII

Teaching Shorthand

ONE of the aims in the previous chapters has been to recall those general principles of teaching and learning which are of particular importance in teaching the skills of shorthand, typewriting and transcription. The aim of the next four chapters is to link those general principles with the practice of teaching. In the case of shorthand, reference is made only to the teaching of Pitman shorthand, as this is the most widely used system in this country.

It would be impossible for any reasonably sized volume to be exhaustive in coverage of methods and material for the teaching of any subject. The methods and types of material mentioned in the following pages are those which the author or other teachers have found effective and they are given as indications of what *may* be used, not of what *must* be used. No teaching situation is static and no two classes are identical; the skilful teacher is knowledgeable about methods and material, but selects according to the needs of the particular classes he is teaching. Some methods are used successfully by some teachers and not by others; some students react favourably, others unfavourably to one type of material. This does not mean that any method, or any material will do; there must always be selection and the teacher needs always to know why the choice is being made. Such questions as: "What benefit do I expect the students to gain from this material?" "Is this method the most economic for student learning?" "Would a shorter method achieve the same results?" "Is this material sufficiently challenging for the stage of attainment reached by the students?" are all pertinent in the task of deciding how and with what material to teach.

THE CLASSROOM AND ITS ORGANIZATION

Shorthand classes require little equipment or special classroom arrangement compared with many other subject classrooms and it is perhaps because of this that even the minimum requirements are sometimes overlooked.

Obviously the room should have good natural and artificial lighting and should not be overcrowded with desks and other furniture. Indeed, the arrangement of the desks is the first priority in a shorthand classroom, for since shorthand is a skill subject, supervised practice is essential. The desks should therefore be arranged so that there are sufficient gangways to allow the teacher to walk round and watch individual students writing. *How* one writes shorthand and the habits formed in the early stages of learning are as important as *what* one writes. If the teacher has not such access to each student, it will mean that some students take longer than is necessary to acquire good habits and to this extent the teacher is inefficient through no fault of his own.

Normally the desks supplied by education authorities allow for a comfortable writing position but teachers of shorthand sometimes accept without comment the fact that the desks are too high or too low and that the students are therefore forced to adopt bad postures.

It is relevant here to mention the question of writing position for the shorthand student. This means a position, not by any means uniform for a whole class, but one which enables the writer to achieve fluency and speed in writing as well as the habit of turning the notebook quickly and automatically.

It must be stressed that good posture and handling of tools (notebook and pen) must become habits, and both teacher and student must realize that habits are not formed in one lesson or by the student being told what to do. From the first lesson the teacher must demonstrate, supervise and guide students until the good habits are well established. If good habits are not formed, bad ones will be. Far too often in elementary and intermediate classes one sees students writing shorthand with the left hand supporting the head instead of being on the book ready to turn the page. A method which should be used frequently and regularly in the earlier stages is to ask students to start writing from dictation on the third line from the bottom of the notebook; the teacher then dictates sentences or a paragraph sufficiently long for the students to turn over and fill two lines of the next page. The blank lines on the previous page can be used later for other appropriate work.

Equipment

Although only a well-equipped shorthand classroom will have all the items in the following list, those marked with an asterisk may be considered essential.

*1. Desks and chairs for teacher and students.
*2. Chalkboard (roller type with two sections ruled for shorthand, lines $1\frac{1}{2}$ or $1\frac{3}{4}$ in. apart).
3. Clock with sweeping seconds hand.
*4. Ample display board provision.
5. Electric points for recording machines.
6. Recording machine(s).
7. Cupboard for stationery.
*8. Bookcase (small, for class reference library).
9. Textbooks and notebooks according to the needs of the classes using the room.
*10. Shorthand reference books (dictionaries, shorthand and English; small encyclopedia; atlas).
*11. Stop-clock (this is preferable to a stop-watch, as it is easier to watch and is less likely to be dropped).

CHOICE OF TEACHING APPROACH

As we have seen in Chapter II, shorthand writing requires both knowledge and manual skill and the teacher of shorthand is therefore confronted with the problem of deciding in what order and in what form each shall be presented. Is it better to give theoretical knowledge first, with examples, and then ask students to apply it to other cases, or should the students be presented with simple shorthand material which they learn through hearing its meaning read to them and through copying work? The first of these methods has become known as the "traditional" method; it is also sometimes called the "analytical" method.

Traditional Method of Teaching

The students are taught the rules in order that they may see the reason for a given outline and so that they will be able to construct outlines for words which they have not seen in shorthand. By this method, too, dictation and speed development are given less emphasis until the whole of the theory has been taught.

Functional Method of Teaching

The second method is known as the "functional" method; its aim is to enable the student to acquire a shorthand vocabulary by mental images of complete outlines in context received from printed shorthand. In some cases no writing is done for several weeks; in others writing is started after a few lessons and the shorthand matter is copied, with and without the teacher dictating it at the same time. The theoretical knowledge is developed gradually and is not emphasized. There is little or no direct application of rules and students are not expected in the early stages of their learning to construct new outlines.

Most research workers and very many practising teachers today (including the author) advocate a great deal of reading and writing of outlines (with and without copy) in context from the earliest stages, with little emphasis on "knowing the rules," that is, being able to repeat them. As Dr. Holland[1] has said—

> if the rule be in the textbook it is not necessarily made the student's own by letting him copy it into his notebook. The sounder plan is to let him use the textbook for extra-class reading or home-work and to take plenty of dictation in class.

Yet the learning of rules by heart (without sufficient opportunities for application) and the writing of them in longhand into notebooks are fairly common practices in shorthand classes; they could with advantage be forgotten.

The author has found that students learn and understand the rules more effectively if "cues" are given during the early application of new knowledge. Thus, if the new knowledge has been the use of upward and downward *r* for vowel indication, when the students are reading Exercise 13 of *Pitman Shorthand New Course*, or the teacher is dictating it, the teacher would say, immediately the outline for "early" is reached, "Remember, downward *r* initially to show the initial vowel"; or, immediately after "injury" the comment would be "ray finally to show the final vowel." This method is also valuable for recalling to students' minds knowledge previously given, especially with regard to position writing, until there is no longer need for such help. This method follows two sound principles of teaching, (*a*) that it is better to prevent errors than to correct them, and (*b*) that students should be given opportunities for over-learning essential knowledge.

Rate of Introduction of Theory

Another problem of approach, especially with the traditional method, is whether to give a quick presentation of the theory, leaving consolidation and other aspects of the skill till the theory has been

[1] Holland, Robert W., *Principles of Teaching Applied to Pitman Shorthand* (London, Sir Isaac Pitman & Sons Ltd., 1952).

covered, or whether to take a more leisurely approach, consolidating and developing the sub-skills concurrently with the theory. For instance, advocates of the first method take only one term (seventy to eighty periods) with secretarial students from grammar schools to cover the theory and simple dictation matter at not more than 30 to 35 words per minute. The second and third terms of a one-year course are then devoted to revision, consolidation and speed development. Advocates of the second method, with similar students, would take one-and-a-half to two terms to cover the theory, but would develop writing ability on a rather wider vocabulary up to 50 words per minute and would give revision and consolidation early so that the third term could be devoted to speed development.

Theory Plus Practice

The methods of reading and copying, copying while the teacher reads the passage, and of acquiring knowledge of the theory in small units interspersed with a great deal of practice, accord with general principles of learning since they contribute to a maintenance of student interest, give an opportunity for satisfaction from achievement, and avoid meaningless, unrealistic exercises. B. J. Davis[1] of Columbia University Teachers' College studied different methods of teaching shorthand in 1936 and the following conclusions which he reached are pertinent to our present topic—

> The learning exercise should take place in the same form as final use. This implies the arrangement of material in context from the start. . . .
>
> The learning exercise should take place in the same manner as final use. This implies dictation from the very start of the learning process. Straight copying of notes is not the same as having the material dictated—the initial stimulus in one case is visual, in the other auditory.

Combining Copying and Dictation

In order to combine the advantages of copying and dictating, a good method is to allow the students to have the correct shorthand in front of them but to dictate the passage slowly. However, there is one danger about which teachers using the method for the first time should be forewarned. Since the whole purpose of dictating the matter is so that the *sound* of the word shall be associated with the *outline*, the teacher must instruct the students not to write *ahead* of his

[1] "A Study of Shorthand Teaching," *Contributions to Education*, No. 693 (Teachers' College Columbia University, 1936).

dictation. The quicker students (or the more careless) will deliberately copy faster than the dictation and, of course, in the process, are training themselves to ignore the sound. The teacher should, therefore, walk round and check any student who is going against the instructions.

The Inductive Method of Presentation

A general principle of learning which is important for all teachers to apply is that students learn more permanently and with more understanding that which they discover for themselves than that which is told to them. This has led to a form of presentation of knowledge known as the "inductive" method. It can be used within either the traditional or the functional approach and by it the students are given a number of examples from which they themselves can discover a general rule. For example, if the following outlines are written on the chalkboard 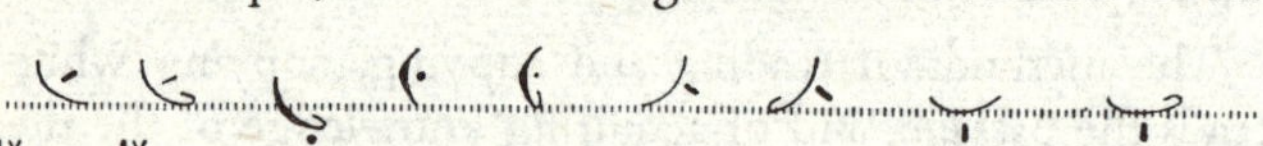 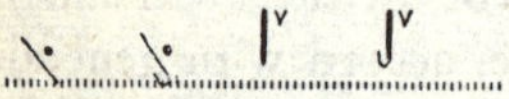 and the teacher reads them to the class, the students will easily discover that the small hook represents *n*. From the next three sets of examples—

2. 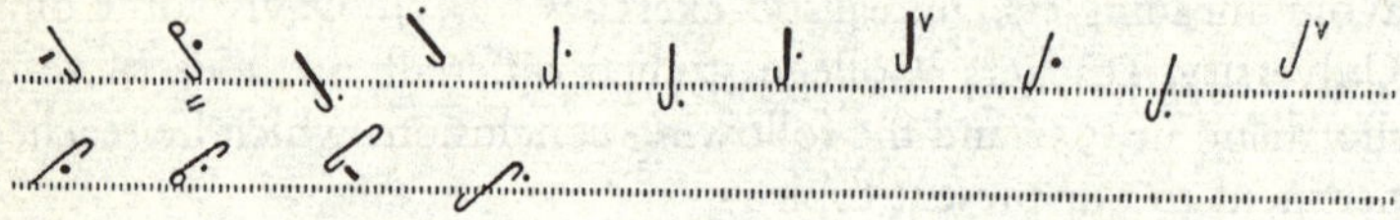

3. 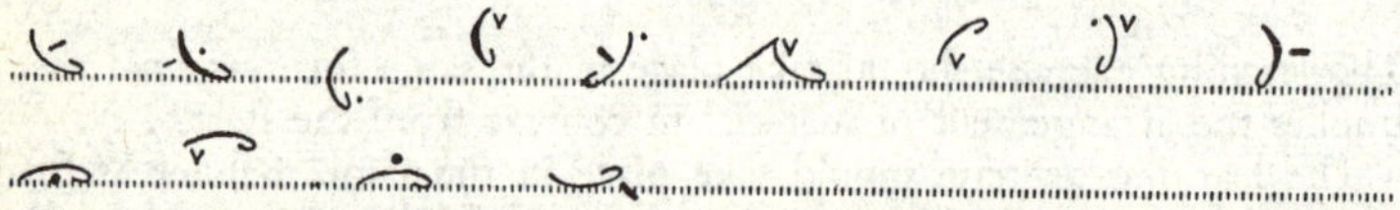

4. 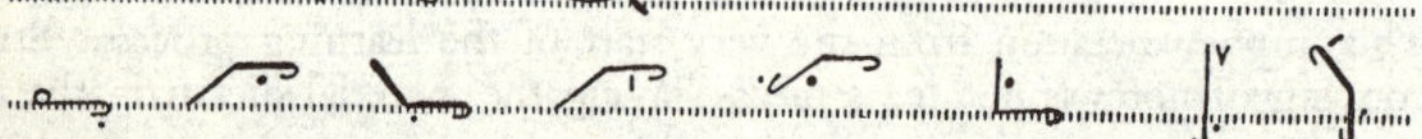

they will be able to discover the position of *n* hook in relation to the respective forms of stroke consonants. The outlines are then practised (both by reading and writing), some as isolated outlines, some in context, with the teacher reminding students, when this seems advisable, of the *n* position. The time required for presentation by this method is rather longer than by the more direct "telling" method, but if understanding is made easier and the resultant learning is more permanent, there will be a gain rather than a loss of time in the long run as less time will be required for revision or for remedial work. However, it is *a* method, not *the* method and all sections of the shorthand theory are not necessarily better presented and learned in this way. The skill of the teacher in deciding when to use this or that method is still of paramount importance.

The Omission of Vowel Signs

Closely allied to the problem of what general approach shall be made is a question inherent in Pitman shorthand, namely, the insertion or omission of vowel signs. Former longhand writing habit interferes in the early stages of learning Pitman shorthand because of the difference in the order of writing the vowel signs in the two ways of writing. Old habits are difficult to modify and it is not easy for a beginner to think quickly of the consonantal skeleton of an outline and then revert to the vowels. After some experience it becomes so easy that one wonders how it was that there was any resistance at all in the first place. But, of course, the resistance was one of habit. Many teachers have found that to avoid this feeling it is better not to emphasize the thorough "learning" and the constant insertion of vowel signs at first, but to explain them for reading purposes (so that they are "recognition knowledge" only) and to require their insertion only gradually as they are useful for fluent reading and are used naturally in note-taking. The author has the habit even in fast writing of always inserting a vowel in certain words, and of never omitting diphthongs, triphones and diphones unless extremely pushed. To train students to be sufficiently mentally alert when taking notes in order to recognize when a vowel sign would be useful to fluent reading is to train good transcribers. If this method is adopted the progress in the early stages is more rapid. Other teachers go so far as to omit the teaching of the vowel signs completely for writing purposes.

WORD FREQUENCY

Shorthand is a linguistic skill and therefore it is not out of place to draw on the experience of language teachers in the matter of the teaching vocabulary. To teach the structure (the theory) of the language a controlled vocabulary is used, namely, the teaching material is confined to words of high frequency. There is abundant evidence from both research workers and classroom teachers to show that it is wrong to teach too many aspects of the language at one time. Therefore new grammar (new theory) is always presented in a limited, known vocabulary as far as possible. New words are introduced with known grammar, and new grammar introduced with known vocabulary.

This principle of a controlled vocabulary has been applied to the teaching of shorthand for a number of years and Pitman shorthand teachers are familiar with the abundant and useful material provided to cater for their needs in "common word" reading and dictation matter. Thorndike's English Dictionary also gives the frequency of all words falling within the first 10,000.

Like all good things, however, a limited vocabulary for shorthand learning has its dangers. It is so easy to continue with "common word" passages beyond the time when they have a solid value, or to use them too frequently. The result of so doing is to give students a false idea of their capacity; when they take the public examination or the test for a post their skill may break down on the unfamiliar words, with unfortunate results. Again, there may be something to be learned from a study of the progress of many students from slow writing, say, 50 words per minute to the level of about 100 words per minute. It is fairly well recognized that very many students seem to reach a plateau at round about 80 words per minute. Some reach 70 but cannot push to 80, others reach 80 but find it extremely difficult to reach 100. The following theory is put forward as worthy of consideration. It is possible to write longhand quite quickly for short periods—in a small experiment carried out by the author some years ago it was found that ex-grammar school students could copy simple material at 35 to 45 words per minute for three minutes without previous practice; that mature students who were used to note-taking for professional studies could achieve 50 to 60 words per minute, and one even wrote at 80 words per minute; younger students from secondary-modern schools achieved only 15 to 20 words per minute. If then, the mind and hand can co-ordinate at these speeds in longhand writing, provided the shorthand symbols are for well-known words and are recalled without hesitation, dictation at 50 to 60 words per minute is not demanding of our secretarial students a greater co-ordination than they are accustomed to. Many teachers will confirm that such students find it fairly easy to write common-word material at 40 words per minute early in their course, provided the dictation is for short periods. It has been said that below 40 words per minute it is almost impossible to grasp the general meaning of dictated matter and the fact that at 40 words per minute the material becomes meaningful may account for this finding. However, when speeds of over 70 words per minute are reached, the students are having to make a much greater effort to co-ordinate mental and manual skills and if at this time we also add a new task, that of dealing with less common and unfamiliar words, are we not giving the students too heavy a learning load? It is for this reason (based on experience) that the author advocates a judicious *gradual* introduction of words outside the accepted 2–3,000 common words. But this *should not be done during the first learning* of the theory. If such words are introduced during revision and consolidation periods, interest is maintained, for it cannot be denied that many students find the common-word material dull. Students from grammar school courses are particularly prone to take a dislike to shorthand in the early stages because of the lack of challenge in thought content of the material used, although they are not all necessarily conscious of the reason for their dislike.

In order to counter this lack of challenge and to prepare for the effort of exceeding 70 words per minute, the list of words in Appendix 1 was drawn up, based on knowledge of students' difficulties with these words from the point of view of (*a*) recognition of the shorthand outline, (*b*) spelling skill in transcription, or (*c*) knowledge of meaning. The list was then correlated with *Pitman Shorthand New Course* and checked against the Horn and Peterson[1] word list. Groups "A" consist mainly of words in the 3,000 frequency range, with some at the level of 4–5,000; Groups "B" fall mainly within the 6–9,000 frequency and Groups "C" mainly outside the 10,000 frequency. The author has used the list with the aim that all students should be able, by the end of their course, to deal with Group "A" words without reference to a dictionary for spelling; Group "B" words would provide vocabulary extension for the less able students, for whom Group "C" would be merely "recognition" vocabulary; for better students and older students Group "B" words should be well known and Group "C" words would be used for vocabulary extension. With the latter types of students little work was usually needed with Group "A" words, yet they were introduced regularly and spot checks made on the students' ability to spell them rapidly.

STANDARDS OF ATTAINMENT

No statistics are available to give a general picture of standards required of students at the end of their course. The reasons are obvious—

[1] Horn, Ernest and Peterson, Thelma, *The Basic Vocabulary of Business Letters* (New York, The Gregg Publishing Co., 1943).

(*a*) the great variety of course duration (anything from two to five or six terms); (*b*) variety of types of students (educational background, previous appropriate knowledge); (*c*) variation in time allocated (anything from one and a half to twelve hours a week); and (*d*) whether an internal or public examination is used as a qualifying test. Nevertheless, from information received from a number of schools and colleges, and from personal experience, one can say that there are standards to which many courses are geared and which may be summarized as follows—

Junior Students

Minimum 60 w.p.m. Some courses aim at 80 w.p.m. in an internal and/or public examination.

Senior Students

Minimum 80 or 100 w.p.m.

It is possible for the aim to be a speed of 80 words per minute on quite difficult material rather than 100 words per minute on less difficult matter. The standardization of test material is another task awaiting interested and energetic shorthand teachers. In spite of this general pattern there are many students who attain speeds of 120 and 140 words per minute at the end of their course and some who attain reporting speeds. Since 80 words per minute is just the stage at which co-ordination of ear, mind and hand is being quickened beyond previous levels, and since it is at this stage that over-learning of the outlines, through use, is only just beginning, it is a dangerous stage at which to stop training. It is the experience of many teachers that students who discontinue training and use of shorthand at about 80 words per minute suffer a greater and more permanent loss of speed and knowledge than students who continue to speeds of 100 words per minute and over before discontinuing the skill. It is possible for a high-speed writer even after a break of six months without high-speed practice, to regain peak form in two or three weeks with about an hour's regular practice each day.

THE SHORTHAND SYLLABUS

this is a separate document from the scheme of work it will consist of—

1. Requirements, if any, for entry to the course.

2. Time allocation, e.g. eight periods weekly of fifty minutes each.

3. Aims of the course, e.g.—

To give a sound knowledge of the theory of Pitman shorthand.

To develop ability to take notes in neat, accurate style, at a minimum of 80 words per minute on matter of average difficulty.

To develop ability to read and transcribe shorthand notes fluently and accurately.

To improve English knowledge (especially vocabulary and punctuation) through shorthand material and exercises.

4. Method—

Dictation will be given from the beginning and theory revision continued throughout the course.

Opportunity will be given for dictation practice from recording machines to meet the needs of students achieving varying rates of speed.

Homework will be given on three evenings a week (thirty minutes each evening).

Both timed and office-style dictation will be given and opportunities afforded for different voices to be recorded on the recording machines, so that students may get used to different styles and voices in dictation.

5. Textbooks—

Pitman Shorthand New Course

A Student's Review of Pitman's Shorthand

6. Other material—e.g. dictation matter, chosen by the teacher or students from current newspapers, periodicals and from literature.

7. Qualifying test at end of course, e.g.—

R.S.A. Shorthand-typist's examination (80 or 100 words per minute).

College practical test combined with typewriting and office practice.

Public speed examination at speed of attainment of student (R.S.A. or L.C.C.).

SCHEME OF WORK

If this is combined with the course syllabus, each item above under Aims and Method will be expanded to indicate particular items to be taught, at what stage in the course they are to be covered and more details of the methods to be used, including time and methods of revision.

Some teachers prefer to divide the work into weekly units, others into monthly, and yet others into terminal units. The most flexible unit is probably the month, but it is a matter of personal preference. In any case, a teacher should always feel free to modify a scheme of work; if a number of parallel classes are involved, the changes will of course be made after consultation with the other teachers, in order to prevent difficulties arising at the end of the term or other period of testing when one class is found to be out of step with the rest.

LESSON PLANS

As we have mentioned in Chapter I (p. 15) lessons are related to each other and to the whole course; they must therefore be planned in such a way that this fact is taken into account. In shorthand teaching account has to be taken also of the principles of skill acquisition; it is never a simple matter of "teaching this or that section of the theory," or "giving speed practice," but rather of deciding what aspects of the knowledge and of the skill are to be introduced, emphasized, practised or touched upon, and through what methods and teaching material. Naturally, in the early stages of shorthand learning more time will be spent on exposition of the theory, reading and dictation of matter exemplifying the principles of the system; at the intermediate stage theory revision and speed development will predominate, while at the more advanced stage transcription and speed development will need most attention. However, that is not to say that transcription has no place in the elementary stage; indeed, transcription training begins in the very first shorthand lesson and good or bad habits, habits which will help or hinder transcription skill, are being formed throughout the course.

Although, as has been said already, lesson notes can be set out in any form preferred by the individual teacher, the following outline, already given in Chapter I, is repeated here on p. 91.

Although it is not possible to say before a shorthand lesson exactly what is to be put on the chalkboard, it is advisable to have the basic chalkboard work planned beforehand on paper. When shorthand theory is being taught the board should show, at the end of the lesson, a very brief summary of the essential points made during the lesson

Class .... Time.................. Date..................

Aims: (Main) ....

(Subsidiary) ....

Approx. Time	*Subject Matter*	*Methods*	*Chalkboard*

Comments

....

....

and the appropriate shorthand examples. It is a good plan, if the chalkboard is large enough, to divide it into three sections to be used thus—

Summary of teaching points (shorthand theory, etc.)	Shorthand examples	Incidental matter (outlines requested by class; longhand of words unfamiliar to class)
	....	

A feature of most shorthand lessons, especially after the introduction of the theory, should be "pace." The students must feel the need for mental alertness and the need to respond from time to time to a challenge, and the teacher must realize that a gentle, even pace throughout a lesson will not provide the stimulus so necessary for speed development.

Homework

A great deal of the homework for a shorthand class will consist of reading and copying work in preparation for dictation practice in subsequent lessons. Exercises can sometimes be given in which longhand is transcribed into shorthand or vice versa, but writing longhand from shorthand is rarely the most beneficial form of exercise for the shorthand student. Shorthand is a linguistic skill and the more one sees, reads and writes it the better. The ability to read shorthand can generally be adequately tested in class orally, and the ability to transcribe shorthand (to cover points of English) is best developed through typewritten work. In order to get a shorthand reading habit established it is necessary to give interesting matter. We cannot really expect our students to become engrossed in reading shorthand for simple business correspondence; but they may respond (and the author has found that they *do*) to short passages on topical matters, on subjects in which they themselves are interested and (for later stages) to short stories.

One type of homework exercise which has been far too frequently used in the past is the learning of short forms or contractions in lists. This does not lead to economy of learning as the material is being presented in an artificial setting. Short forms are used singly, or in small groups, *in context* and they are most easily learned by *being written in context*; therefore a better homework exercise is to present students with short sentences containing a selection of short forms, have them fair copied for homework, and to dictate them the following day several times at increasing speeds. The same remarks apply to phrases and contractions.

Possible Student Activities in the Shorthand Class

Certain activities or techniques tend to become associated with the teaching of particular subjects, so much so that they become what may be termed "teaching clichés" and, like verbal clichés, lose their original force and effect through over-use. In the shorthand class, dictation and reading back must of necessity be two of the standard activities, yet they need not be standardized. Dictation can take a variety of forms, and reading need not be confined to reading dictated notes. Variation wisely made is likely to maintain or enhance interest; it also enables the teacher to focus attention from time to time on particular knowledge or elemental skills of the total skill which need reinforcing. The following list of activities, with comments on their purpose and their value to the shorthand class, is given in the hope that it will be useful to any readers who may be new to shorthand teaching.

Reading Shorthand from the Chalkboard. This enables the teacher to have the attention of the whole class directed to one focal point and to combine reading the exercise with the explanation. The matter used can be a variation of that in the textbook. Single outlines can be used for developing quick outline recognition, the teacher controlling the pace of reading by using a ruler to point to the outlines (in random order or in sequence).

Copying Shorthand from the Chalkboard. Copying from the board is not as easy for the student as it might seem; small points of detail (hooks, vowel signs, etc.) do not always "register." The constant looking up and down interferes with fluent writing. The teacher should watch what the students write and should not assume that they are copying accurately. When passages longer than one or two sentences have to be copied, individual copies of the shorthand prove more efficient than the chalkboard.

Fair Copying from Printed Shorthand. This is valuable (*a*) in the earliest stages for building up a mental image of correct outlines and (*b*) at later stages preparatory to dictation in order to prevent outline errors. Its disadvantages are that students may either write so slowly that they "draw" the outlines, or that they may copy carelessly, without thought, and therefore inaccurately. There is no guarantee that students read as they write. Printed shorthand does not give sufficient emphasis to position writing—first and third position outlines need to be respectively higher and lower for fluent reading. The teacher needs to be vigilant while students are copying.

Reading in Unison from Dictated Notes. This is a useful technique provided that the teacher notices who are the "passengers." This method saves lesson time and often helps the weaker members.

Timed Drills on Single Outlines (Including Phrases). This is a good morale and confidence booster. Drills should not be for too long (fifteen seconds is usually enough). Repeated drills should generally be for improvement of previous *individual* achievement, not competitive with other members of the class. This technique gets much necessary repetitive work and over-learning done "with a purpose."

Copying from the Textbook (or Duplicated Shorthand) while the Teacher Dictates. This is a good technique for controlling the pace of work. Care must be taken to see that students keep up with the dictation, otherwise some students will be writing ahead of the teacher. The purpose is to associate the sound of the word with the sight of the outline.

Tracing Outlines in the Air. Some teachers find this useful; the author is doubtful of its value as no teacher can check *all* the students (if the whole class traces the outline) and some students will make movements out of proportion, or completely wrong. A better method would seem to be to ask the students to write the outline in their notebooks while the teacher walks quickly round and makes a spot check.

Over-writing Printed Shorthand with the Blunt End of a Pencil, or with a Pen. These are useful techniques if done carefully. They give the students a feeling of writing quickly and fluently. Dictation should be given immediately after such an exercise as the fluent hand movement is likely to "carry over."

Individual Reading of Printed Shorthand or Dictated Matter. This can be very time-consuming and should not be carried on for long periods. The problem is whether to let a student "worry out" an outline, or allow other members of the class to prompt. Discretion is necessary. Reading of shorthand in class is for teaching, not testing; it is reading practice, therefore help from the teacher or another student should be permitted, but not before an indication from the teacher.

Copying Shorthand, Leaving Two Lines Blank, for Future Dictation. This is a very useful technique, especially as homework preparation for the next lesson. Care must be taken to ensure that the copying is correct. The first dictation can be at a slow speed in order to give the teacher time to walk round and glance at the books. If inaccurate copying is discovered, the dictation should be stopped and remedial work given instead.

Selecting Words for Use in Sentences Composed by Students. After completion of the theory, students are asked to compose and write in shorthand one sentence to introduce a selected word (one word for every three students); students dictate (in turn) sentences to the class. This method consolidates vocabulary work, gets the students actively involved in shorthand writing, and provides for purposeful repetition work (short forms and the selected words are written more than once). It is useful for homework preparation.

Copying and Slow Dictation for Shorthand Style. These are useful techniques for stimulating pride in workmanship. They also help to focus attention on detail of shorthand outlines, on size and spacing.

Through such exercises students can also be made aware of the relationship between the number of words, the lines of shorthand, and the lines of type.

Visualizing Outlines. After a few correct outlines have been written on the chalkboard and read by the students (especially as remedial work), students are asked to close their eyes while the teacher reads a word and the students indicate, by raising a finger, when they have a mental picture of the outline. Those outlines on which there is a delay are then practised again. This technique makes students aware of the difference between seeing an outline on paper and being able to recall it from writing. As a check on what has been visualized, the words should be dictated in context and corrected if necessary.

"Cold" Note Reading. This is a technique which should be used periodically in every course. It stresses the importance of reading ability and helps to develop confidence.

"Delayed" Writing. Students listen to dictation of a sentence and write shorthand after dictation is finished (the length of the sentence can be gradually increased). This technique is popular with students and helps to develop ability to retain words and to write behind a speaker. A variation of this technique is for students to take down a sentence, the first half of which is dictated slowly and the second half so quickly that they must write from memory.

Students Dictate to the Class from Shorthand which has been Previously Read. This technique provides purposeful shorthand reading. Variation of voice and style of reading is also provided; some students gain confidence and learn how to project the voice. The teacher can write the passage on the chalkboard.

Students Choose Short Prose Passages for Reading to the Class. This technique often reveals the outside interests of students and provides greater variety of dictation matter.

Two-minute Speeches by Students "Reported" by the Rest of the Class. Again, this provides variety of subject matter and style of dictation.

Students Dictate the Reply to a Letter. At first the students can be given time to prepare the reply; later, if they are capable, spontaneous replies can be given. A different letter for reply can be given to every four students. One letter is sufficient for any particular lesson.

The above list is not, of course, exhaustive; there are the more general activities of prepared and unprepared dictation, question and answer on points of theory, etc., and every teacher will discover others.

TEACHING AIDS

At one time the shorthand teacher probably had no other aid than the chalkboard and one textbook; today there is a plethora of textbooks and, in addition, most of the following aids are available on request—

1. Recording machines.
2. Charts.
3. Pictures of shorthand personalities.
4. Shorthand books and periodicals.
5. Films.
6. Film strips.
7. Tape-recorders.

Of all these aids the most important is the chalkboard; good demonstration by the teacher of movement, size of outline, direction and manner of writing, is one of the most inspiring and effective teaching aids in the shorthand class. The important point to remember, of course, is that the students should be asked to watch while the outline is being written and all outlines should be written *as one unit.* Inexperienced teachers sometimes ask a student for an outline and as it is being described will start to write the strokes, stopping when the student hesitates and starting again when the student has decided what should be written. Students unwittingly imitate this kind of writing instead of forming a mental image of the *complete* outline first and then writing it fluently. Shorthand material written by the teacher and other expert shorthand writers and duplicated is also invaluable, as it gives the necessary practice in reading more cursive styles of shorthand than the printed textbook style and serves as a link between this and the student's own notes.

Material for film strips can be prepared fairly easily by any teacher. Special exercises (not available otherwise) can be prepared for additional oral reading in preparation for transcription problems such as inserting punctuation, capitalization, etc. If the material is wisely selected for its content value, film strips can, over a period, save teaching time. They also need less space for storing than books or individual student copies.

Sources of Teaching Material

Every teacher will want to choose his or her own textbook and it frequently happens that the choice is determined by the book from which the teacher himself learned the subject. This is sometimes unfortunate, for not all textbooks are ideal class books. There are several shorthand textbooks which are unsuitable for a functional teaching approach. *Pitman Shorthand New Course* has become popular because it presents the theory in a clear, simple manner and does not go beyond 2,000 common words. Most of the matter is in shorthand and it leaves ample scope for teachers to supplement lessons with other material of their own choice to suit the needs of their particular classes.

Since it is easier to read shorthand than to take notes from dictation, there are excellent opportunities for extending the students' knowledge of English or other subjects through the *reading* material specially prepared by the teacher. One useful method is to have a short passage discussed in the English class for points of sentence structure, punctuation, content, etc., and for the shorthand teacher to present it for shorthand reading and to question the class quickly on spelling, meanings of selected words, and reasons for punctuation. Later in the course, when the students are more proficient at reading, they can have the shorthand copy in the English lesson while the English teacher holds the longhand copy. For the English class this is good material for practice in short oral summaries. For dictation matter anything topical, or of subject interest to the students, is valuable. It often happens that only part of a passage is too difficult for note-taking and this can easily be made suitable by substituting easier words and phrases. Another source of drill material is to ask students to compose and submit in shorthand sentences incorporating selected words (e.g. from the correlated word list, Appendix 1) and to use them, after checking for accuracy of construction, for speed bursts. Students can dictate their own or other students' sentences to the class so that two more purposes are served, namely, that the class has a change of dictating voice and that the teacher is free to walk round and watch students writing. If a teacher is responsible for a more advanced and also an elementary class, the former may be very pleased to prepare such material, in shorthand, for the other class to read. This provides purposeful shorthand revision and writing practice for the one class and saves the teacher some homework!

CHARACTERISTICS OF PITMAN SHORTHAND

The teacher needs to view his subject with insight, that is, with "mental vision, discernment . . . apprehending the inner nature . . ." as the dictionary defines it. With shorthand a teacher needs to reflect on how the system is constructed and why the rules exist. Any good system of shorthand must be built up on three basic principles, namely, *fluency* and *brevity* (contributing to speedy writing) and *legibility* (contributing to speedy and accurate reading). In order to achieve these basic aims different methods (rules) will be devised which will form the characteristics of the particular system. That the Pitman system of shorthand is a good one no one can deny. What then are its characteristics which emerge from the rules? Briefly they are—

1. Suggestiveness (many words having the same or similar consonantal structure are given different outlines).
2. Linearity (outlines are kept near to the line of writing to give the minimum of hand movement).
3. Sharp angles (joined consonants and hooks are allowed only if each is easily distinguishable).
4. Similar motion (circles, loops and alternative forms of consonants are used to avoid awkward changes of direction).

These characteristics are obtained by the application of certain rules, and an appreciation of the relationship between the rules and the structure of the system gives teachers and students a better understanding of the skill; they can see *why* as well as *how* the outlines are written. The following examples (not exhaustive by any means) of this relationship are given to amplify the point—

Basic Principles and Characteristics of Structure	*Rules of Pitman Shorthand to Implement the Principle*
FLUENCY	
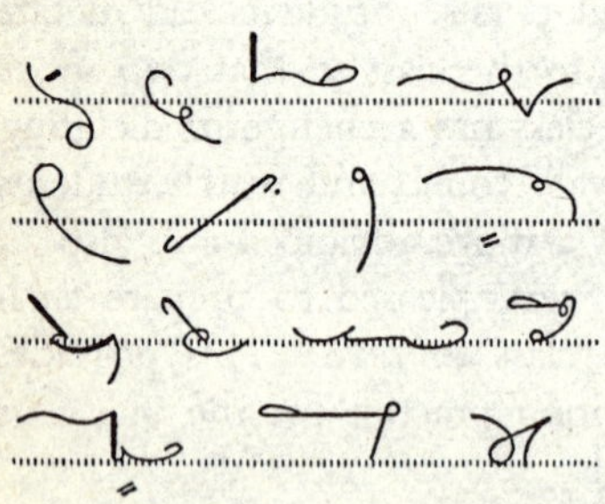	Use of circles, hooks and loops; doubling; use of medial hooks; phrasing.

Basic Principles and Characteristics of Structure — *Rules of Pitman Shorthand to Implement the Principle*

BREVITY

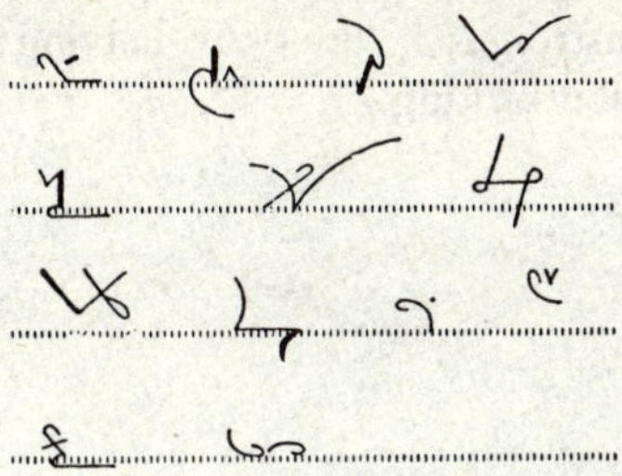

Use of hooks, circles; omission of vowels; halving; phrasing; intersections; contractions; use of alternative forms of consonants and vowels.

LEGIBILITY

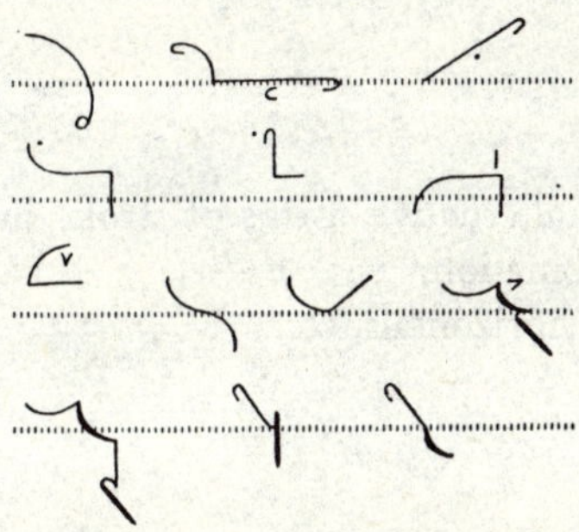

Doubling; two strokes of unequal length may be joined only if both can be clearly seen; use of alternative forms of consonants.

SUGGESTIVENESS

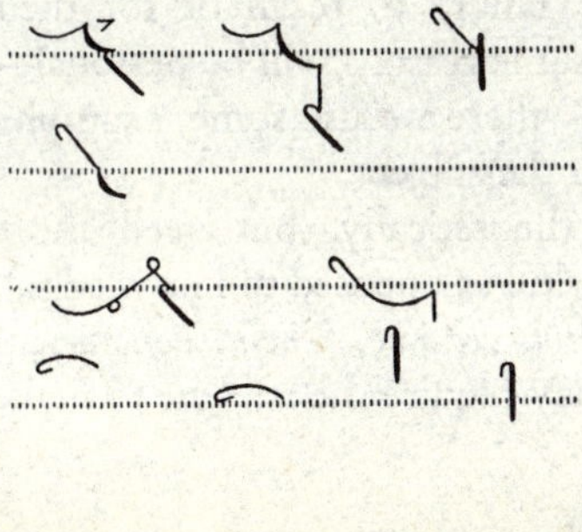

Distinguishing outlines for words of similar structure; position writing; use and non-use of hooks; etc.

Basic Principles and Characteristics of Structure	*Rules of Pitman Shorthand to Implement the Principle*
LINEARITY 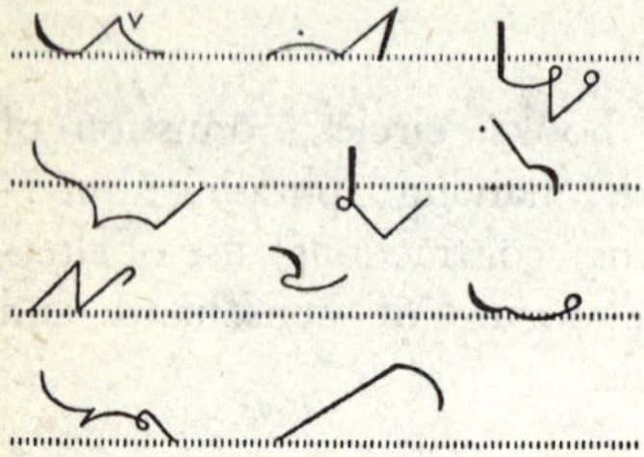	Use of medial *ray*; avoiding three downstrokes; use of halving; position writing.
SHARP ANGLES 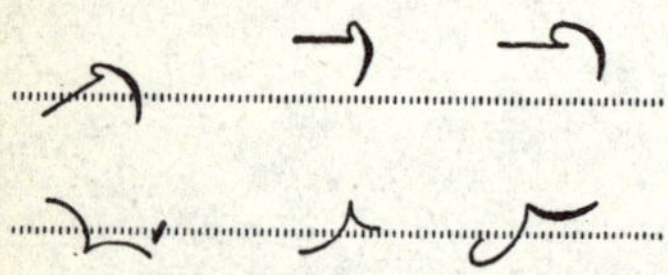	Use of alternative forms of *r*, *fr*(*vr*), *thr*(*THr*), *sh*.
SIMILAR MOTION 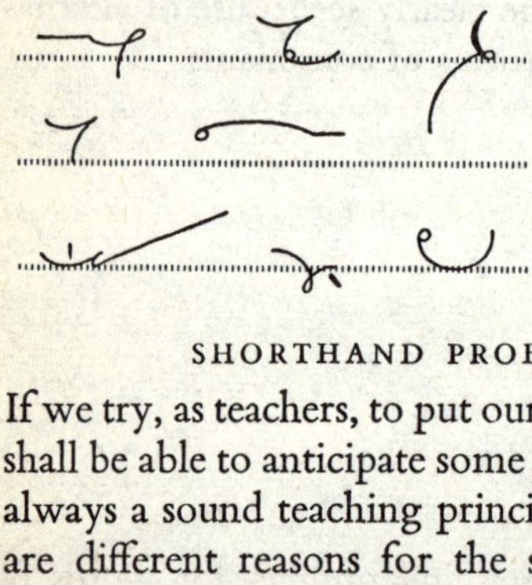	Use of alternative forms of stroke in combination, e.g. *n* + *l*, *r* + *m*, *ls* + horizontals, etc.

SHORTHAND PROBLEMS AND THE LEARNER

If we try, as teachers, to put ourselves in the position of the learners, we shall be able to anticipate some of their difficulties and prevent errors—always a sound teaching principle. We shall soon discover that there are different reasons for the students' failure to recall or for their writing imperfect outlines. Although some reasons will be personal—reasons of capacity, interest, mood, etc.—there are also some, examples of which are given below, inherent in the subject.

1. Some outlines may be simple theoretically, but need more practice than others for fluent writing (skill as opposed to knowledge), e.g. *bungalow*, *securely*, *York*, *narrow*, *debt*, *accurate*, *benefit*, *honorary*.

2. The theory may be simple, but may require the student to make

a mental jump ahead. For instance, it is not difficult to grasp the rule that certain vowels cause an outline to be written in the first or third position, but the application of this rule sometimes needs more practice, e.g. in words where the first downstroke is preceded by one or more horizontals and the student must think ahead in order to start the outline in the right position. Examples of such outlines are: *map, Nile, cash, manage, catch, kitchen, move.*

3. Application of the theory may suffer because of the interference of old longhand habits, e.g. with prefixes it is a common error for students to write—(connected) 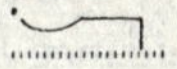 (community) 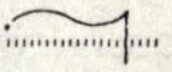 (disconnect) 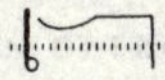 (commemorate) 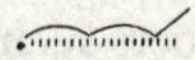 (reconnoitre) 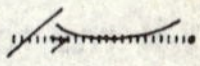.

4. A habit is fairly well established through a sizeable unit of work and then a modification is made, and the textbook gives insufficient practice material for the modification to be established, e.g. after eight pages of examples and exercises with circle *s* on the right hand side of straight downstrokes, there are ten examples of circle *s* written outside the angle formed by two straight strokes. These are given but slight application in only one following exercise. The student will know the rule and be able to repeat it "word perfect," but it takes more than one exercise to establish the right response to the new words.

5. Another possible source of confusion in learning is not inherent in the system but is one of teaching method; that is, the too early use of technical terms. It is better to write examples on the chalkboard, to explain in simple terms and use the technical term (if necessary) only after the students have seen examples and understood the rule. A case in point here is the "*-shun*" hook. To start by telling a class that "today we are going to learn the *-shun* hook" is to mystify them for the first few minutes of the lesson—and, incidentally, to miss a good point of correlation with spelling. A better way to start is to ask the class for words like "fa-shion" ending in the sound of *-shun* so that they can be written on the board in longhand to show the different ways of spelling the same sound. This reinforces the knowledge that shorthand must be written according to sound. Beneath the longhand words can be written the shorthand outlines and the simple ones (*-shun* inside curves) chosen for the students to practise. If the students do not provide sufficient words of the structure required, they can easily be added by the teacher. If the outlines are written without explanation of the hook, the students can discover it for themselves

(inductive method). In any case technical terms should not be used unless there is no plain alternative.

6. A source of difficulty in reading and transcribing outlines lies in the word meaning, or spelling. There are about two hundred homophones, most of them common words, and it needs practice to recall immediately the appropriate spelling. There is a natural tendency to recall the more common word "there" instead of "their," "soul" instead of "sole" (in one class fourteen out of twenty-four students transcribed "soul trader" instead of "sole trader"; there, obviously, was a case for guidance *before* the transcription).

Yet if the teacher remembers such points, remembers to look at all the teaching material with the eyes of a learner, it is not difficult to prevent the errors by an appropriate amount of explanation, guidance and supervised practice. This is, in fact, the difference between *teaching* and just *giving a lesson*.

THE TEACHING UNIT

This topic can be considered from two aspects. Firstly, how much, in terms of subject matter, should one present in a lesson (what one may call the lesson unit), and, secondly, what should be the form and size of the teaching or learning units within the lesson? In a subject like shorthand, where much of the basic knowledge has to be used automatically, there is need in each lesson for much practice; it is therefore obvious that the amount of new knowledge which can be presented will be less than in a descriptive subject like history or commerce.

As was said earlier, there are teachers who prefer to present the theory in a short period of time and to revise and consolidate concurrently with speed development work; and there are others who prefer to have small units of theory thoroughly practised before moving on to new work. Whichever method is used, the teacher still has to decide how much theory and how much practice shall constitute the lesson. An inexperienced teacher may think that the chapters of the chosen textbook are a sufficient guide, but textbooks are not necessarily method books. They give the text of all the subject matter which may be taught; they should never be used without reflection to determine the order of presentation and they cannot determine *how* the matter shall be taught. To take an example, almost at random, the subject matter for alternative forms *fr*, *thr*, *fl* and their corresponding heavy strokes (four main rules) is linked with the provision of  for *ng-kr* and *ng-gr*, making five points of theory in all. If all these are presented as *one* unit of knowledge before any practice is given, students will find it much more difficult to learn than if each item is given separately, followed immediately by reading and writing practice. The teacher needs to prepare supplementary material on each individual section, but the extra preparation means more effective learning and thus a saving of class time in correction and remedial work. Some of this supplementary material will be of a purely temporary character, suited to the immediate needs of a particular class, but through experience the teacher will collect some material which can be used over quite a long period with different classes, either because it meets common needs, or because the material has an intrinsic value apart from the shorthand aspect. This principle of several small units of work to cover theory and practice also accords with general principles of lesson planning, i.e. variety of activity and of work pace within a lesson.

Working in Meaningful Units

All research workers into the process of learning are unanimous in stating that meaningful context assists learning; therefore current practice in shorthand teaching (as in language teaching) is that "the sentence is the learning unit." Ann Brewington[1] states—

> little economy in learning results from using the shorthand symbol or the word as the learning unit . . . [it] remains too small to permit continuous, rapid writing. . . . The use of the sentence as the learning unit marks one of the most important stages in the organization of materials. It afforded opportunity for studying the effects of various sizes of the learning unit and it encouraged increasing the size of the paragraph. . . . It provided opportunity for incidental learning, which teachers had previously deemed impossible and undesirable in shorthand, thereby making it possible and desirable to devote time and energy to the systematic construction of new and infrequently used words and phrases, since a large number of the high-frequency words and phrases were mastered through incidental learning.

Harm Harms[2] of Columbus University, Ohio, reports—

> Sufficient evidence is now on record to warrant the statement that new words should be introduced in contextual (sentence or paragraph) form in order to

[1] "Classroom Techniques in Teaching Shorthand," *Proceedings of* 1945 *Business Education Institute* (Teachers' College, University of Cincinnati).
[2] *Methods in Vocational Business Education*(Cincinnati, South Western Publishing Co., 1940)

secure most efficient learning. This means that word lists and drills on individual words should be used sparingly. Such word lists can still be used effectively as a review teaching device and in connexion with blackboard illustrations.

The experience of the author has been that word drills are certainly effective if performed with a definite purpose, e.g. to develop manual dexterity (see point 1, p. 100) or for remedial work if students are drawing instead of writing outlines. In this latter case the outlines should be carefully chosen—any outline will not do, but those which will quickly give the students a feeling for movement, such as .... form/farm .... fair/fare (useful also for reminder of possible alternative renderings) .... matter .... scatter .... reminder .... fact .... ours .... yours sincerely .... mostly .... of which .... to which (useful also for consolidating short forms) .... receive .... scale .... meanwhile .... useful.

Other outlines may be chosen because, although they may seem difficult to a beginner, if they are practised with focus of attention on improving the rate of writing, they become easy. Examples of this category are—

.... shell .... detailed .... afford .... likelihood .... specifications .... unfortunately (if a contraction is not taught) .... let me know .... hundred .... splendid .... beginning .... shoulder .... straightened .... acquaintance .... campaign .... imbued.

A third group may be chosen because it is a common tendency for beginners to form them badly, e.g. .... printed (n is shortened) .... incorrectly (2 k's shortened to 1½) .... looking (k too short or too long, or slanting upwards) .... relief (not compactly written and therefore taking too much space and writing effort)  cargoes (k too short) 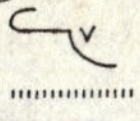 qualify (kway used instead of kl).

Finally there are the outlines which do not seem to "stick" on first or second presentation and need drilling. To teachers with experience it becomes almost instinctive to give extra practice and revision on the following words—*beyond*, *entire*, *start*, *system*, *though*, *indicate*, *quiet*, *wave*, *refer*, *disease*, *article*, *discovery*, *behaviour*, *publication*, *operation*, *somewhat*, and others.

Teaching Short Forms

This last topic brings one to a vital part of the subject matter for all shorthand writers, no matter what system they write. All systems of shorthand provide specially short outlines for the commonest words and these are listed as "short forms." At one time it was the practice (following academic learning methods) to ask students to learn a given list of short forms for homework, but a little reflection should show us that this is a most uneconomic way of learning. It certainly does not follow the principle of economy of effort. It is the experience of many a student that a list can be learned as required as homework, but that when the words occur in dictation they are not, as expected, at the pen tip and in addition a bad habit of recall has probably been established. If the list—say, *according*, *acknowledge*, *advantage*, *advertisement*, *all*, *an*, *and*, *any*, *anything*—has been learned and the word *advantage* occurs subsequently in the dictation and the response is not immediate, there is a tendency for the mind to recall all the outlines from the beginning of the list until *advantage* is reached. Meantime, of course, attention to the dictation has been interrupted and a gap in note-taking results. Short forms are not used in lists and therefore if we recall the general principle that "the learning exercise should take place in the same form as final use," we shall not ask our students to practise short forms in lists, but in sentences. As a by-product of the textual method, we can secure the active co-operation of students (and, incidentally, more learning) if we ask them to compose a number of short sentences made up mainly of short forms as far as they have gone in the theory. Examples of such sentences are given below and on the following page.

We hope to be of service to you.
The task is beyond our ability.

His desk is beyond hers.
We shall acknowledge your cheque tomorrow.

However, as a form of drill, it is an excellent plan to ask students to revise about 10 short forms preparatory to the teacher's dictating them two or three times in different sequences at speeds which demand an all-out effort from the students. This is the method used in the *New Course Intensive Workbooks* (Pitman). Even at the earliest stages the speed of such dictation can be 40 words per minute. This gives the students a challenge (to which they generally respond with enthusiasm) and it also ensures some over-learning of essential knowledge as well as prevention of "drawing" the shorthand outlines.

Another method for phrasing, boosting speed and consolidating ability to write short forms without hesitation is to take from the textbook, or compose, sentences in which there are fewer *outlines* than *words*. The outlines and words are counted and the sentences are dictated at *so many outlines* per minute, with previous exhortation to the students to make a special effort to get everything down. After two or three attempts (usually they are successful at the third), the *words per minute* can be announced. Such sentences are—

How-can-we keep in-touch with-them when-they go away? (7/12—7 outlines, 12 words.)
Why-do-you think it-would-be-the wrong thing to-do? (6/12)
I-believe that a large-number-of members of-our-society were surprised to-learn of-the views of-the speaker. (13½/21)
We-believe that-we-shall-be-able-to do more-business if-we-are allowed to-reduce our-prices. (8½/19)

(In the last two sentences the intersection has been counted as half an outline since it requires a lifting of the pen.)

This technique often results in the students suggesting other phrases or shortening of outlines, and a healthy discussion, student-initiated, can lead to more effective learning of shorthand theory.

What has been said of short forms applies equally to contractions.

Phrasing

There are several important points to bear in mind when teaching phrasing. One has already been given—namely, that the students must see for themselves the benefits of phrasing.

Secondly, to teach the *principles of phrasing* is more important than to teach *phrases*. Certainly there are some phrases which occur so frequently that they may be considered as standard outlines and should be taught as such. On the other hand, whether a shorthand writer phrases or not depends as much on where he is in relation to the speaker as on whether he knows a phrase. If a writer is keeping up with the speaker, then phrasing will be missed because the hand will have moved from the previous outline too quickly for a phrase to be written. In slow speed work, therefore, it would seem wrong to consider non-phrasing as a mistake and to blame students for it. Rather should they be trained to keep behind the speaker, even if the speed is slower than their "cruising" speed and to listen for possible phrases. Although in examinations it is not permissible (or desirable) that the reader should indicate phrasing, yet in the early stages of shorthand learning when the dictation has to be slow and untimed there are many opportunities for helping the students to acquire a feeling for the right kind of phrasing, by reading the words together a little more quickly. The students should, of course, be told beforehand that the teacher expects them to "register" such phrases. After such reading it is also necessary to read the matter again in natural form, just as all speed bursts should be followed by writing at least some of the same material more slowly for style as a corrective to badly formed outlines.

WRITING FOR SPEED AND FOR STYLE

It will be useful here to say a little more about writing for style. Employers naturally do not normally mind what kind of shorthand their employees write, provided that the transcripts are correct and mailable. The shorthand teacher, however, cannot take such an attitude. High speed is never built on careless, shapeless notes and we cannot be certain that none of our students will wish or be able to go beyond the mediocre achievement of 80 or 100 words per minute. Moreover the ultimate purpose of shorthand writing—transcription—is likely to be far better served, by more accuracy and expedition in production, if the notes are easily and therefore fluently read. Both shorthand teacher and students should aim at style as well as speed, but neither should be sacrificed for the other as this is certainly not necessary.

One way to encourage attention to style is to choose a passage of not more than two hundred words on a topic likely to interest the students, duplicate the shorthand text (the teacher's own good style notes) and allocate it for a reading and copying exercise. Give the students an opportunity to work on it as homework and as classwork. Follow this with dictation of the passage at a comfortable speed for all every day for three or four days. Finally, give one more dictation at the same speed and take the shorthand notes in for assessing writing style only. Shorthand errors can be noted and dealt with in subsequent lessons. These assessed copies can then be kept in a folder and the progress of the students will be apparent to them. The author used to have the final dictation taken on a loose-leaf sheet (exercise book size) with a wide margin on the left-hand side.

ENGLISH AND SHORTHAND

There are three fundamental reasons why shorthand teaching cannot be separated from English teaching, namely (*a*) the fact that shorthand is a linguistic skill and therefore words are the very stuff of which it is made; (*b*) a well-developed skill in English is a contributory factor to success in the total shorthand skill (both writing and transcribing); and (*c*) shorthand is another means of writing and therefore of communication. The content of dictation matter will vary in quality, and as educators we should seek to use the best. The oft-quoted comment in the McNair Report that "all teachers are teachers *of* English because they are teachers *in* English," is true in a very special way of shorthand and typewriting teachers. The very quantity of material, the innumerable opportunities for unwitting learning, and for over-learning through repetition cannot leave a student's English knowledge in the same state at the end of a shorthand-typewriting course as at the beginning. Whether the influence is good or not depends on the quality of the material in which the student is asked to work and that is in the hands of the teacher.

The shorthand teacher can obviously help students to improve their skill in English, and thus their skill in shorthand. Secondly he can make a contribution to their general education. The extent to which he can do either or both of these things will depend on the type of students, the time allocation to the subject of shorthand, and his own vision.

Improvement of English Skill

The weaknesses in English which prevent a shorthand-typist from being efficient are (*a*) punctuation, (*b*) spelling, (*c*) general English vocabulary. Although no shorthand lesson should be turned completely into an English lesson, neither should any shorthand lesson pass without some reference to English. It is the constant help, the unexpected opportunities for recall, the favourable comment on success and the regular "backing up" of the work of the English and typewriting teachers which are so valuable. Therefore the shorthand teacher should plan his points of correlation, should consult with the English and typewriting teachers, and should show the students that he is interested, even enthusiastic, about English as well as about shorthand. The following are some of the more obvious methods of linking English with shorthand. Individual teachers will doubtless devise others and prefer them, but as long as the material and methods are used naturally and through a sincere desire to help, they will be effective.

Elementary Stage. (Before theory is completed, and with speeds at under 50 words per minute.)

1. The correlated word list (Appendix 1) is used for consolidation of shorthand and for checks on spelling and meaning of words, e.g. when students are working on Chapter V of the *New Course* as new matter, some consolidation on Chapters I–IV can be given through sentences such as the following—

(*a*) They may manage to *effect* the change they ask for.
(*b*) They will weigh the *package* and *check* the *mail.*
(*c*) Ask him to *attach* the envelope to the *agenda.*
(*d*) May they give the *cheque* and the memo to the bank?
(*e*) The damage may *affect* the checking of the mail.
(*f*) They say the delay may *affect* the job.
(*g*) Can the chalk *affect* the watch?
(*h*) They may have to check the *effect* of the *damage* to the shop.
(*i*) Ask him to lay the *package* on the *envelope.*
(*j*) They may be *delayed* by the *damage* to the boat.

Method

A. The sentences are presented in shorthand on the chalkboard (prepared before the students enter the room), the class read each sentence, spell and/or give the meaning of selected words (e.g. those in italics above). Students then take the sentences from dictation.

(If appropriate, they can be asked to transcribe their notes for homework.)

B. The sentences are written in shorthand by the teacher and duplicated so that each student has a copy. (This method is necessary if the chalkboard work cannot be done before the class arrives.) Method A is then followed.

C. Teacher dictates the sentences at a speed within the capacity of the class; students read from their notes and give spelling and/or meaning of words as required by the teacher.

An important feature of spelling in the shorthand class is that it should be rapid—at the speed of the competent typist, not of the slow longhand writer.

2. When reading exercises from the textbook or chalkboard, spot checks are made for punctuation, spelling and meaning of words.

3. Short sentences are dictated or read from the chalkboard to introduce homonyms and to check on spelling.

4. Sentences containing items of useful knowledge are used for dictation and reading (e.g. A4 paper is 8¼ in. wide by 11¾ in. long. There are 480 sheets of paper in a ream).

5. Sentences should be composed by the teacher (*a*) to cover common errors of shorthand students with the aim of preventing rather than correcting; (*b*) for remedial work on errors in particular classes.

After Completion of Theory. (With speeds of over 50 words per minute.)

1. Material is prepared by the English teacher, dictated and taken in longhand, then discussed in the shorthand room, taken from dictation and transcribed on the typewriter. (The passage must be short.)

2. Short passages of literary merit are used for intensive work, i.e. theory revision, outline practice, phrasing, spelling and meaning of words, drilling outlines of words new to the class, dictation at varying rates (timed and untimed). Individual students may be asked to give an oral summary of the passage (either in the shorthand lesson or later in the English lesson).

3. Students are given two or three words each and asked to write, in shorthand, sentences incorporating the words. The sentences are checked for English and used in class for dictation, especially speed bursts.

4. Students are given, in shorthand (to read for homework), extracts

from good writings. Individual students are asked to dictate (from shorthand) to the class the next day.

5. Students are asked to choose a passage from a set book, or any other book of literary merit which they are reading, and put this into good shorthand (with dictionary); the passages are put on the bulletin board for spare-time reading, and are later distributed to a class as a reading exercise.

6. Students are asked to extract, or compose, short notes or prose passages on a selected topic (their own selection or the teacher's) and to illustrate these. (Work on foolscap paper can be posted on the bulletin board.) Topics might be: present-day fashion; a modern author; a favourite sport; a foreign city; etc.

7. Passages chosen by the teacher as examples of well-punctuated passages are presented in longhand in English lessons for discussion. They are then dictated in the shorthand lesson, read back with punctuation, and the students are asked for comments on the use of the punctuation marks.

8. Beginnings and endings of books of different styles (e.g. novel, biography, thriller, etc.) are read to show how style achieves purpose. Passages are dictated, read back and brief comments are made on style. The passages are then passed to the English teacher for discussion. (In the latter case the students would work from their shorthand notes and the English teacher would have the longhand version.)

USE OF LITERARY MATERIAL

Recalling the general principles of learning on which the acquisition of skills is based, we remember that immediate response to a certain stimulus is not established by one reinforcement; we also know that over-learning of knowledge is necessary if it is to be retained for any length of time. The material through which we learn a system of shorthand and through which we acquire the skill of writing and reading it fluently must therefore provide opportunities for developing the immediate response, and for over-learning. As has been pointed out, the shorthand writer needs to respond immediately to a very large number of words in a great variety of contexts, and if our teaching is confined to repetitive work the student will not be prepared to deal with the changes of stimuli which the variations of context present. In developing shorthand writing ability, it is necessary to have practice in taking down matter on a variety of topics, but also a variety of matter on the same topics. For instance, it is far more valuable, both for the shorthand and the ancillary learning, if a series of letters, or short passages, is used for dictation over a period of, say, two or three days, or even a week, than if all the dictated passages are unrelated to each other. In the later stages of a course a sequence of work can be used for transcription practice so that there is some degree of reality in the work.

In the elementary stage of learning the consolidation of the theory should be given through different material from the original presentation and practice. Although some repetition is valuable in revision and consolidation, variation of matter and method is essential, for we know that boredom can quickly set in.

In the later stages of speed development and transcription training, extensive material is essential if the English and shorthand vocabularies of the students are to be developed to the required standard and, again, if interest and effort are to be maintained.

Difficulty of Material

It is sometimes tempting to keep to repetition for extra practice because it is difficult to find material which is of a similar grade or because we think only in terms of dictation as the form of practice. However, just as ordinary reading widens one's English vocabulary, so shorthand reading, involving the seeing of many outlines a number of times, can help to ensure that the outlines pass from the recognition to the active vocabulary stage. Consolidation of theory can with advantage, and often with pleasure, be given through reading only, and a wider choice of matter is thus immediately available. For instance, the following passages are all worth using as reading matter for three important reasons—(*a*) they all contain useful shorthand vocabulary; (*b*) they are likely to interest most students, and (*c*) they provide good opportunities for the teacher to comment on the content and perhaps add to the students' general knowledge.

1. Extract from *Great Men of Science* by Philip Lenard (G. Bell & Sons Ltd.).

Michael Faraday (1791–1867). Here again we have one of the greatest men of science, of his kind incomparable, and unique in the endowment with the peculiar mental constitution which makes the investigator, who uses his senses to penetrate into the unknown, and actually expects to see everywhere new things in plenty. He detects the smallest sign of anything peculiar or not fully understood, and then applies to it a mind already schooled by the thorough study of nature, and completely adapted to it, exhibiting the greatest patience in the pursuit and multiplication of his observations, until the new thing has been understood in its essentials, and this has become a new mental possession.

The innumerable occasions on which Faraday brought these gifts to bear in his laboratory had to do with things of very varied importance; from discoveries of the greatest possible range down to small explanations, which are a necessity for the thinker, even if they do not always reveal anything essentially new. In this connexion we see that even the most gifted investigator is unable to see ahead far into the unknown, and that his value rather consists in exerting his gifts faithfully and with the greatest industry, quite uninfluenced in his steady course by the desire for public success, purely from love of the depth of nature, and—as was the case with Faraday especially—simply from sheer delight in the observation of nature.

2. Extract adapted from an article in *The New Statesman and Nation*, 26th January, 1957.

Bernard Shaw and Spelling. Bernard Shaw, as we all know, was very anxious to reform our alphabet in order to make the spelling of the English language more logical and, consequently, easier. The chief argument in favour of reform is that there are more sounds in the English language than there are letters in the Latin alphabet with which to write them. We therefore have to use some of the letters for more than one sound each and also have some illogical two-letter combinations. Bernard Shaw made an analysis of the language to show that we needed a minimum of forty letters in order to represent all the sounds; he considered the present alphabet led to tremendous wastage of time, energy, material and money because two letters have to be written instead of one millions of times every minute. He wanted the old letters to be discarded altogether and a completely new alphabet to be launched for use as an alternative until either the new or the old proved the fitter to survive.

3. Extract from *Ghosts of London* by H. V. Morton (Methuen & Co. Ltd.).

Shepherd Market. Shepherd Market (to which many people add an inaccurate "s") is one of the most satisfactory ghosts of a London that existed a hundred and fifty years ago. It is satisfactory, I think, because it is still vigorously fulfilling the functions which created it; the selling of potatoes and cabbages, beef and mutton, leatherwork and china teacups; and all the rest of it.

It is a pity that so many other fragments of an older London have departed from their original intentions. They have fallen prey either to lawyers or business offices, or have otherwise been converted to uses never contemplated by their makers. But Shepherd Market owes its human interest and its vitality to an unbroken succession of small shopkeepers, who carry on, within a few yards of one of the world's most expensive thoroughfares, as if they were in Ipswich or Faversham. You might, indeed, remove the whole of Shepherd

Market as it stands, with its fishmongers, butchers, fruiterers, to any old country town in England; and no one would guess that it was the very heart and core of Mayfair.

The disreputable fair in May which gave its name to this part of London, was a fair that in medieval times used to take place once a year round the gates of what eventually became St. James's Palace. This palace began life, perhaps in Norman times, as a hospital for female lepers. It was a good way out of London, among fields, and was dedicated, not to St. Giles, the patron saint of lepers, but to St. James-the-less. The annual fair of St. James was granted for the upkeep of the institution by Edward I in 1320 and, with the tenacity of a fair, it continued to be held in St. James's long after Henry VIII, having pensioned the last three leprous maidens, had turned the lazar house into a royal residence.

Selecting Material for Interest Value

As an example of presenting a topic through a variety of passages, the following quotations are given. They were selected to show that writers of different nationalities and of different periods in history had expressed similar ideas on the question of one's judgement of literature. They have been used with many different types of students and for different purposes in the subjects of English, shorthand and typewriting. They have invariably given pleasure, or enlightenment, or provided a stimulus for reflection beyond the original subject.

It is suggested that the quotations be presented to students in shorthand for reading with the teacher—not as reading tests, but as passages to read and discuss.

Virginia Woolf, *The Common Reader*, The Hogarth Press Ltd. (Twentieth Century).

The only advice, indeed, that one person can give another about reading is to take no advice, to follow your own instincts, to use your own reason, to come to your own conclusions.

Most commonly we come to books with blurred and divided minds, asking of fiction that it shall be true, of poetry that it shall be false, of biography that it shall be flattering, of history that it shall enforce our own prejudices. . . . Do not dictate to your author; try to become him; be his fellow-worker and accomplice.

Perhaps the quickest way to understand the elements of what a novelist is doing is not to read, but to write; to make your own experiment with the dangers and difficulties of words.

To read a book as it should be read calls for the rarest qualities of imagination, insight and judgment . . . literature is a very complex art.

Montgomery Belgion, *Reading for Profit*, The Cresset Press Ltd. (Twentieth Century).

As far as my observation goes, the great majority of readers read solely for the momentary entertainment, relaxation, or distraction which a book affords them. In other words, they read solely in order to pass the time agreeably.

The conscious profit to be had from reading derives as much from what we may think and feel after the reading is over as from what happens to us while we actually read. . . .

Too many people, it is obvious, have no real understanding, no awareness, of life.

Whether or not our reading can affect us, whether or not it can colour our lives, influence our character and influence our conduct, must depend to a very great extent on our own susceptibility and sensitiveness to the written word. And in large measure our susceptibilities to the written word are functions of the quality of our own individual experience and of our ensuing intuition of the nature of actual life.

Cervantes, Preface to *Don Quixote* (Sixteenth Century).

. . . I will not earnestly beseech you, with tears in my eyes, dear reader, to pardon or dissemble my child's faults: for what favour can I expect from you, who are neither his friend nor relation? You have a soul of your own and the privilege of free-will, whoever you be, as well as the proudest he that struts in a gaudy outside; you are a king by your own fireside, as much as any monarch on his throne; you have liberty and property, which set you above favour or affection, and may therefore freely like or dislike this history, according to your humour.

Coleridge (Nineteenth Century).

Four classes of readers—

1. Sponges, who absorb all they read, and return it nearly in the same state, only a little dirtied.
2. Sand-glasses, who retain nothing, and are content to get through a book for the sake of getting through the time.
3. Strain-bags, who retain merely the dregs of what they read.
4. Mogul diamonds, equally rare and valuable, who profit by what they read, and enable others to profit by it also.

R. L. Stevenson (Nineteenth Century).

To know what you prefer, instead of saying Amen to what the world tells you you ought to prefer, is to have kept your soul alive.

Oscar Wilde, *Intentions* (Nineteenth Century).

The meaning of any beautiful created thing is at least as much in the soul of him who looks at it as it was in his soul who wrought it. Nay, it is rather the beholder who lends to the beautiful thing its myriad meanings and makes it marvellous for us, and sets it in some new relation to the age, so that it becomes a vital portion of our lives, and a symbol of what we pray for.

D. L. Sayers, *Begin Here*, Victor Gollancz Ltd. (Twentieth Century).

Our reading and thinking are undisciplined. We read at random a book about religion, an article about social conditions in the Rhondda Valley, an angry newspaper correspondence about red-tape in government offices, a piece of poetry and a novel about big business in America; we approve and disapprove of them all in separate compartments of our minds, and it never occurs to us to put the whole lot together and see what bearing each of them has on the rest. . . .

T. S. Eliot, *Points of View*, Faber & Faber Ltd. (Twentieth Century).

Wide reading is not valuable as a kind of hoarding, an accumulation of knowledge, or what sometimes is meant by the term "a well-stocked mind." It is valuable because in the process of being affected by one powerful personality after another, we cease to be dominated by any one, or by any small number. The very different views of life, cohabiting in our minds affect each other, and our own personality asserts itself and gives each a place in some arrangement peculiar to ourself.

Such examples of interesting material could be multiplied in many fields, and it adds to the interest and fun of teaching and learning when teachers and students themselves discover and use such passages. One of the important points to remember is to give the source—author and title of book or periodical. In shorthand (and typewriting) classes we tend to shroud our teaching material in a mist of anonymity which can become a fog and prevent our students from keeping that alertness of mind which is so desirable in note-taking. It is also important for the reasons for the choice to be given, or some comment to be made on the material either before or after reading so that it is not looked upon merely as a reading exercise but as something which has intrinsic value.

Intensive Use of Material

If we decide to use material intensively, the first requisite is that the passage shall not be too long—150 to 200 words is generally found to be a useful length. If the passage is longer, too much time is required to deal with it thoroughly and both teacher and students are likely to become bored with it—any intensive work should be given up immediately there are signs of boredom. The main purpose of intensive work is to cause over-learning and if interesting material and varied or challenging methods are used, and if the period of time devoted to such work is wisely controlled, there will be little chance of boredom or fatigue setting in.

The following two examples of material and method are offered only as an indication of what has been found effective; every teacher will discover for himself material and methods to suit his particular classes.

Intensive Work Plan on a Passage to Enable Students whose Average Speed is 80 *Words per Minute to Take it at* 100 *Words per Minute* (or more, according to their capabilities). The passage is from an R.S.A. shorthand-typist's examination at 80 words per minute, with a small addition in the last paragraph in place of the name and address which was dictated in the original.

Dear Sirs, We have received this morning your letter containing[10] your plan and *estimate* of the cost of making the[20] *alterations* for *converting* the large house in East Lane into[30] three fairly large flats.

We think the plans have been[40] carefully and well thought out, and they *undoubtedly* provide for[50] three very convenient flats, but on further *consideration* we should[60] like to have your opinion on the following changes.

First[70] of all we are anxious to know whether the large[80] room on the ground floor could be made into two[90] rooms, one of which could be a bathroom. If so,[100] the room at the back now containing a bath, but[110] which was not *originally* a bathroom, could be turned into[120] a kitchen. This would mean that each *tenant* would have[130] his own bathroom.

Secondly, would it be possible to have[140] a passage from the garden-room to the side door?[150] Although even a *narrow* passage would make the room somewhat[160] small, it would give an *entirely separate entrance* to Flat[170] Number 2.

Perhaps you would let us know at once[180] if these plans could be carried out without upsetting the[190] plans as a whole or *incurring* extra cost. Yours faithfully,[200]

Method: first lesson.

1. Read the letter to the students while they listen and jot down words for which they are not sure of the outline.

2. Take one word from six different students (dodging about the class), put an outline on the board and mention any point of theory, e.g. *turned*—strong vowel, therefore *t* and *stroke r*; finally hooked *r* following another consonant represented by *ray*. Add other examples, e.g. *returned, patterned, adjourned, churn, curved, modern, assertion*.

3. Drill *turned, returned, adjourned, modern,* by dictation, and other outlines asked for.

4. Put on the board any outlines of italicized words in the letter not covered by the first and second points above. Dictate these new words to the students once or twice and then dictate sentences including some of the words, at the same time walking around the classroom and watching the students as they write.

The following are examples of such sentences—

Will they make the alterations?
There are undoubtedly many alterations to be made.
The tenant will undoubtedly wish to be consulted.
I wish to convert the house into flats.
Please convert the dollars into sterling.
The cost of rebuilding would exceed the cost of converting.
This is our second tenant who has asked for a small room to be turned into a bathroom.

5. Drill phrases: *we have received, this morning, your letter containing, of making the, we think the, first of all, we are anxious, could be made, would make the, let us know.*

6. Dictate the letter at irregular speed, but in two, or not more than two and a quarter minutes.

7. Students read back and any further outline queries are answered.

8. Dictate at 100 words per minute.

Homework. Poor and incorrect outlines should be practised and the whole letter written in good shorthand twice.

Method: second lesson.

1. Dictate the letter in sections at 100, 110 and 120 words per minute.

2. Dictate the whole letter at 100 words per minute, at 110 words per minute and, if students wish, at 120 words per minute.

At a further lesson a week or two later dictate the following passage at 100 words per minute without any preparation. Follow up with remedial work as necessary, after checking either immediately after dictation by having students read back while the teacher writes on the chalkboard, or by taking in the students' notes for correction.

If we are fortunate enough to secure this property it[10] would certainly be worth while converting it into flats and[20] we ought undoubtedly to take the opportunity of doing so.[30] A surveyor friend of ours has estimated that alterations to[40] this ten-roomed house would cost approximately £1,500[50] if the conversion were into three entirely separate and self-[60]contained flats. We do not consider that this would be[70] exorbitant in view of the return which we could expect[80] ultimately to secure. We should certainly have to provide separate[90] bathrooms and kitchens for each tenant; this might be difficult,[100] but if the alterations are carefully planned, we think it[110] could be achieved.[113]

Intensive Work Plan on a Passage Suitable for a Speed Class of Any Range from 70 plus to High-speed Short One-minute Burst. This passage is adapted from *Sir Rowland Hill*, by Norman Wymer (Oxford University Press).

To a person like Rowland Hill the inefficiency of the[10] postal system was a challenge.

Not only was the service[20] inefficient and expensive, but it was also very unfair. The[30] poor people had to pay the very heavy charges, while[40] a great many rich people were able to avoid paying[50] them at all. For instance, members of the House of[60] Commons and the House of Lords were allowed to post[70] their letters free, provided they addressed them themselves and signed[80] them on the outside.

There was no uniform rate of[90] postage, but many different rates, the charges depending upon a[100] number of different factors. To begin with, letters were graded[110] according to the number of sheets of paper used. When[120] a letter was handed in at a Post Office it[130] was taken into a dark room and held before a[140] bright light to see how many sheets of paper it[150] contained. It was then given an initial charge. In addition[160] to this, a further charge was made according to the[170] distance it travelled, and this had to be paid by[180] the person receiving the letter.[185]

Method: first lesson.

1. The teacher duplicates enough shorthand (photographic or spirit duplicator process) for each student to have a copy. Shorthand is read by the class individually or in chorus (with the help of the teacher as this is not a reading *test*, but reading in preparation for intensive work).

2. The class practises outlines which the teacher selects and dictates, i.e. contractions and phrases.

3. The teacher writes outlines for the following words on the board and discusses theory (question and answer technique)—*postal*, *postage*, *system*, *provided*, *factors*, *dark*, *bright*, *initial*, *distance*.

4. The passage is dictated at a comfortable speed for the class.

5. Individual students read back from their own notes, or by exchanging notebooks.

Homework. Students practise their own weak outlines and copy the passage at least twice.

Method: second lesson.

1. A student is selected to read the passage, from the duplicated shorthand copy, to the class at a fairly slow rate; the teacher walks round and watches what is being written.
2. Remedial work is given by the teacher on any weaknesses noticed.
3. The passage is dictated at 70, 80 and, if desirable, 90 words per minute (or at whatever range of speeds the class is working).

PLATEAUX OF LEARNING

Whether plateaux *must* be a feature of learning is still a debatable point. Harm Harms[1] says "Plateaux are a common component of learning, though not always necessary," but quotes A. J. Gates's opinion that plateaux will always be present in most learning situations. The following extracts from Harms's book are also worth quoting—

> The reasons for plateaux are many: fatigue, emotional disturbances, wrong technique in connexion with some particular phase of the work, etc. The basic observation in connexion with plateaux is that it represents a stage in learning when the organism is endeavouring to change from one level of reacting to a higher and better organized level. Psychologists maintain that if the skill is presented in such a way that the higher level characteristics are embodied in the beginning techniques, then the organism will not have to unlearn one set of patterns to form another. . . .
>
> Woodworth gives the causes of plateaux as—
>
> ". . . (1) undue attention to one part of the task, (2) oscillation of attention from one part to another, (3) conscious effort to co-ordinate, (4) carrying over of errors from one part of the performance to another (as in a two-handed performance), and (5) lack of balance between the skill attained in different parts of a complex skill."
>
> Commins urges "Many plateaux may be broken by an increase in the strength of motivation. The fact that improvement may not be as great as originally expected may give rise to discouragement and a subsequent 'going stale.'"
>
> Smith, in a study of the causes of plateaux in learning came to the conclusion that about 60 per cent of them are due to such factors as failure in motivation, emotional strain, weather, light, illness, and re-learning after a period of inactivity, and Gates has said—
>
> "It is particularly important in the early stages of learning to detect errors, which, if allowed to persist, may become difficult to break and may impede progress or make it impossible. By controlling motivation, the organization of

[1] Harms, Harm, op. cit.

units of instruction, and learning procedures, teachers and pupils together may prevent many plateaux."

In shorthand the errors which are likely to cause plateaux are more often than not errors of technique; for instance, if students are allowed to draw outlines in the early stages, speedy writing is likely to take longer to acquire than if the students are given a clear idea first of what to write in *complete* units (not *b* joined to *k*, or *m* joined to *n*, but the *outline* for "bake" and the *outline* for "many"), and then shown how to write it quickly and fluently. Again, if students are not shown *how* to form circles to straight strokes (particularly where to begin the circle) many of them will be making unnecessary movements and producing outlines like 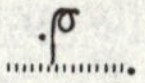. If students are not trained from the outset to turn the pages of their notebook quickly, a habit may form of slackening the right-hand movement at the end of a page to allow the left hand to work at its accustomed slow level. A good left-hand technique helps a writer to maintain the writing speed of the right hand.

If, however, plateaux are observed (they will be at different stages with different students) the teacher can only be vigilant of the students' work and manner of working in order to try to discover the reason and take appropriate action. It may be a lessening of work tension (in the case of fatigue, poor health or emotional upset), the heightening of challenge (when a student does not realize she is capable of greater effort or better work) or variation in method or material (to re-stimulate interest), or revision may be needed to fill in important gaps in knowledge.

Although mention was made earlier (p. 86) of the common plateau at the 70 to 90 words per minute stage, it is, of course, possible for plateaux of learning to occur at any time during the learning process.

DICTATION

There are two main aspects to the question of dictation, i.e. the skill of the teacher as a reader and the style of dictation to be adopted.

The Skill of the Teacher

Since the dictation should be heard by every student in the room without strain, and since the purpose of the dictation is for the students to write a shorthand symbol for every word, it is understandable that the teacher may (perhaps unconsciously) give an unnatural reading. This results from pitching the voice too high (this happens more often with women teachers than with men) instead of projecting the voice more strongly, and by giving almost every word in the passage equal emphasis. The effect is sometimes so to kill the meaning of the passage that it is a hindrance rather than a help to the students who are taking notes. Another problem for the reader is the similarity and the differences between grammatical phrasing and shorthand phrasing. Where the grammatical phrase coincides with a shorthand phrase (e.g. *there-is-no-need*, *we-do-not-know*, *in-the-first-place*) no difficulty arises, but the teacher has to guard against developing the habit of reading shorthand phrases (seen almost instinctively while he reads) where there is no grammatical phrase, (e.g. *we-have-reason* [break] *to-believe*; *there-are a number-of* [break] *excellent*; *rate-of* [break] *learning*; etc.).

It is helpful to very elementary students to have training in hearing common shorthand phrases and therefore permissible for a teacher from time to time to read with emphasis on shorthand phrasing, but only for very short periods and certainly not when the students have acquired a feeling for phrasing—which is generally well before they have reached the 50 words per minute stage. The reading should, of course, be intelligent, natural and given as a reading to the class of a meaningful piece of prose which conveys ideas. Most of us are not aware of our particular weaknesses in reading unless we hear recordings of it and all shorthand teachers should make a point of doing this.

The Style of Dictation

The second aspect of dictation is that of timed and untimed, or examination and office style dictation. The main object of most shorthand courses is to train office workers who will take dictation from a number of different people, at different rates, and in many different manners. Never, except in proficiency tests, will the office shorthand-writer be called upon to take dictation at a regular speed, timed by a stop-watch. This important fact is often overshadowed or even forgotten because of the dominance of the qualifying test at the end of the course. If all students are to be assessed, obviously there must be a common yardstick and the timed test has been, and to a large extent still is, the only means of giving a test which will be equally fair to all. With the greater use of tape recordings it is to be hoped that untimed, irregular dictation will take its rightful place in the training and testing of our future shorthand writers (*see* p. 178). For the moment it is possible and reasonable to hold the balance between the two: the following approach has been found by the author to do just that.

In the first term of a one-year course, when the students are spending most of their time acquiring knowledge of the system, most of the dictation should be untimed and given as a dictator would give matter to a new junior in the office. The matter is dictated in intelligent, grammatical phrases, pauses are made to allow students to write and the teacher to watch what is being written. In every lesson, however, a small portion of matter *which has already been written in shorthand*, will be given at timed rates, so that the students can be challenged to put their knowledge into practice without hesitation and so that they can have the satisfaction of "knowing where they stand." In the second term the amount of timed dictation can be increased, but there should still be a great deal of untimed, and irregular reading, especially when typewritten transcription begins. In the third term, most of the dictation should be office style except that for an appropriate period just before the speed examination there should be an intensive attack on taking notes from timed dictation. In other words, the timed test or examination should be regarded as a hurdle for which special training is necessary; the main work of the course is to prepare students to take irregular, untimed and amended dictation and to produce typed transcripts from it as intelligently and as expeditiously as they can.

Closely allied to the manner of dictation is the question of providing variation of voice, and perhaps accent, so that the students are not handicapped when they take an office test or an examination where another teacher reads. The recording machines will help in this problem but even without them a good deal can be done. It has been the experience of the author that if students dictate to the class (from shorthand, prepared beforehand) there is not only the advantage of a different voice, but many students gain confidence which was lacking before. Any hesitancy to dictate is usually overcome when it is pointed out that in the office they may be required to test potential new staff and that if they are nervous because it is a new experience to them, that nervousness may be communicated to the candidate.

Needless to say, no teacher should undertake to read for an examination (either internal or external) who has not practised reading to time. It may be helpful to add that a stop-*clock* is easier to use than a stop-*watch*. Whilst all test reading should be faultless and clear enough for all to hear without strain, the students should be given an opportunity during training of taking dictation which has some of the faults of much office dictation, i.e. interruptions, mumbled words, amendments, external noises, etc.

Audio in Shorthand Speed Development

After the theory of shorthand has been covered and the stage of speed development and theory revision is reached, the value of audio work remains. Sound-tapes enable the teacher to put on practice passages of any length in which the dictation is flawless, and which can be repeated as often as necessary.

The use of sound-tapes can be extended so as to include all the necessary preparation material (e.g. one-minute dictations, vocabulary and short-form work). Then passages may be repeated at higher speeds. Several persons may work on the same tape so that the students get practice from different voices. Extemporized and office-style dictation may be recorded. A situation may be dramatized so that a conversation is recorded. The possibilities are numerous of very effective skill development, through the use of sound-tapes at this stage.

TESTING AND MARKING

This is a topic on which it is very difficult to provide any general information or idea of standards. Public examination bodies, for very sound reasons, do not publish their marking schemes, and schools and colleges are apt to be equally secretive. In shorthand, there is the perennial question of allocation of marks to shorthand notes and to transcript; there is a school of thought which pays little heed to the quality of the notes, as its adherents take the view that the businessman is not concerned with the means, but only with the end—the typed document. This view is the extreme opposite from the older approach to the teaching of shorthand, when all the emphasis was put first on sound theoretical knowledge, when theory tests were given (from longhand, not from dictation) and when speed practice was delayed until a satisfactory standard in theory was attained.

The author believes strongly in a "happy medium," for the following reasons—

1. A good knowledge of shorthand theory, and a good writing style, are the basis of speed work and fluent transcription. The better

the note, the more likely is the student to transcribe it intelligently and expeditiously.

2. If notes are poor, they will only be useful if transcribed quickly (where immediate memory can assist), or if the matter is familiar to the transcriber. Neither teacher nor students know at what level they will be called upon to work; they may be in a post where the vocabulary is wide, where the speed is also fairly high and where a high degree of accuracy is insisted upon. Such work can never be achieved on poor notes.

3. The old saying that "every soldier has a marshal's baton in his knapsack" can be used of shorthand writers; no teacher can say that he has no potential high-speed writers in his class and it is wrong educationally to withhold from students anything which may help them to achieve their maximum potential.

4. Good shorthand notes are likely to engender a pride in the subject and in workmanship. The author has always found a willing response to the challenge of a good style in writing; indeed it often enables the student who writes in good style, but is not so good on theoretical knowledge, to gain confidence and a desire to work harder on her weaknesses.

Just as in typewriting it is helpful to strive for speed separately from accuracy so that they finally merge, so in shorthand writing it is possible to strive for style as something apart from speed or theoretical knowledge. Students fairly soon acquire the habit of writing good outlines and this carries over into speed work. With evening students who have rather slow dictation in the office, it has proved an excellent method of getting more "practice" (focus of attention) to ask them to concentrate on style whenever the dictation was below their normal writing speed.

Having decided, then, that both style and speed are to be assessed, we come to other aspects of testing and marking. It will be convenient to deal with them at the two stages which, for the sake of convenience, we will call the "theory" and the "speed" stages, although speed will come into the first and theory will come into the second.

There will, of course, be definite purposes in the testing, based on the general principles given in Chapter V, and the tests will be informal and formal, according to the aim at the time.

In shorthand, more than most subjects, testing is really taking place for most of the lesson, since chalkboard reading, note-reading, questions on theory, and the teacher watching the writing of students, all serve the purpose of making the teacher aware of the progress and weaknesses of the students. None of this work is, however, rated by a mark and therefore the teacher must have rather more formal tests. At the theory stage these should still be through the dictated word so that the response is to sound, not to sight. The tests will also have to take place at fairly regular intervals and not merely on the completion of the theory. The problem then is what theory shall be tested for marking and what other aspects of the skill shall be allocated a rating?

On the matter of what shall be tested in theory, teachers will have different views and in the long run it probably does not make much difference whether there were three tests on, say, the halving principle, two on the representation of *s* and one on *-shun* hook or whether these numbers were reversed. The most practical way to proceed is to decide on the number of tests which it is desirable to give during the session, to allocate the theoretical knowledge into sections to correspond to this number and then to decide how much of each section shall be covered in each test. The first item in any record would be theory, but the other aspects of the subject should be tested and the author has found the outline given on p. 127 to be a useful form of record to show progress.

It is impossible to include in the tests all items of theory, all short forms, or all contractions. The teacher must therefore be vigilant during his teaching to discover what the students have already learned so well that it is unlikely to be forgotten. For instance, it would be a waste of time to give a test on the individual consonant strokes, since these are learned by constant use and any remedial work is best done spontaneously in the course of teaching; likewise, it would be unnecessary to include in a test on *s* circle such simple words as *safe*, *sum*, or *face*, but *lace* would be included because of the possibility of the *l* being written in the wrong direction. Important principles and important exceptions will be covered, but minor points should be omitted.

At the intermediate stage, that is, when the students have covered the theory and are writing at speeds between 50 and 70 words per minute, the emphasis in teaching will be on the development of writing and reading speeds and of transcription skill. In formal tests, therefore, these aspects will predominate, although some testing of theory (especially principles of contraction and phrasing) will also be included. At this stage some checking of spontaneous writing of short forms should take place during each lesson, so that immediate remedial work can be carried out.

As much typewritten transcription as possible should be given, but formal typewritten transcription tests should be kept to a minimum since at this stage the students need guidance and help in *preventing* errors. They also need guidance and practice in good work habits in this more complex skill.

At the advanced stage, the objectives will be increased writing speed, reading speed and proficiency in typewritten transcription. Formal tests should ideally be in the form of typed transcripts. However, because of the demand on typewriting facilities, this may not be practical. For examination some longhand transcription practice is essential.

The number of tests to be given will vary with the length of the course and the needs of the class. Some students respond well in effort when frequent tests are given; others do better if testing is kept to a minimum. As in so many other things in teaching, it is unwise to generalize.

Shorthand Progress Tests

Names	Theory Tests 1 2 3 4 5 6	Reading Tests 1 2 3 4 5	Shorthand Style 1 2 3 4	Short Forms 1 2 3 4	Speed Tests 1 2 3 4

CHAPTER VIII

Teaching Typewriting

THE fact that the typewriting classroom is a specialist room is both advantageous and disadvantageous from the point of view of the typewriting teacher and student. The advantages are obvious: in the first place the room is often carefully chosen for siting so that it receives good natural daylight; secondly it is usually adequately equipped with tables and adjustable chairs, although the latter do not solve all the problems of seating even one class of twenty to twenty-five students of varying heights. Varying table heights would be an asset in most typewriting rooms.

TYPEWRITING ROOM EQUIPMENT

Apart from tables and chairs, stationery and textbooks, the following items of equipment are desirable and the author considers the items marked with an asterisk to be essential.

*Typewriters and Copyholders.** If only one typewriting room is available, it will be necessary to have at least one-third of different makes and the remaining two-thirds of the same make.

If two or more rooms can be fitted up there is a distinct advantage in having one equipped with machines of the same make for the beginners' classes.

In the variety of typewriters there should be included some with elite- and some with pica-size type, some with different lengths of carriage and some electric machines.

*Demonstration Stand.** This is standard equipment with some education authorities.

Duplicating Equipment. Rotary ink duplicator,* spirit duplicator* and photocopiers are examples of this.

*Filing Cabinets.**

*Bookcase and Stationery Cupboard.**

*Dictating Machines.**

*Record Player.**

Labour-saving Devices. Examples of these are the guillotine, stapling machine,* punch* and pencil sharpener.*

Reference Books.

Display Board.

Lintograph or Plastograph Board.

Lettering Stencils. ("Econasign.")

Large Map of Great Britain.

Tape-recorders.

CLASSROOM ORGANIZATION

It is customary to seat twenty to twenty-five students in a typewriting room, but at all levels it would be better to have smaller groups as is the custom in other practical subjects. Fifteen would be an ideal number at any time but is a necessity at production work level.

One of the possible disadvantages of the typewriting room being a specialist room is that it is likely to be in use for every period of the day and evening, and unless there is strict supervision and good organization with regard to tidiness, machine maintenance, etc., it can become one of the most neglected rooms in a school or college.

Frequently, too, in order to accommodate the required number of students, the tables are minimum in size and give no opportunity to train students in placement and handling of papers or other work accessories. It also sometimes happens that too many tables or desks are put into the room with the result that it is not possible to have gangways to enable the teacher to see each student at work. The typewriting teacher needs to work with elementary students all the time and individual supervision is essential to good progress.

The following are given as essential points of good organization for a typewriting room—

1. Each desk and machine should be clearly numbered and a rule established that machines are not to be moved without the permission, and *under the supervision*, of the teacher in charge of the class at the time.

2. A "Repairs Book" should be kept, preferably on the teacher's desk, and any machine requiring the attention of the mechanic should be entered in it as soon as the fault is noticed. A suitable form for such book would be—

Desk No.	Make of Machine	Fault	Date repaired and checked (Teacher's signature)

3. If space allows, storage cupboards, duplicating machines, filing cabinets, etc., should not be placed in one area, but the different working areas separated in order to avoid congestion when students are working at different things. There should be one area for duplicating work, one for students' filing cabinets, another for the teacher's filing cabinets, etc.

All typewriting rooms should provide storage space for—

Practice material	Business documents (examples)
Test material	Reference books
Students' files	Small office tools
Textbooks	Current paper stocks

4. As in any other classroom, the chalkboard should be left clean at the end of each lesson. If roller type boards are installed, it would be reasonable to leave material on one section, with the request that it should not be erased.

It is assumed, of course, that the typewriting teacher, in common with other teachers, will have access to film and film-strip projectors when desired.

THE SCOPE OF THE TYPEWRITING SYLLABUS

The brief account of the development of typewriting as a subject given in Chapter I showed that today typewriting embraces a wide range of skills and also some ancillary subjects. The typewriting teacher today, in drawing up a syllabus and scheme of work for any particular class or group of classes. will have to decide which and how much of the following items shall be included once the students have learned to manipulate the machine—

1. Straightforward copying of continuous matter (from perfect or amended copy).
2. Copying of tabulated matter.
3. Preparation of business documents (from typescript, print or manuscript), e.g. legal documents, specifications, minutes, bills of quantity, etc.
4. Speed development from perfect copy.
5. Preparation of masters for various duplicating processes.
6. Use of duplicating machines (including photocopiers).
7. Audio-typing.

These are nearly all major topics, requiring, if satisfactory standards are to be achieved, more than a superficial knowledge and skill.

The typing of continuous matter forms the basis of the development of a typist's skill and of her speed of operation once the basic ability to manipulate the typewriter has been learned. Some teachers feel that a good proportion of class time should be spent on this type of work before students are allowed to embark on work calling for ability in display. In a one-year secretarial course such teachers would probably not introduce the typewriting of business letters until the second term, and in a more junior course, in which the weekly time allocation to typewriting would be less, keyboard work would probably occupy two terms. Other teachers feel that in order to create or sustain interest it is better to introduce simple display work in the first term, allowing the perfecting of the keyboard skill and general machine manipulation to take place side by side with it. It is not possible to be dogmatic on such questions—at any rate until valid evidence is produced as a result of research work—as so much depends on the capabilities and the attitude to work of the students, on the relationship between them and the class teacher, etc. It can, however, be said quite definitely that until the students can manipulate the machine without hesitation as to finger reaches and with some degree of confidence, it would be wrong to interfere with the acquisition of this basic skill by introducing problems of display.

A typewriting course then, in essence, falls into two parts—(*a*) learning to manipulate the machine, and (*b*) developing speed and accuracy in the production of typewritten documents. The latter is the more difficult task and requires the longer time, since the degree of difficulty of such work can vary tremendously. It is not always recognized that it is not necessarily the kind of document which determines the degree of difficulty; it is not possible to establish a hierarchy of difficulty merely by establishing an order of presentation according to type or form of document.

Any piece of typewriting work may be easy, of medium, or of considerable difficulty because of one or more of the factors given below—

1. The medium in which the copy is presented (typescript, print, manuscript, shorthand).
2. The extent to which and the manner in which the copy is amended; whether the amendments involve taking in matter from other documents.
3. The length of the document.
4. The "typewritability" of the copy (some matter, such as formulae, abbreviations and technical matter, involves awkward combinations of movements which prevent the typist from maintaining a continuous, fluent rhythm).
5. The extent of the matter to be displayed (tables, etc.).
6. The extent to which the display of the copy corresponds to the desired final form.
7. The language content (whether the vocabulary and style are familiar to the typist).
8. The number of carbon copies, if any.
9. The stage of attainment of the typist in relation to the copy (whether the student is ready for the particular type of work to be done).
10. The time allowed for producing the fair copy.

In a word, the teacher has to provide practice material for the development of the skill of machine manipulation and for the skill of applying that ability to the speedy production of accurate and well-displayed documents.

A Basic Plan

The following is an outline which incorporates the ideas given in the points above and which could serve as the basis for a detailed scheme of work.

THE PRESENTATION OF TYPEWRITTEN WORK

Stage 1	*Suitable Material*
Machine manipulation— (*a*) Learning finger reaches. (*b*) Learning to manipulate other moving parts of the typewriter—	
Parts of machine. Keyboard work. Machine manipulation in general. Posture.	Word, phrase and sentence exercises.
Stage 2	
Typing continuous matter in order to consolidate finger reaches and machine manipulation—	
Margins. Line-end division of words. Capitals. Paragraphing. Typing on lined paper. Some speed development.	Alphabetic sentences. Paragraphs (informative matter). Short articles. Short reports.
Stage 3	
Copying with simple display— (*a*) From typescript. (*b*) From print. (*c*) From manuscript. (*d*) From chalkboard shorthand. (*e*) Audio-typing (where appropriate).	
Centred headings. Hanging paragraphs. Side headings. Centring to page. Equal column display. Continuation sheets. Completing forms. Speed development. Use of carbons.	Articles. Simple letters. Notices. Memoranda. Simple forms. Short Minutes. Simple tables. Simple invoices. Staff work, if suited to attainment of class.

Stage 4	*Suitable Material*
Copying with display of medium difficulty— (*a*) From typescript. (*b*) From print. (*c*) From manuscript. (*d*) From good shorthand copy. (*e*) Audio-typing (where appropriate).	Letters (with tabulated inset).
Centring headings to copy. Unequal columns. Erasing. Arranging own display. Preparing stencils and masters. Duplicating. Ruling. Speed development. "Production" work.	Agendas. Menus. Minutes (more difficult). Wills. Declarations. Financial statements (fairly simple balance sheets). Specifications. Programmes. Statistical tables, etc. Staff work, if suited to attainment of class.
Stage 5	
Copying with difficult display (from any medium, including shorthand notes and machine dictation)—	
Vertical headings. Two-page matching. Units of work, including several different documents. "Cold" shorthand notes. Estimating space from crowded manuscript. Direct typing of letters, memos, etc., of own composition from brief notes. "Production" work.	As for Stage 4, but more difficult presentation; also from shorthand. Staff work.

The types of material given could, of course, be extended, but it is suggested that what has been indicated is sufficient for the general run of typewriting courses.

Lesson Planning

In typewriting, as in shorthand, the general principles of lesson planning for a skill subject apply—small units of theory are followed by practical application; supervised practice and remedial work are selected to suit the needs of the individual student; subjects are correlated where appropriate; and the students are given the opportunity of using their initiative and of developing good work habits and attitudes.

Homework

It has been suggested that typewriting as a subject precludes the setting of homework, yet a moment's thought and reflection on the nature of the skill shows that this is not the case. As we have seen, typewriting calls constantly for the application of knowledge in several different fields. Students may not be able to practise the manual movements as homework, but the working out of typewriting problems (e.g. calculating display layouts, reading manuscripts, preparing manuscripts to be typed by fellow students, reading subject matter on stationery and equipment connected with typewriting, etc.) saves class time and can make the difference between failure and success in the subsequent classroom exercise.

TEACHING MACHINE-MANIPULATION

The references in Chapter I to research work on the learning of typewriting are sufficient to lead anyone to the conclusion that word patterns, phrase patterns and sentence patterns make the learning of the keyboard finger reaches easier than do meaningless letter combinations. A second point of interest which such studies bring out is that it is helpful to the student to look at the keyboard first to see as well as feel the movement required. Of course the eyes must be kept on the copy while actually typing. The author supports these findings from her own experience in the classroom and also strongly recommends that the earliest exercises should be written boldly on the chalkboard. The need for the students to keep the head well up when copying from the board minimizes the temptation to "glance" at the keyboard. Students thereby gain confidence in typing by touch more quickly than if the copy is at the side of the machine. The method is also helpful in securing the habit of good posture. The point is sometimes made that to ask students to copy from the board is not a good technique because students will never need to do so in the office, but this point is not relevant provided that the chalkboard exercises are not carried on until a strong habit is formed.

The first presentation of the typewriting skill to any class will, of course, be in the form of a demonstration of touch typewriting by the teacher, at a rate sufficiently high to give the idea of ease, fluency and speed, but not so rapid that the students gain the impression of a task impossible of attainment by them.

Electric Typewriters

Most schools and colleges now include some electric machines in their equipment—in the United States and Canada entire classes are taught on electric machines. The question which any education authority will ask when confronted with a request for expenditure on these more expensive machines is whether they are likely to justify the additional cost. In America there is no doubt about the answer: quicker learning, higher speeds and better quality work. In this country several colleges have carried out experiments in initial teaching on electrics versus initial teaching on manuals, and in alternating the initial teaching (changing each fortnight or so) on electric and manual machines.[1] Although the total number of students involved is relatively small, the results are similar to those obtained in the United States. What is undeniable is that electric machines cause less fatigue. It is obvious that a typist who has been using only manual machines for a number of years will find it more difficult to change to an electric machine (negative transfer of training), but new typists do not find it difficult to be adaptable in their skill.

Copy on Right or Left

After the first week or two the students can be expected to copy some exercises from the textbook (or sheet prepared by the teacher). The question then arises as to the position of the copy and the use or non-use of copyholders. On the latter point it is strongly recommended that copyholders be used during the training period as they give a better reading position and help good posture. There is some difference of opinion on whether the copy should be placed on the left-hand or the right-hand side of the machine. Some teachers maintain that if it is placed on the left-hand side the vision is interfered with when the left hand returns the carriage; others say that this movement makes no difference. It is further suggested that if a typist has a markedly strong or weak eye, this will determine from which

[1] See article in *Shorthand Teachers' Supplement*, Vol. 27, No. 6 (March 1965).

side she prefers to read. There does not seem to have been any recent study of the problem, nor any reference to it in the earlier books and periodicals on typewriting method. L. J. West,[1] although he makes no mention of choice of side, states that—

> devices which hold the copy behind the typewriter (e.g. Line-A-Time) have not been acceptably evaluated. There are slight benefits from tilting the copy so that the line of vision is at right angles to the middle line of the page (instead of leaving the copy flat alongside the typewriter) that is, at an angle of 41 degrees from the vertical.

He then, somewhat surprisingly, adds—

> Since stands may be fabricated cheaply, their use would appear sensible.

In view of the detailed nature of his study, the omission of the topic of copy position is to be regretted.

Order of Presentation of Keys

The next decision which a typewriting teacher has to make when preparing to take a beginners' course is the order in which he will present the keys. There are two well-known methods—the *horizontal* and the *vertical*. When the horizontal method is used the keys are learned in "banks," in the following order—first, the home row (asdfg hjkl;); next, the third bank; then the bottom bank; and lastly the top bank. In the vertical method, the keys are learned in files. The teachers who favour the former method probably do so for the following reasons—

1. All fingers are used from the start.
2. It enables the hand position to be established by using the first and fourth finger keys as anchoring positions.
3. The correct stroking is established before the student is confronted with finger reaches.

The vertical method advocates make the following points in support of their preference—

1. As the first fingers are more flexible and independent, and, since the reaches with them are easier, it is wise to proceed from the simple to the more difficult.
2. The use of two fingers at a time on four keys is easier to establish than that of four fingers, especially for the reaches.

[1] *Review of Research in Typewriting Learning with Recommendations for Training* (Texas, U.S.A.F Personnel Training Research Center, 1957).

3. In this method the vowels are introduced sooner and therefore more words and sentences can be practised than with the horizontal method.

The author has found that a combination of the two methods is definitely advantageous. By establishing the staccato stroking movement on the home row and then introducing the reaches vertically, or in a "skip-around" order (see below), confidence is gained more quickly and the more meaningful material which can be used for practice work maintains interest. E. G. Blackstone[1] in 1940 studied the work done in evaluating typewriting teaching methods and on the question of the keyboard approach made the following points—

1. Three methods of teaching the keyboard are used: one starts with the home row; one starts with the first fingers only; and one skips around the keyboard apparently without any logical plan of approach. Such evidence as there is seems to favour the skip-around method.

2. The keyboard may be taught as a whole or broken into parts. Experiments made thus far have shown little difference in the results of the procedures.

3. There is some evidence to promote the use of words in a meaningful context rather than nonsense syllables or the repetition of a single word. When the material is interesting, accuracy appears to increase.

Rate of Keyboard Introduction

With the earlier "accuracy before speed" method of teaching, it was customary to introduce the finger reaches gradually, consolidating the skill on one bank of keys before moving on to new reaches. In some courses fifty to sixty hours were spent on keyboard learning and simple copying. With what today is called the "skill" method, the keys are introduced rapidly—in some cases in as little as two hours, though the average is about ten hours. Words and phrases are introduced from the beginning and simple display work is started anywhere between the fourth and eighth week of the course (taking a one-year course as the average). It would seem from the experience of many teachers that the more rapid introduction is suitable for older and more intelligent students, whilst the younger and less bright students do better with the more gradual introduction coupled with a fair amount of consolidation.

[1] "Summary of Research in Typewriting," *The Nationa Business Education Quarterly* (Washington, D.C., Spring, 1940).

Blank Keys

The author had the experience of teaching a number of beginners' classes with the machines "blanked" and later having to transfer, rather unwillingly, to visible keyboards. After one session with the latter the value of the blank keyboards was shown to be extremely small. Blackstone[1] reports that "blank keys and wall charts of the keyboard seem to be inferior to the use of visible keyboards at which the students may look temporarily while learning the locations and reaches." The expression "while learning" does not mean during practice, but only to give a visual impression of direction immediately before the practice of the new reach. Many other authorities confirm this finding.

Keyboard Shields

The use of this device is fortunately disappearing. Today the emphasis in typewriting learning is on technique and no teacher can observe the finger technique of students if the hands are hidden under a shield. Moreover, there is another most important principle of skill acquisition which cannot be applied if shields are used, namely, that no movement should be allowed at the learning stage which is not required at the expert level. If shields are used to cover the keyboard, then the learner has to make an entirely wrong movement for the carriage return. Instead of the "continuous path" movement, the shield forces the left hand to retrace the path from the keyboard to the carriage return lever.

One would hesitate to mention the deplorable habit of providing students with "aprons," yet it seems that at the time of writing these so-called aids are still in use. It must take students a good deal longer to gain confidence in their ability to type when such restraining devices are employed.

Layout of Practice Material

The next question is the form in which the copy should be presented to the student. Most modern textbooks have been arranged to avoid the cramped, printed copy of some of the earlier books. Instead they present the elementary exercises in imitation typescript, with good, simple display, helpful illustrations and instructions on good technique. Many of the exercises are also on the lines of the modern trend in teaching, namely, to train the student to be competent in production

[1] Blackstone, E. G., op. cit.

work. There are, however, still examples to be found of form and layout which hinder rather than help the student. As we have already said, copy which students can recognize immediately as having meaning will aid learning; secondly, the eyes must be guided easily along the line of copy and anything which hinders steady progression hinders finger movement. For these reasons exercises such as the following should be avoided—

> or for or for for he the the an and an and he the and for he
> us if he us of it me so me to he an go an he an do by do by me

If the teacher wishes students to type words more than once, it is better to write the word on the board, giving the instruction "Type this word until I ask you to stop." In this way students will be able to work at their own pace and will not need to wait, inactive, until the slowest member of the class has finished the exercise. The instruction to type a certain number of perfect copies of an exercise is also one to be firmly rejected, for as soon as a student makes a mistake and has to start again, a fear tension is set up and the skill gradually, or perhaps suddenly, breaks down. From time to time it is a good technique to say to a student "Try to let me have a perfect copy of this short passage. You may not manage it the first time, but you may start again on another sheet of paper." This is a challenge and if the teacher is careful to stop the work after a reasonable time and give the student a different task, no harm will be done. Blackstone mentions the requirement of perfect copies as a device which should be avoided, and compares it to "some of the torture devices of the Inquisition." Time and again teachers of typewriting have found that one of the best ways to get accurate work is to give students copy which is within their capacity but which is "purposeful," i.e., is going to be used. This is not to say that all work must be "production" work; if the purpose of an exercise is understood by the students and there is willingness to co-operate, the exercise will be as beneficial as any "job." It must also be stressed that, in spite of the value of material which is to be used as an incentive to accurate work, such tasks must always fit in with and not be allowed to take the place of the graded work of the course.

Speed Versus Accuracy

This is still a topic which arouses lively discussion, yet there would now seem to be sufficient evidence from researches and from the experience of practising teachers to indicate that both can be achieved if attention is paid to both, and not to one only, from the earliest days. The authors of *Typewriting Behaviour*[1] stress again and again a finding in research studies that—

> Fast, correct stroking is not mastered in slow practice. A queer bias for petty accuracy hinders uncounted typing classes. "Copy" rather than "technique" is wrongly made the objective. . . . The Gilbreths are fully justified in their stress on correct motions first, speed second, accuracy last. Losses in accuracy with greater speed are relatively slight, unless the speed waxes excessive. Any errors slow up the speed, as the usual error is a transitory breakup in the sequence pace.

In a movement away from the "accuracy before speed" attitude, there has been developing the recognition that "speed and accuracy" should be the aim and that different types of exercise should be given for each. Thus, in what is now widely known as the "skill" method (popularized by Alfreda Patten in this country) or as the "simplified" method (introduced into America by L. A. Leslie and P. S. Pepe), one-minute timed writings are advocated, the first for accuracy, followed by several for speed, and concluding with a final writing for accuracy. With older students who can quickly appreciate the need for technique and control, this method may be used for a good proportion of the practice or drill periods. With younger students, who are more prone to develop speed without control and therefore without technique, the teacher needs to be more cautious in the use of timed writings. There is a danger that students may develop excessive hand movement and uneven stroking in their effort to force the speed.

It is perhaps understandable that typewriting teachers and students who are accustomed to the idea of speed developing after the establishment of accurate stroking habits, should find it difficult to accept what appears to be a contradictory concept; the fundamental point, however, is that a fast movement is different from a slow movement and is not the slow movement speeded up. This is true of all skills. Miss Elizabeth Sidney[2] in an interesting paper quoted the case of the improvement in skill of hosiery workers in a Scottish town. It was found that a "different, more complex neural pattern was established

[1] Dvorak, A., Merrick, N. L., Dealey, W. L. and Ford, G. C., *Typewriting Behaviour* (New York, American Book Co., 1936).

[2] "The Theory of Learning and Management Training," *Education and Commerce*, No. 18 (January, 1957).

in performing a job at great speed compared with the pattern of the same job performed slowly. The solution was to concentrate a great deal on speed. He [the experimenter] guessed that if the general pattern of extremely fast work was established, accuracy would soon develop, and his results have borne this out. . . ." This general principle of skill acquisition, then, is worth noting and if both teacher and students know the definite aim of each exercise or drill, and if the three elements of technique, speed and accuracy are kept in balance, there will be no point of controversy.

Supervised Practice

At the learning stage of machine manipulation and consolidation, and at all times during speed development work, the author is strongly of the opinion that the most important function of the teacher is to observe the students and note individual strong and weak points. Confidence is one of the basic necessities for any learner of a skill; therefore, if the teacher is observant and can say to a student "That was a good movement," or "Your fingers moved very nicely then," or again, "Yes, that was better"—no matter how slight the improvement—there is more likely to be an upward trend in performance than if the teacher concentrates solely on the weaknesses. Supervision of practice is also necessary in order to take account of the general principles of learning, of prevention of errors and the catering for individual differences. If a teacher does not see how the individual students are performing, work cannot be graded to suit progress and some students will be held back or others pushed ahead too quickly. The worst kind of typewriting period (it cannot be called "lesson") is that in which the procedure is for the students to type an exercise, have it corrected at the teacher's desk, and to continue with the next exercise, or repeat the first one if required to do so. Unless the teacher works with the class during most of the class period until such time as all students have established effective practice habits, the students' technique and even their attitude to work will deteriorate and the best use will not be made of the typewriting class time.

By working with the class and being vigilant in watching for improvements and weaknesses, the teacher is also allowing another general principle of learning to operate, namely, that immediate knowledge of progress is conducive to effective learning.

Errors

In all work which is designed to develop accuracy, any errors made should be studied and, if possible, the reason for any persistent ones discovered. Error analysis is useful, but need not be over-emphasized. Again, a few minutes watching a student will often tell the teacher more about the remedial work required than any detailed correction of the typescript. It is obvious from the studies made at different times that there are certain stroking errors which are common to many students and it is helpful for the teacher to be aware of them so that preventive or corrective work can be given. On page 395 of *Typewriting Behaviour*[1] the authors state—

> The delusion that students learn to typewrite by mastering an accurate letter stroke leads many to think of errors as false letter strokes. To count isolated letter errors is artificial and fruitless. Typing errors are signs of interference, due partly to drills on isolated letter strokes and nonsense combinations, partly to relative dominance of common sequence signals, partly to chance slips in technique, and partly to underlying keyboard arrangement. [And] it may be stated as a general principle that the wider the delay between strokes in sequence, the higher is the chance of error.

Blackstone[2] found that different kinds of errors were made by bright students and dull students, the former failing more on spacing, omissions, additions and stroking, and the latter more on "centring, tabulating and other situations involving planning rather than technique habits." This is a finding which most teachers will confirm from their own experience and which might well be borne in mind when students are selected for typewriting courses. What cannot be stressed too often is that the typewriting skill for the future office worker does not consist only of ability to produce rapidly a copy of straightforward matter from a perfect original. On the question of typical typewriting errors, Blackstone adds that from several studies of these it has been found that the most frequent are "substitutions of one key for another (most frequently *i* for *e*), incorrect spacing, strikeovers, omissions, transpositions, and incorrect hyphenization."

Elimination of Errors. When errors have been diagnosed and practice is required on those involving faulty reaches, care should be taken to give the right kind of practice. It is rarely effective to drill the single word, as it frequently happens that the error has been caused through

[1] op. cit.
[2] Blackstone, E. G., op. cit.

faulty anticipation, or through a difficult word-to-word letter sequence. The best drill is for the sentence or phrase to be repeated and for further drills with the same letter combinations to be given for subsequent work. Although West[1] does not mention error elimination, he does say—

> there is no reason why practice on *frf* or on *for* should help much for the subsequent typing of *are*, *run*, *prefer*, or any of the many thousands of words containing *r*. It is far better to have extensive practice on a lot of materials than to have intensive practice on a more limited set of materials. While this stricture against excessive repetition applies throughout the learning (including, for example, speed-building materials), it is perhaps particularly relevant to the large amounts of repetition on small units of material so frequently built into the keyboard-learning stages of typewriting training.

On the point of overtyping, it may be said that all teachers consider this kind of error worthy of the heaviest marking penalties. It must certainly be prevented from developing into a habit. A method which the author has found to be effective is to explain to the students very early in the course why such errors are unacceptable and to announce the penalties which will be strictly imposed, namely, that every overstriking will be counted as two errors in the first term, as three in the second term, and as five in subsequent terms.

Capital Letters Out of Alignment. This type of error should rarely occur (except through machine faults) after the first few shift-key exercises. If a good demonstration is followed by appropriate practice and by the teacher watching the hand action of *every* student and giving additional help where necessary, there should be no difficulty. In the matter of appropriate exercises, the author has found that better shift-key operation is obtained more quickly on short sentences which enable fluent typing action to be maintained, than on artificial, rhythm-breaking sequences which do not have a meaning. Even an experienced typist finds that the latter type of material slows down speed; a learner, who cannot be expected to be able to modify her newly acquired stroking skill, finds such material irksome and frustrating. Anyone wishing to prove this point should type each line of the following exercises three times and note the difference in rhythm and movement between performance on Group A and on Group B—

Group A. Short sentences

(16 shift-key operations in 207 key strokes, covering 12 letters.)

[1] West, L. J., op. cit.

Quarto paper measures 8 inches by 10 inches.
The share market in London is called the Stock Exchange.
A Peseta is a Spanish coin.
William Caxton gave us the first printed book in England.
The largest public library in Britain is in the British Museum.

Group B. Artificial matter

(58 shift-key operations in 156 key strokes, covering 44 letters and characters.)

aA bB cC dD eE fF gG hH iI jJ kK lL mM
nN oO pP qQ rR sS tT uU vV wW xX yY zZ
Has Gap Man Vue Nip Box Had Gas Map Vox Nod Box
a";) s/l(d@k' f£j& J7F5 K8D4 L9S3 :-A2
Zero Frame Itself Match "Press" Small Whom

Teaching the Figure-character Keys

Some years ago the author decided that the traditional method of teaching finger reaches to the top bank of keys produced awkward movements and seemed to be an unnecessarily difficult method of learning. Since expert typists' hands hover over the keyboard and make swift movements up to the figures and back to the home position, it was thought that it would help learners if they were allowed to move the *hand* up and, in the very earliest stages, establish a "guide position" as one does on the home row. Rapid return to the home row immediately the figure key had been struck was stressed and practised. The improvement in the rate and accuracy of learning was considerable in every class in which the method was used. In recent years this method has been reported as one which is favoured in America and which is there called the "pipe-organ" method. The authors of *Methods of Teaching Business Subjects*[1] report a third method which they describe as "'a modification' of the pipe-organ method—the 'we-23' drills, in which the typist works from the last row of alphabet keys rather than the home row in making reaches."

TYPEWRITING RHYTHM

Ideas about rhythm in typewriting have changed as a result of psychological studies. Harm Harms[2] reports Jane E. Clem as saying—

[1] Tonne, H. A., Popham, E. L. and Freeman, M. H., *Methods of Teaching Business Subjects*, 2nd ed. (New York, McGraw-Hill Publishing Co., 1957).
[2] *Methods in Vocational Business Education* (Cincinnati, South Western Publishing Co., 1940)

Metronomic rhythm has been replaced by a new conception of rhythm. Rhythm is now interpreted to be a flow of writing in which the many combinations are typed faster than the hard combinations.

West[1] confirms the view that rhythm does not mean equal time intervals between strokes. "Objective measurements of these time intervals," he says—

> show positively and clearly—beyond all possible argument—that the interval between strokes depends mainly on the ease or difficulty of making the particular motions involved. Intervals are short between easy or well-practised combinations of motions and longer for more difficult or little practised stroking sequences. . . . It has been shown, even for the very simplest of skills, that the human organism is incapable of maintaining "perfect rhythm." . . . Any improvement in working at even tempos, resulting from the imposition of such a tempo, takes place in the very early trials, is quite small, and does not appear to be permanent. In other words, the variety of rhythms used in typewriting do not appear to be teachable.

Nevertheless, most teachers will agree that even tempo key-stroking is valuable in the earliest stages of learning as it helps to develop a staccato movement and an even pressure.

The consideration of rhythm brings one naturally to the question of the use of music in the typewriting lesson. There are undoubted advantages if music is used with discrimination and a *definite aim*, which must be understood by both teacher and students. One has heard of extreme cases where music has been used in every lesson, for the *whole* period, during the first two months of a course, or where it has been used "just to make a change." H. E. White gives the possible aims as—

1. Class control.
2. Speed control.
3. Stimulation of rhythmic movement.
4. Rapid establishment of the necessary required reflexes.
5. Pacing.

For class control the main advantage of music for the students is that in their earliest efforts of rather uncoordinated movements, the external stimulus helps to "keep them going" and to relieve or prevent boredom. In all muscular actions the human organism tends to perform with greater ease to the stimulus of music. For the teacher the obvious

[1] West, L. J., op. cit.

advantage is that he is free to observe individual students at work, to give encouragement and advice on the *manner* of performance and thus prevent bad habits forming.

When a degree of facility has been acquired on the machine, some students tend to adopt a somewhat slow, deliberate pace for all their work and find it difficult to increase their speed; others tend to do the opposite and force their speed too soon. Short periods of typing to music are excellent forms of control for both types of students; the slow performers should be required to type to a beat faster than their normal, while the more rapid but uncoordinated operators should be required to type to a slower beat.

The stage at which a student will move away from the regular, even tempo stroking to the rhythmic pattern dictated by the ease or difficulty of the required movements will be an individual development; however, there is not likely to be a great variation in a class until a fair degree of automaticity has been established in the finger movements. Some authorities maintain that the individual rhythm does not (or should not) develop below 50 words per minute. Others, including the author, believe that it develops sooner, at about 35 words per minute (if, indeed, it is possible to generalize at any speed). However, if discrimination is used in deciding on the frequency, duration and purpose of typing to music, the question is purely academic. Music can certainly be used at all stages of a typewriting course, provided that the following points are kept in mind—

1. The matter to be typed should have been practised first without music so that frustration is not caused through unfamiliarity of the required movements.

2. The period during which music is used should be short—ten minutes is generally sufficient in any lesson.

3. Typing to music does not need to be a feature of every lesson; the time may be more beneficially used for other work.

4. In almost all classes there will be one or two students, at least, who dislike this form of work; some may never acquire the ability to type to a regular tempo.

5. The volume of sound should be kept at a level to avoid disturbing other classes. The students seated farthest away from the record player generally pick up the beat from the class.

6. The aim which the teacher has in mind should be explained to the students on each occasion that the music is used.

For a fuller treatment of this topic the reader is referred to H. E. White's book already mentioned.

AUDIO AIDS

Although, as has been said above, music is helpful in the keyboard learning stage, the author is convinced that the newer methods using recording machines are superior. Audio-typing is now part of most typewriting courses (see section on Audio-typing, pp. 174–81) and is an examination subject in its own right. The stimulus of the spoken word and, when individual transcribing machines are used, the fact that each student works at her own pace, give a more realistic situation than music and certainly help students to progress more quickly at all stages.

PRACTICE MATERIAL

In selecting practice material for the typewriting student a number of factors have to be considered. It is rarely possible, or desirable, to use a textbook from cover to cover; within the scope of the subject matter textbooks must be designed to appeal to the widest possible public and are never intended to be the only source of material for a particular class. But, apart from the economic aspect of textbook appeal, the application of some important general principles of teaching and learning will demand that other sources be used. How otherwise can we provide individual remedial work, utilize student and teacher interests, correlate with other subjects in the curriculum, or cater for individual rates of learning? We therefore come back again to the point that all teaching involves selection and if we have to select we must know why we are choosing this or that material.

Choice of Word and Sentence Exercises

In the early stages of machine-manipulation learning and consolidation, the main purpose will, of course, be to develop manual skill, and since we know that meaningless matter is more difficult to type (even for the experienced typist), artificially constructed matter will be avoided. There is no virtue in setting the type of exercise in (*a*) overleaf, when the same reaches can be practised naturally and in meaningful form, as in (*b*).

(*a*) *Figure Exercise* (artificial).

fr4567uj fr4567uj fr4567uj ju7654rf ju7654rf ju7654rf
;p-; sw2a 1091 de3s ki8k fr4d ju7j fr5f hy6h

(*b*) *Sentence Unit* (meaningful).

The 45 rubber balls will cost 5p or 6p each.
The 75 folders will certainly hold 645 discs.
They have already sold 4,567 copies of this article.
When ordering 5p or 6p balls please quote reference JU745.

Even at the word and short sentence stage of keyboard consolidation, vocabulary and general knowledge can be linked with practice material. The following types of exercises have been found to be particularly useful for this purpose—

1. Select and dictate about six words which will be useful for keyboard and vocabulary, e.g. for younger students—

occupy career seized ceases accede cancel

and for older students—

anomaly census quorum gazette excise liquor

Check for spelling and typewriting, either orally or from chalkboard copy.

Students then spend five minutes typing one line of each word in which they had an error.

It will be noticed that the words for the younger students are of the same length and give practice on the bottom row of keys.

2. A development of these exercises a little later, when the use of the tabulator key is to be consolidated, is to ask the students to set the left-hand margin stop at 10, and tabulator stops at 30 and 50. The instruction then is—

"Type the first word when it is dictated and *immediately* use the tabulator key to the next column; similarly, after the second word. After the third word, *immediately* return the carriage to the next line."

At this stage nine or twelve words may be dictated. More than twelve is not desirable as too much remedial drilling may result for the time available, since chances of error are increased with the increase in the number of words.

3. A third development of this exercise is to dictate *short* sentences (about eight standard typewriting words) incorporating selected words, and give the instruction to start typing *after* the whole sentence has

been dictated, using the tabulator key in order to type the next sentence as a new paragraph. It is advisable not to include in each sentence more than two words likely to give rise to misspellings. The students must be instructed to keep their eyes on the teacher, or on the chalkboard.

The following are examples of suitable sentences.

For younger students—

One ream of paper contains 480 sheets.
The copyright of the book was inherited.
My colleague has been paid £50 by cheque.

For older students—

A customs and excise officer seized the goods.
To assess the deficit will be an immense task.
They were loath to admit their negligence.
The estimate for the renovations is not accurate.

Remembering that the skill of the typist is a complex one (see p. 33) the good teacher will select teaching methods and materials so that there is a balance between the acquisition of the necessary knowledge and the acquisition of the manipulative skill. One way which the author found of ensuring the over-learning and quick recall of essential knowledge without using too much class time was the "short answer" test. These were informal class tests, used frequently, taking no more than five minutes, and generally checked immediately so that each student could revise those facts which she did not know. The following are examples of such tests—

Short Answer Test No. 1

1. An average line of elite type gives about .... words.
2. Pica type gives .... and elite type .... characters to the inch.
3. Octavo paper measures .... × ....
4. A stitching margin is ....
5. A bichrome ribbon is one ....
6. The continuation sheet of a letter should show ...., ..., and ....
7. If there is sufficient room leave .... line spaces between the subscription and the writer's designation.
8. 19, 40, 58, 92 are represented in Roman numerals thus ...., ..., ..., ...
9. l.c. means ....
10. "Messrs" should not be used before ....

Short Answer Test No. 2

1. Absorbent type paper is used for .... duplicating.
2. Elite type gives .... lines of type to the inch.
3. Justifying in typewriting means ....
4. An engrossment is ....
5. International A4 paper measures .... × ....
6. A folio = ... words.
7. cf. means ....
8. In matter for the printer footnotes should be typed ....
9. Show a good division for these words:

comparison	adjustment	accentuate	remittance
....	....	....	....

10. Write the correct form of the following words if they are incorrectly given:

proffessor	relevent	embarrass	exorbitant
....	....	....	....

It is to be noted that none of these questions refers to points of machine operation which, of course, should always be tested by the teacher observing the student typing. However, such points of technique should not be tested while students are on "production" work tests. In the latter case students should be left to work as they would be in an office, without unnecessary interruptions.

Choice of Continuous Matter

At the stage of continuous matter the scope of choice is greatly widened and passages can be chosen which are of interest, representative of good use of punctuation, or informative in the field of general or business knowledge, etc. The following are given as examples—

1. *Informative Paragraph* (practice on underscoring and brackets).

Carbon paper. In choosing the particular kind of carbon paper to use for any typewritten work four points should be kept in mind: (1) the number of copies usually taken and the thickness of the typewriting paper; (2) the importance of the carbon copies; (3) the type of machine to be used; and (4) the colour required—it will usually be black.

2. *Interest Paragraphs* (practice on capitals).

Shepherd Market

Between Curzon Street and Piccadilly in London there has somehow survived a quaint little village which dates from the days when sheep fairs were held on land which is now part of Hyde Park.

Piccadilly Circus

The centre of London is Piccadilly Circus, "the hub of the world." At its centre stands the famous statue of Eros, and from it radiate some of London's best-known streets—Piccadilly, Regent Street, Haymarket and Shaftesbury Avenue. The origin of the word Piccadilly is dubiously connected with "pickadil," a ruff or frill.

3. *Extracts from Books* (longer passages to convey ideas).

There can be few words of more various meaning than crack and the present popularity of "get cracking" as an incitement to almost any kind of activity shows that crack is still a favourite. Crack in Shakespeare is a gay urchin as well as that rending and menacing noise, the crack of doom. As a brisk child, crack does, I think, survive in some pastoral English. Thieves have long had crack in their cant for house-breaking. We need not bother about crack's conventional use for a blow. More interesting is its employment for forms of talk, usually exaggerated, lurid gossip-talk. That links us up with the modern wise-crack, a word which would have been understood more easily by a man of the eighteenth than of the nineteenth century.

Extract from *I Give You My Word* by Ivor Brown (Jonathan Cape Ltd.).

An illustrated book is a partnership between author and artist to which the artist contributes something which is a pictorial comment on the author's words or an interpretation of his meaning in another medium. This partnership works in a numder of different ways. In a few rare instances the author and the artist are identified in a single person who himself carries out the designs. This union, as in the case of Blake, can result in a masterpiece comparable with the great achievements of creative art. But usually the illustration is the work of another hand, ideally, a hand which itself carries out the design in whatever medium has been chosen.

Extract from *English Book Illustration* by Philip James (A King Penguin Book).

4. *General Knowledge Passage* (practice on letters *c,v,b,n,m*, and capitals *B,C,G,H,I,L,S,T,W* and ").

Big Ben

Big Ben is the name given to the bell of the large clock at Westminster. The sound of this great bell is heard all over the world, making us feel at home wherever we may be. It was called Big Ben after Sir Benjamin Hill, the Chief Commissioner of Works when the bell was cast. He was a very tall, stout man whose friends had nicknamed him Big Ben. The name is very suitable because the bell—now over ninety years old—weighs thirteen and a half tons and the hammer that strikes it four and a half hundred-weights. Each of the dials of the clock measures twenty-two and a half feet in diameter and the figures on them are each two feet long. The minute hands are fourteen feet long and weigh two hundred-weights. They travel at the rate of one foot per minute.

If you want the right time, remember that the first blow on Big Ben tells the exact hour. Although Big Ben is the most famous bell in England, two others beat it in years. The biggest is "Great Paul" of Saint Paul's Cathedral, which weighs seventeen tons, and the second biggest is the huge bell in Liverpool Cathedral which is one ton heavier than Big Ben.

From a newspaper article.

It cannot be too strongly emphasized that in presenting such work to the students their attention must be drawn to its purpose; they can, for instance, be asked to read the passage silently before typing in order to know what it is about and to ask any questions they wish. Many students have been encouraged to follow up points of interest in copy material.

Choice of Displayed Matter

At the stage when display of medium difficulty is given, the main emphasis will be on teaching conventional forms of display and of developing speed on other exercises consisting of straightforward continuous matter. Drill work will be concerned mainly with individual weaknesses.

Choice of "Production" Work

At the next stage, that at which students are being prepared for the more realistic work of the office, (the "production" stage) sequences of work should be given when possible in order that students may have continuity of work and the opportunity to realize the importance of finishing interrupted work. For this purpose the following topics have been found to be of value and are given as examples only.

The first is the obvious sequence of a business transaction, which can be started as revision of earlier, simpler work and be continued with the more difficult documents.

Business Transaction Sequence. It is advisable to treat this as a fairly intensive sequence of work, otherwise interest may wane.

1. Internal memorandum (containing instructions to a buying manager to obtain estimates for certain goods).
2. Letter asking for quotation.
3. Reply from suppliers, giving quotation and enclosing order form.
4. Order form completed and sent with covering letter to suppliers.
5. Letter of acknowledgement from suppliers giving delivery times.

6. Invoice from suppliers.
7. Letter containing further order.
8. Statement of account from suppliers.
9. Letter from suppliers enclosing statistical table of new lines, prices and delivery delays.

Committee Work Sequence.

1. Copying exercise on committee terms.
2. Convening notice (or letter) to send out Agenda and Minutes.
3. Agenda.
4. Chairman's agenda.
5. Financial statement.
6. Minutes.

Arranging a Meeting (for example, of a social club). This sequence can be adapted to apply to a number of social events, such as lectures or concerts, and may include preparation on programmes, invitations, etc.

1. Writing to a speaker.
2. Speaker's acceptance.
3. Booking local hall by letter.
4. Circular to members.
5. Notice of meeting for posting in club headquarters.
6. Notes for speaker's talk.
7. Brief report of meeting for local press.
8. Secretary's report to club committee on success of meeting.

In these sequences the class can work in two groups, each student being paired with another to "receive" and "reply" and the work can be in the form of an assignment, to be completed by a certain date. The work should be presented in a folder. Alternatively, the teacher can see each piece of work as it is done. The necessary stationery for the business transaction can be prepared beforehand by stencil. If the college authorities will provide the money, electronic stencils can be prepared and letter headings, invoice forms, etc.. duplicated.

TEACHING DISPLAY

If we ask ourselves why we take the trouble to display matter in this or that way we find that it is not merely in order to make the typescript look attractive; the fundamental reason for display is that it shall convey the information to the reader in the most effective way. This means that the reader must be able to read it easily to see which are the important items, their relation to each other, and to be able to refer back to any section quickly and easily when necessary. Therefore the *first* criterion for the choice of display is the *purpose* of the document. This will determine what items need emphasis, what margins are desirable, what variations of line-spacing should be made, etc. Even for documents which are commonly used in most business offices there is often no definite right or wrong display formula; but there is frequently the "style of the house."

It is this variation of style which causes difficulty for the typewriting teacher, when dealing with the question of display. Textbooks say one thing, examining bodies may seem to require another and the business houses say many different things. What are the students to be told? They will certainly learn how to display more effectively if they can understand what the document is trying to convey and how emphasis and relationships can be portrayed in typescript. As a practical measure the author has told the students, when display work starts, that variations exist and that in the office there may be a style of the house which must be adhered to, or the typist may be left to adopt her own style, but in that case she will be expected to produce work which has a good appearance. Therefore, in class, the students will be given a style of the house which will be used for at least the first half of the session. Later they will be given the opportunity to vary display and decide for themselves, according to the basic principles of purpose, emphasis and good appearance, the style they wish to adopt.

In introducing students to the typing of specific documents it is important to lead up to such work. Trial and success is better than trial and error, for it saves time and frustration for both teacher and students. The document must, then, be looked at from the point of view of its typing content. For instance, many students find that their first invoice does not reach an acceptable standard, or even match their normal standard of work; they have produced a good letter, a good memorandum perhaps, at the first attempt, but a near failure with the invoice. This is not because the display has not been understood; it is probably because they were not ready, because they had not been sufficiently prepared with the sub-skills required for success. For instance, they need to have consolidated the typing of figures, the typing of sums of money, perhaps also fractions, the use of the tabulator key, and the typing of totals. All these things need to be revised and practised in advance of typing a complete invoice. Again, it is sometimes the custom of typewriting teachers to combine the understanding of the layout of an invoice with its typing, and if there are no printed invoice forms the students are required to rule one up. This takes some of them so long that they have to rush the main task of the lesson, the actual typing, in order to complete it within the lesson period; alternatively, they leave a half-finished exercise which may or may not be completed later. As they are hardly likely to be asked to prepare their own invoice forms in the office, and since it is a simple matter to have a form duplicated (either by the teacher, or *one* student), it is wasting precious teaching and learning time to give the task to every student. Some local education authorities have recognized the need for printed standard documents and have provided these as normal stock for typewriting classes.

Tabular Work

Another occasion where there is a need to analyse the task and see what sub-skills need developing or consolidating before the whole job is undertaken is in column display with headings. At one time, through the influence of the examination tests, it was customary to give a complete page of tabulated matter as an exercise. This meant that in any one lesson the students would have the opportunity of making one set of calculations only; the rest of the period would be taken up with typing the long list of items. The basic skill for column work, however, is to calculate *quickly* and *accurately* the starting points for the various headings and columns. The current practice is to give three or four short exercises instead of one long one so that the students have more concentrated practice in calculation. This exercise of planning display is also a useful type of homework.

When tabulated work is first introduced chalkboard diagrams are, of course, essential. If the statement is a simple one, to be displayed with an equal number of spaces for the margins and between the columns, the method of adding the number of type spaces required and deducting from eighty (pica type) or ninety-six (elite type) and dividing the remainder by the number of blank spaces required, is easy to teach and learn. However, as we have said before, the display must depend on the relationship between the parts of the document and the emphasis required. In this case the number of spaces required between the columns must be decided individually and added together. This may be done either before or after the margins have been decided upon, according to their relative importance. If it is essential that a certain number of spaces be given to the left-hand margin, for example, then that must be taken into account before the spaces between the columns are allocated.

Display of Documents

There is today such a variety of technical work and so much specialization that it is no longer possible to find one right way of setting out, say, a specification or estimate, and since textbooks cannot always be up to date it behoves the teacher to try to be knowledgeable about current practices. This leads to the next important point in teaching display, namely, that if an understanding of the document is to be gained, then the students should see the actual document whenever possible. In legal work, for example, it is possible for the teacher to buy document forms for wills and conveyances from law stationers and to type perfect copies. Typewriting teaching affords many opportunities for the students to be inspired by examples of work done by their own teacher. Most teachers display examples of students' work in the classroom, but one rarely sees examples of *expert* work by the teacher. (Is modesty the only reason?) It may be that typewriting teachers have done themselves and their subject a disservice by not emulating their colleagues in other fields (art, dressmaking, cookery) where it is normal practice not only to tell students what to do, but to let them see it being done at the expert level and also to see the finished article. Just as every typewriting student should build up a folder of her own acceptable work during the course, so the teacher should have a range of specimens (renewed from time to time) to illustrate and enrich the teaching. Textbook reproduction can never give an adequate image to the mind even of the simplest of business documents—the letter on headed paper of a quality never seen in the classroom. In other practical subjects good materials are used; why do typewriting classes not have a small stock of good typewriting paper and good letter headings for special work? How can students take a pride in their craft—and be cost conscious—if "practice paper" is the only quality on which they are allowed to work? Even the skill of erasing cannot be adequately acquired.

TEACHING ERASING

At one time many teachers considered it quite wrong to allow students to use an eraser, and it was certainly not regarded as a skill which needed to be taught. Today opinions are divided, but the general trend is towards teaching erasing. The question then arises as to when it shall be first introduced and the extent to which it shall be allowed. The author adopts the following plan which seems to work satisfactorily.

Students new to typewriting are told that until they have acquired the basic skill of operating the machine and can achieve a reasonable standard of copying skill no erasing will be allowed since it is important that both they and the teacher should be able to see the kind of error made. They are told that in the early stages they are bound to make some mistakes (which will not be considered a crime) and appropriate remedial work will be given. This "no erasure" stage usually applies to the first term in a one-year course. In the second term the students are taught how to erase and allowed to erase in one piece of work at each lesson for a week. From then to the end of the term they may only erase on occasions indicated by the teacher. In the third term (their last) they erase *except* when they are told not to do so. In this way they are encouraged to produce accurate rather than corrected work, and the question of erasing is kept in perspective.

TEACHING DUPLICATING

The office worker today needs to have some knowledge of a wide range of reproductive methods for documents and the typist will certainly need practical experience during her training in the two traditional methods, i.e. ink and spirit duplicating. In many schools and colleges one teacher is in charge of the practice office and will be responsible for teaching duplicating. If this teacher is not the typewriting teacher there should be close collaboration in order to ensure a balanced course for the students and especially to avoid unnecessary overlapping of teaching.

The teaching of ink and spirit duplicating has inherent difficulties for the teacher which can only be overcome by good planning and organization. The main problem is of teaching, say, all twenty to twenty-five students of a class with one ink duplicating machine and one spirit duplicator. Secondly, there is the question of the cost of the materials and, thirdly, there is the fact that to become efficient one needs to operate the machine for more than one or two copies, so that the amount of duplicating paper to be used is another problem.

There are three methods of organizing the instruction and a teacher may have to use each of them at different times according to circumstances.

1. If the theory of spirit and ink duplicating is taught at the same time, the teacher can set students to work preparing spirit machine masters and ink machine stencils while he supervises two or three students at a time using the ink machine. When he is satisfied that they can continue on their own, he can transfer to the spirit machine and supervise the working there. He thus alternates between the two machines. In the meantime the rest of the class have been given an assignment of work for submission at the end of the lesson.

2. A second plan is to teach two students each machine (four students in all) and they in turn teach two more until all members of the class have worked both machines. Those not engaged on duplicating may be preparing masters or stencils or be occupied on other work. This method gives more time to the teacher to supervise the work of any member of the class instead of concentrating only on those at the duplicating machines. In an evening class this method is particularly useful, since there is nearly always one member of the class who already knows how to operate one of the machines and who may be quite proud to be called upon to teach the others.

3. The third method is the easiest for the teacher but not always possible to arrange. It is for the college (or school) administrative office to undertake the tuition of two students at a time, or during any period when students are with them for practical work, if such a scheme is operated.

It is obvious from the above that most of the students cannot acquire real competence in duplicating; however, they can be given sufficient practice in preparing masters and stencils. To overcome the problem of expense with the latter, the teacher will in the first lesson use only one or two stencils for the whole class, allowing each member to type two lines with her initials at the side. The stencil is rolled off and the students can see the quality of their own contribution.

In addition to classroom teaching there may be, of course, visits to the showrooms of the machine manufacturers, to business efficiency exhibitions, and of representatives to the college or school to carry out a demonstration.

CORRELATION OF SUBJECTS

In addition to the opportunities afforded by doing practical work in the typewriting class for other members of staff, it is important that there should be an association between the curriculum subjects so that consolidation and over-learning may take place in a natural way. A few examples of the ways in which correlation may be organized are given below. It must be stressed that the benefit to the student of accidental, unplanned and unnoticed correlation will be minimum.

Correlation with English

The link between English and typewriting is, of course, the widest, the most natural and therefore the easiest form of correlation. Typewriting is another form of writing; therefore, anything which can be written (apart from special technical symbols) can be typed on the standard typewriter. The main areas of English knowledge which are directly relevant to the typist's skill are vocabulary extension, punctuation, summarizing and composition. In some cases work can start with the typewriting exercise; in others with the English. All the following ideas have been put into practice and found to be helpful to the students.

1. This exercise is designed to develop ability to recognize words from their consonantal skeleton—necessary for Pitman shorthand writers—and to consolidate spelling ability.

Exercise. Present the following material in typescript and ask the students to type the definition in the first column and the complete word in the second—

official count of the people of a country	c.n..s
easily broken	fr.g.l.
acknowledgement of money	r.c..pt
to set apart from others	s.p.r.t.

(In the above example each omitted letter is indicated by a full stop, but in later exercises this help need not be given.)

2. Sentences, faulty grammatically, can be typed with appropriate amendments, and the typed exercise given to the English teacher for marking.

3. Sentences which are in the active voice can be typed out in the passive voice.

4. English homework, written at home, can be typed in the typewriting lesson for submission to the English teacher.

5. Sentences can be composed and typed, each introducing *one* of a list of words, for example—

eligible, credible, stationery, precede, beneficiary.

6. A list of words which have difficulties of English (e.g. spelling or meaning) *and* typewriting (e.g. words beginning with the same letter or containing a difficult reach) is placed on the chalkboard to be copied; the material is then used in the English lesson. Such a list might contain the following words—

ingenuity	practice on *i* and *e*
anonymous	practice on difficult reach
connoisseur	practice on double letters
zodiac, zigzag, zenith	use of weak finger

7. Copying material for typewriting chosen by the typewriting teacher is passed to the English teacher for *intensive* study in the English class—vocabulary, punctuation, literary worth, ideas, etc. Similarly, the English teacher passes material to the typewriting teacher for copy typing, perhaps asking students to add their own notes taken in the English class.

8. Notes of a communication required to be expanded (composed for homework), are typed and are then taken to the English teacher for marking.

9. A letter copied in the typewriting room is taken to the English class for discussion or for the composition of a reply; students exchange manuscripts and type the reply.

10. Class compositions are exchanged and taken to the typewriting class to be typed as manuscript exercises; the necessary English corrections are made by the typist and recorded on the original. The English teacher has the typed copy to mark.

THE STUDENT'S FILE AND FOLDER

The question of what to do with exercises typed during the course needs more consideration than it is sometimes given. It is not uncommon for all work to be put in a folder (more or less tidily) and for the sheets to accumulate until the time when the teacher or the student feels compelled to throw some away. There is certainly no benefit to be gained by an indiscriminate collecting of all typed work. A simple and workable plan of selection must therefore be devised. The following is offered as one which has worked.

All work should be regarded as either practice work or work to be filed. From the very beginning the teacher should indicate to the students which category of work she is asking for; the earliest efforts on the keyboard exercises will mostly be practice work and the teacher will need to take in only one or two pieces of work in each lesson in order to check on touch and stroking accuracy. Later, some examples of good work in the progression from the simple to the more advanced documents should be retained for a period so that reference can be made to see the extent of the progress. There should, however, be a sorting-out at regular intervals, and when this is carried out there can be a transfer of all work which is worth keeping to the permanent folder to be kept by everyone. This folder could have three sections: Section 1 to take informative material provided by the typewriting teacher during the course (notes on typewriting display, office materials, business procedure, office machinery, etc.); Section 2 for examples of mailable work typed by the student—preferably an organized selection of different documents; and Section 3 for those passages of interest value given by the teacher or discovered by the student (or students) which the student thinks are worth keeping. This last section would include any project undertaken during the course.

PROJECT WORK

This type of work gives many opportunities for correlation and for linking typewriting with the individual interests of the students. The term "project" in the sense of "an undertaking, an enterprise" has acquired a significance in education which typewriting teachers may find a little difficult to connect with their subject. Yet a project need not be an ambitious affair; it is an "undertaking"—what one "takes upon oneself." As we have said earlier, shorthand and typewriting teachers are mainly concerned with teaching future office workers. Those workers will be expected to work intelligently, neatly and expeditiously; their skills are complex and they will have to use them in a variety of situations. It is therefore necessary that the students should be given opportunities of undertaking something which they themselves will organize. If there is only little time available, it need be no more than finding some information from books in the library, summarizing it and typing it in the appropriate form. This might involve a few pages of typescript. It could also be the composition, and illustration, of an article on a subject of interest to the student. This kind of project has been given frequently and the following is a selection of the topics chosen by students. The results are invariably neatly, and often charmingly, illustrated--

Messing About in Boats
Pig Breeding
The Royal Ballet School
Silverware
Our Nearest Neighbour (The Moon)
Breeds and Points of Horses

Such work is often carried on outside class time and is most valuable to the teacher as an indication not only of the typing skill of the student, but of her attitude to and responsibility in carrying out a task. A third point of value is that this work frequently leads to ancillary subjects or to the filling in of gaps of knowledge in the primary subject—gaps which might not otherwise have been discovered. Finally, it gives opportunity for choice, and consequently for understanding display. Students learn and retain far more about display when they are confronted with the task of arranging their own material than when they are told what to do. (Another case of discovery being better than rote learning.) Some employers have shown interest in seeing such work when they interview candidates for employment; if such interest could be more widespread it would undoubtedly help colleges and schools to raise standards, and employers would be less willing to accept low standards.

Sometimes projects are carried out individually, and sometimes by small groups of students. They can also be linked with other subjects in the curriculum. For example, in one college it was a feature of the secretarial course that during the first term the students should be introduced to topics under the title "Social Studies" with a specialist lecturer. At the beginning of the second term each student, in consultation with the staff, chose a topic within that field and began reading on it; by the end of the term she had prepared material for a small booklet. This material was then typed in the third term (one or two periods a week were allowed from the typewriting class time to supplement the free time of the student devoted to the work). The work was assessed by both the social studies lecturer and the typewriting lecturer—for content and for form of presentation. A number of the studies produced work that would have done credit to first-year university students. In some cases the improvement in the typing skill was quite marked.

Consultation with other members of the staff concerned with the teaching of related subjects will enable the typewriting teacher to link her lessons to what has already been taught in other classes. For instance, the theoretical knowledge about invoices can be taken by the commerce teacher and the typewriting teacher will follow it up by introducing the typing of invoices; more time will thus be available in the typewriting class for practical typewriting.

TESTING, MARKING AND EXAMINATIONS

From all that has been said in the previous sections it is not difficult to realize that the public typewriting examinations cannot ever include certain aspects of the student's typewriting skill. The time factor, practical considerations of the examination itself, and the exigencies of assessment all make impracticable the inclusion of anything more than fairly straightforward copying tests. Problem situations, the collating of information from different documents, the finding and insertion of additional information (to mention but three of the everyday situations in the office) are not tested at the level of the typist or the shorthand-typist; they are only beginning to be tested at the level of the private secretary. If, then, the typewriting teacher bases his course and final testing entirely on the public examination, the student is not going to be as prepared as she should be for her first office work. College or school tests should be used to supplement the public test, to cover those aspects of the skill which the latter cannot cover. They should not be set merely as "trial runs" to indicate likely success or failure in the public examination.

The Accuracy Test

Internal testing should not be too frequent, but should cover a representative section of the course work without a heavy bias on any one aspect. At the present time there is a tendency to pay too much attention to the so-called "accuracy test." This test is badly named, as although it is timed it is neither an accuracy nor a speed test. Many students tend to do less well in it than in their normal work. When it is administered with a deductive penalty for errors it is no more than a faulty imitation of championship tests (from which it is derived), wrongly used. Championship tests are competitive and must therefore involve standard penalties for errors; tests during training are not competitive (or should not generally be). Their purpose is to show what progress has been made and to indicate the standard achieved. The advocates of reducing the speed by a given number of strokes for each error maintain that, were the errors corrected, the quantity typed would be less. But a standard reduction has no relation to the time which a correction may take. Some errors would be put right in a fraction of the time that others would need. If, therefore, a standard penalty by reduction is imposed, the so-called "net speed" is purely artificial. Furthermore, championship tests are not training tests: no remedial work is called for afterwards; the errors are not analysed; every error is given equal weight. In training, however, before the student has reached the level of the expert, she is entitled to assistance from the tests. It is for the student and teacher together to consider the type and frequency of the errors made so that appropriate remedial work may be carried out.

A better method for assessing the speed of each student is for the teacher to decide at the various stages what percentage of error she will allow for the speed to be accepted and recorded. If the number of errors is below the figure set (e.g. no more than 3 errors in a period of 5 minutes' typing, or no more than 5 in a period of 10 minutes) then the gross speed is accepted.

The worst feature of over-emphasis of accuracy tests is that the speed produced from them is given as the typing speed of the student. It is comparable to saying that if one dressmaker can stitch so many inches or yards in ten minutes, and her neighbour stitches so many inches or yards less, the first dressmaker will make a dress faster than the second and be the better dressmaker. (It is worth remembering, too, that accuracy tests are now being discontinued by some typewriting examining bodies, and a "warming-up" test substituted.)

The modern trend in teaching is to train the student to use her basic knowledge and manipulative skill in the production of mailable copy. Both during training and in public examinations students are required to think rather more about the particular task, to do rather more planning in display, and to be on the alert for uncorrected errors in the "copy." In order to help the students reach such competency the teacher of typewriting must use supplementary material of her own selection and make an appropriate choice from the many new typewriting textbooks available.

Class Testing

Since it is a well-established general principle of learning that immediate knowledge of results leads to greater and better effort, and that praise and reproof also affect subsequent performance, the method of the teacher supervising as much practice as possible and giving advice, praise and reproof during the lesson, saves a good deal of laborious marking outside the classroom. This time can be much more profitably used in preparation of teaching material. West[1] reports that—

> praise appears to be best for poor learners; for good learners, reproof for inadequate performance (i.e. for performance below obvious capabilities) has produced more improvement than has praise for good work.

In the early stages of the typewriting skill development, the testing will be to determine progress in two areas—(*a*) machine manipulation, and (*b*) accuracy of key stroking. The first area *must* be assessed by the teacher during performance and a good deal of the second can be, and should be, checked by the students themselves. In any office the responsibility for ensuring that only work which has been checked and corrected is submitted for signature will lie with the typist herself and she must be trained for it. It is therefore recommended that the teacher takes in for correction and assessment selected exercises only (including some, of course, for double-checking). Other work will be seen by the teacher during the lesson periods so that the students have immediate knowledge of the standard achieved. A useful way of helping students to be self-critical and to see how their work can be improved (especially in display) is for the teacher to start by asking the individual student what she thinks of the work and how she suggests it might be improved. The teacher can add points here and there and give detailed advice where appropriate. In this way the assessment of the work is a co-operative effort and not a "pulling-to-pieces" by the teacher.

Material for tests of ability to type accurately from straightforward copy will be selected according to the needs of the students, but in any

[1] West, L. J., op. cit.

case it will never be so loaded with particularly difficult reaches or "typing demons" that it is artificial and meaningless. Research workers have stressed again and again that students do their best work when the material is natural and in a normal setting.

Criteria for judging the difficulty of material for problem typing, —the production of fair copies from imperfect originals—have been referred to on p. 132, but how should one classify as "easy," "of medium difficulty," or as "difficult" the unamended typescript or printed matter to be used for the testing of speed, accuracy, or both? West uses the term "typewritability" and the author has found that, empirically, a helpful method of assessment is to type the matter oneself. As West states "probably the major determinant of speed has nothing at all to do with the language characteristics themselves, but concerns instead, the ease or difficulty of making particular series of motions. For example, "start" is a common word and a monosyllable, yet because it is a one-hand word, it cannot be typed as rapidly as many other longer, polysyllable, uncommon words." If we consider the language characteristics referred to by West, we find that many criteria of difficulty have been sought by research workers (see bibliography, p. 227). These criteria concern word length, word frequency, average number of words per sentence, number of punctuation marks, number of capital letters, number of syllables, etc. West gives an analysis of one simple sentence as follows—

Sentence. Type the materials so that the top and bottom margins are even.

Analysis.	Total words	= 12
	Frequent words (among 1,000 commonest in the language)	= 9
	Total strokes (including spaces between words)	= 63
	Total strokes (excluding spaces between words)	= 52
	Total syllables	= 18
Therefore—	Percentage of frequent words	= 9/12 = 75%
	Average letter per word	= 51/12 = 4·25
	Average strokes per word (stroke intensity)	= 63/12 = 5·25
	Average syllables per word (syllabic intensity)	= 18/12 = 1·50
	Average strokes per syllable (syllabic stroke intensity)	= 63/18 = 3·50

What to Assess

The progress made by each student in the general skill of machine manipulation should be periodically assessed and recorded. Straightforward copying ability should be tested regularly and the gross speed, with the number of errors, recorded. In the earlier stages of display work a series of tests can be given to cover the main types of documents or forms of display on which instruction has been given. In the later stages, however, the work should be assessed with output as well as mailability in mind.

All teachers of typewriting, and certainly all employers, will find themselves in agreement with the comment of Albert C. Fries[1] that "while we are emphasizing the factors of speed and accuracy as essentials in attaining typing skill, the ultimate aim is the development of typing power, or the ability to *use* the skill acquired." So much attention has been paid to the aspects of speed and accuracy in the typewriting classroom that it is easy to overlook the fact that these terms mean different things to different people. Because of the traditional forms of testing speed and accuracy, the typewriting teacher and the typewriting student think almost exclusively of "words per minute" with no more than the permitted number of errors for a "pass" (or recorded speed) achieved on copy material which rarely includes more than two keys from the top bank. The employer, on the other hand, thinks almost exclusively of the number of letters or other documents which are typed and can be signed or approved for use in the course of the day. At the end of the course every student should have a fair idea of her output standard on the types of work most commonly given in offices.

A teacher's record book for a typewriting class might, then, contain plans for establishing progress records such as the example given on p. 169.

Marking Schemes

The allocation of marks to most kinds of typewritten work seems to be very much a matter of individual judgement. There is no doubt, however, that the majority of teachers would welcome information from organized studies of desirable and practical standards to be expected from different types of students and courses, and about generally

[1] "Developing Speed and Accuracy in Typewriting," *Proceedings of the* 1945 *Business Education Institute* (Teachers' College, University of Cincinnati).

Progress Record

FIRST TERM

(Stages 1 and 2—Learning machine manipulation, finger reaches and consolidating these in typing continuous matter.)

Name	General Manipulation	Keyboard Tests	Copying Tests on Continuous Matter	General Comments
	1 2 3	1 2 3 4	1 2 3 4 5 6	

SECOND TERM

(Stages 3 and 4—Development of speed in straightforward copying, elementary and intermediate display work.)

Name	Timed Tests	Letters	Memoranda and Other Work	Invoices	Tabulated Display	Other Work
	1 2 3 4 5 6	1 2 3 4	1 2 3	1 2 3	1 2 3 4	1 2

THIRD TERM

(Stage 5—Further speed development, more difficult display work, "production" work.)

Name	Timed Tests	Documents	Timed Shorthand Transcription	Copy Typing Output	Shorthand-typewriting Output
	1 2 3 4 5 6	1 2 3 4	1 2 3 4	1 2 3 4	1 2 3 4

acceptable marking schemes. At present most schemes are evolved empirically and few, if any, are published. On the question of output employers do not seem able to give guidance on what might be a generally acceptable standard. The best one can do is to quote from the literature or other sources of knowledge which are available and to hope that this field of study will not remain neglected much longer. It cannot be stressed too often that the typewriting skill involves much more than copying a perfect original, and that the ability to use the manipulative skill intelligently, and with adaptability, is what is required *at all levels of attainment*, not only at advanced levels. Marking schemes will be concerned with typographical accuracy, knowledge and judgement in display, with the carrying out of instructions.

Typographical Accuracy. This is an aspect of assessment on which there is a good deal of information available. Lists of "errors to be penalized" are available and they invariably include the following—

Transposition of letters.
Omission of letters.
Incorrect letter.
Transposition of words.
Omission of word(s).
Capitals out of alignment.
Incorrect division of words at line ends.
Unnecessary space between letters in word.
Faint impression.
"Shadow" impression.
Inconsistency of line spacing.
Ragged left-hand margin.
Very uneven right-hand margin.
"Crowding" or "piling" of letters.
Overtyping.

For these errors, except that of overtyping, one penalty is usually imposed. Whether this penalty is represented by one or more marks depends on the number of marks allocated to the test. If it is a simple copying test without any consideration of display or amendment, the mark deduction may be different from that in a test where display has also to be marked, according to the weighting given to the different aspects of the test.

Assessment of Display. Here again it is only possible to indicate the types of error which are usually penalized and not the actual penalty (in marks) imposed. In every typed document there are some or all of the following general points of display—

Even and appropriate margins (left, right, top and bottom).
Centred headings and sub-headings.
Appropriate line spacing after headings.
Good underscoring or line ruling (where appropriate).
Balanced spacing of column work.
Line spacing in money or other totals.
Good use of leader dots (where appropriate).

Other points which may have to be considered are—

Carrying out instructions (insertions, spacing, transpositions, etc.).
Quality of erasures.
Quality of touch (especially on punctuation marks and leader dots).
Judgement in display (where opportunity for this is given).
Use or non-use of abbreviations.
Knowledge of general practice in display (conventional display of common documents).

The most important point for the teacher to remember is that unless the work is studied beforehand and a marking scheme worked out in detail, the task of assessing the students' work will be made much more difficult. On the other hand, a complicated scheme is not necessary and the experience of the author has been that apart from errors of over-typing, very poor erasing and careless checking of work (all of which can be avoided by the student), a simple uniform penalty for every error brings about much the same result as a complicated system of progressive penalties. It is suggested that all teachers should, on some of the more common forms of exercise, mark the same sets of papers according to two different schemes and compare the results.

Assessment of Production Work. In this case the most important factor to consider is whether the work is "usable" (that is, whether it is acceptable as a good piece of work). Any work which could not be accepted for use in the actual business situation should not be awarded any marks at all and should be repeated. Penalties would be imposed for—

Poor erasures.
Omitting to carry out instructions (provided the work was still usable).

Errors which could be put right.
Smudged carbon copies.
Poor appearance of work (creased or smudged paper).
Crowding the page.
In shorthand transcription, substitution of words by others which do not change the sense.
Low output level.

Progress Charts

In addition to the records kept by the teacher, most typewriting students like to see their progress recorded on charts displayed in the classroom. It is also true that such charts have the disadvantage of causing a sense of frustration to the less able students and, perhaps, a degree of self-satisfaction to the more able students which prevents them from making as much effort and progressing as far as they are capable of doing. However, most classes do seem to use wall charts—all too often for one record only, the "words per minute on ten-minute accuracy tests." The disadvantage of the charts just mentioned is often overcome if records are kept of other forms of work, e.g. letter typing, document typing, shorthand transcription, and production work. It is often on the last count that the "slow but sure" student can score higher marks.

For the recorded speed the question arises of the standard to be selected for acceptance. One fairly common standard is that a speed achieved with 2 per cent of error or less qualifies for recording. Another method, and that favoured by the author, is that for a ten-minute test five errors or less are allowed, irrespective of the number of words typed; the speed recorded is, of course, the gross speed, not an artificial net speed (see p. 165). The reason for keeping the same number of errors for all speeds is to give a slight advantage to the beginner who is less experienced in the skill. In any case, the five errors give a 2 per cent margin for a speed of 25 words per minute and as much of the early practice work is carried out at about 24 words per minute this is a good point at which to start timed tests. There is little value in testing for recorded speeds before 20 words per minute. As the speed increases, so should the standard of accuracy and up to 50 words per minute the margin of five errors is reasonable, since 2 per cent error is too high for any practical work. Another point in recording the speed achievement is whether at the end of the course the student should be credited with the highest speed acheived, even though it has been reached only once, or whether the passing of two or more tests at the same speed should be required. In view of the chance factor in the grade of difficulty of any test, it would seem logical to require more than one performance or, alternatively, to reduce the emphasis put upon this one aspect of the work. The public typewriting examinations require only one performance, it is true—and some examining bodies, in fact, have discontinued the "accuracy test" as such—but the rest of the examination is drawn up on the assumption that the speed will be more or less maintained throughout the whole examination, and in any case, the speed test is not an entirely separate examination.

Examinations

Figures were given earlier (p. 42) of the striking difference between the number of entries for the R.S.A. single subject examinations in shorthand and typewriting and those for the combined skill of shorthand-typewriting. If the students cannot or do not wish to enter for the latter type of examination, it is the duty of the college or school to devote time to transcription training in those courses where it is appropriate, and to establish an internal test or examination so that the students (and the teacher) may know what standard has been reached in this more complex but more important aspect of their studies.

CHAPTER IX
Teaching Audio-typing

THE use of dictating machines is increasing rapidly in business and many schools and colleges include audio-typing in their business studies curriculum. As the introduction of this subject on any scale is relatively recent a great deal of experimentation has had to be undertaken to try to find the most efficient and least costly equipment suitable to class instruction, as well as appropriate teaching methods. On some points of equipment and aims opinions differ and may continue to do so for a long time. What is important, however, for any teacher concerned with this subject is to be able to decide on aims, equipment, standards of attainment and teaching methods suitable to the students he or she is going to teach.

AIMS

In the practical office situation audio-typing means transcribing dictated matter from recorded media. The medium may be a plastic belt, sheet, disc, wire or tape; the dictation may have been to a personal dictating machine, by means of remote control dictation, or over the telephone to a recording machine. The audio-typist will necessarily have her own transcribing machine and may do no other kind of work. Other typists or secretaries may spend only part of their working day transcribing from recorded dictation.

The first question to be decided when setting up a course for typists is whether the students are to be trained as audio-typists, as audio- and copy-typists, or as shorthand-typists who are also competent in transcription from recorded dictation. The general trend in schools and colleges is to add audio-typing to all typewriting courses.[1] The idea that audio-typing is a subject suitable for those who would be unsuccessful in learning shorthand will be quickly dismissed by any knowledgeable teacher. The audio-typing skill has many similarities with the skill of shorthand transcription. Both the shorthand-typist and the audio-typist need aural acuity, mental alertness, rapid comprehension of words, and speed in accurate spelling and punctuation.

[1] See articles "A Survey of Audio-typing" by B. W. Canning (Pitman) in *Shorthand Teachers' Supplement* (Issues February–June, 1966).

Both also need to be able to retain words in their mind while listening to the next part of the dictation and both need to make quick decisions on display, word division at line ends, etc. As with shorthand-typists, weakness in English is one of the main factors for lack of success in audio-typing. It cannot be stated too often that office workers concerned with communications need a knowledge *and skill* in English well above average, and that it is the duty of any teacher of business studies, but especially of the teachers of English, typewriting, audio-typing and shorthand to help the students reach the necessary competency in English so that the other skills are not hindered or made less effective.

A second question to be decided is when to begin the audio-typing course. Should the student be taught typewriting by audio-methods, or should, as some authorities think, audio work be left until a competency in typewriting of about 35 words per minute has been reached? On this point there will probably always be more than one opinion.[1] It would not seem to be a matter on which one can be dogmatic.

EQUIPMENT

Since the provision of individual transcribing machines for all students involves heavy expenditure, many colleges have experimented with multi-point systems of relay, and commercially developed systems are also in fairly wide use. The general plan is to have one or more master machines on which the matter is recorded and by means of "junction boxes" connect the students' headsets so that each student or group of students hears the same dictated matter.

With some systems there is progression from Stage I, where the whole class work on the same material, to Stage II where four groups or more can have different material, the student in the back desk of each row sometimes having a foot control so that if any student in the row fails to hear a word or phrase she indicates by raising her hand and the girl positioned at the foot-control depresses the pedal and so reverses the recording by a few words to allow the student time to regain her place in the passage. Stage III can then allow for individual control by the student of her own transcribing machine.[1]

Although in the initial stages of any course the dictation of material to the master machine and the dubbing of it to the students' machines

[1] See also articles in *Shorthand Teachers' Supplement* by J. Campbell, J. R. K. Lyall, and D. L. Flockton, (June and Nov. 1964, and Feb. 1965).

in the later stages will be time consuming, once a good library of material is available only periodic revision and renewal will be necessary.

STANDARDS OF ATTAINMENT

As with equipment, there is, and is likely to be for some time, great variation in the standards required of audio-typists. Schools and colleges are still feeling their way, each examining body has its own standards, and the requirements in individual offices vary according to the type of work and what is regarded as a reasonable average for a day or a week. Some firms give bonus payments for output exceeding the "average" set. The following figures are of interest—

R.S.A.	720 words to be transcribed, plus one letter (about 160 words) to be composed from dictated notes. Time for all work $1\frac{1}{4}$ hours.
Scottish Council	167-word passage to be transcribed in 12 minutes.
Civil Service	360 words to be transcribed in 10 minutes.
Commercial Firm	3,000 lines per typist per week (average output). Typists recruited with a minimum speed of 50 w.p.m. (preferably 60–70) and at a minimum age of 18.

As with copy typing, in assessing a student's speed, the teacher must compare like with like and decide whether the speed is to be assessed on straightforward matter, requiring the minimum of display and no carbon copies, or on "production" type work. In other words, there should be two assessments, i.e. words per minute and output rate.

TEACHING METHODS

Much of what has been already mentioned under teaching methods for typewriting (Chapter VIII) will be equally relevant to teaching methods needed for audio-typewriting.

There are, however, special problems associated with audio instruction, as mentioned in the *Preface* to this edition.

Thus a student, while perfectly familiar with taking dictation—and thus listening to the human voice—and equally familiar with transcribing from shorthand and typing directly on to the typewriter may become apprehensive when first confronted with a transcribing machine.

The first thing for a teacher to do, therefore, is to give the students instruction in the operation of the master machine, so that they feel perfectly confident both in stopping and starting it. Care should be taken to mark the RECORD control of the recorder when it is used in the classroom. (This difficulty does not occur if students are initially taught typewriting by audio methods.)

Some students dislike the feel of headsets, partly because they feel they spoil hairstyles. This dislike can be easily overcome by the use of light-weight plastic headsets, whose ear-pieces fit into the ears, and which do not touch the hair at all.

There are specially prepared sets of tapes available, both for shorthand and for audio-typists. These do *not* supplant the teacher for by using audio methods there is clearly—

(*a*) a substantial saving of effort. The teacher is freed for more important work. Instead of being for part of the time a human dictating machine, the teacher can now more truly teach by guiding and encouraging individuals while they are actually developing the skill and by discovering and eradicating weaknesses and wrong habit formation right at the start. There is more time available for checking and correction of written work and for maintaining proper records.

(*b*) a considerable gain in the use of time to the best advantage. The audio programme has been worked out with great pains taken over its grading. More care and attention to detail has gone into its compilation than is possible in the conventional course. Every item has been timed according to a scheme of tested validity and precision. Except according to the needs of the scheme, the standard of work required is consistent and unvarying.

(*c*) a better motivation. Good sound-tapes are compulsive. Young learners find a challenge and a compelling power about the disembodied voice, and this is the more so when they are—as with this method of hearing—listening and learning simultaneously.

The students have a clear goal in each stage of their work. Two essential conditions of learning are met. The students know exactly what they have to do, and they know precisely why they are doing it.

It is not surprising to find, therefore, that in an audio course, students who are for any reason obliged to miss part of a day's work will go to great lengths to make up for the lost time.

DICTATED INSTRUCTIONS

A matter on which there will probably rarely be unanimity of opinion is the extent to which the audio-typist is to be given information on punctuation, spelling, etc. Methods vary in offices, and at present also in examinations, and whether it is desirable to have uniformity is perhaps a moot point. The following examples of examination passages are quoted for comparison—

Scottish Council for Commercial Education
Audio-typewriting Endorsement
Stage II
SECTION ONE

Material to be dictated: (To be dictated in about 3½ minutes)

The passage I am going to dictate is to be typed in double-line spacing on A4 paper. I will dictate some of the punctuation; other punctuation you will insert where you consider it necessary. You may re-hear the passage as often as you wish, but at the end of twelve minutes you will be asked to stop typing and to hand your typescript to the supervisor.
Now set your margin stops for a 60 letter line.
Here is the passage:
Schools break up for the summer soon and many motorists will be preparing for the holiday (quote) "ordeal," wondering where to pack all the luggage and how to withstand many hours at the wheel cooped up with restless children (paragraph) A roof rack is the answer to most luggage problems (sentence) Trial packing of the car, some days prior to departure, is advisable (semi-colon) not only does it avoid thoughtless (quote) "panic packing" (end of quote), but it enables the head of the house to take a firm stand on what can (dash) or cannot (dash) be taken before it is too late (sentence) Planned packing makes for the maximum use of the space, and attention can also be given to weight distribution (paragraph) The rack brackets should be positioned as far forward on the roof as secure fixing will allow to even out the loading on the front and rear suspension (sentence) Heavy trunks and cases should be packed in the boot (dash) preferably forward (dash) and the lighter luggage on the roof rack (sentence) The rack luggage should be kept as low as possible to reduce the tendency to roll on corners and to minimize the increase in wind resistance which adversely affects speed and fuel consumption (paragraph) The back seat is the best place for children (sentence) Unless the rear door locks have the external lever type of (initial capitals) Safety Catch built into them, or some other type of child (hyphen) proof lock, an adult or capable elder child should sit with them (sentence. Quote with initial capitals) "Free Wheeling" (end of

quote) safety handles (bracket) obtainable for less than (figures) £1 each from garages and accessory shops (bracket) can be fitted in less than half (hyphen)an (hyphen) hour by the least mechanically minded motorist (passage ends)

SECTION TWO

Material to be dictated: (To be dictated in about 3 minutes)

The letter which follows is one sent from a firm which hopes to sell goods to another. The purpose of the letter should be borne in mind when displaying it. Use the headed paper supplied, and type the letter in (with emphasis) SINGLE SPACING. The letter will occupy about 8 inches of the paper's length. Use equal margins.

Here is the letter:

Our reference HL (H Harry L Lucy) oblique S (S Sugar) oblique 12 (one two). Use today's date.

The letter is addressed to Mr. S. (S Sugar) Robertson, Electrical Supplies Limited, High Street, Montrose.

The letter reads: Dear Mr. Robertson (Now a subject heading; centre and use initial capitals) Power Tools (heading ends) When our representative, Mr. Green, called on you recently, you expressed interest in our (initial capitals) Power Drills (sentence) Since your trade is mostly with the home handy (hyphen) man, we feel that our (initial capital) Models (figures) D (D David) 500 and D (D David) 720 would be most suitable for your purposes (sentence) We give below the descriptions and recommended retail prices of these models (sentence) On these, you would, of course, receive the customary (figures) 20% mark (hyphen) up. (Indent and display) Model D (figures) 500 (sentence) A sleek all (hyphen) purpose tool (sentence) Drilling speed (figures) 2,600 r.p.m. (revolutions per minute) (sentence) Chuck size (dash. Figures) ¾″ (sentence) Drives all attachments (sentence) Price (figures) £6 19s. 6d. (paragraph) Model D (figures) 720 (sentence) This is a (figure) 2 (hyphen) speed drill (sentence) Chuck size (dash. Figures) ¼″ (sentence) The fast speed (dash. Figures) 2,400 r.p.m. (dash) for drilling, sawing or sanding (colon) slow speed (dash. Figures) 900 r.p.m. (dash) for drilling masonry and large holes (sentence) Drives all attachments (sentence) Price (figures) £11 19s. 6d. (paragraph) There is, of course, a very wide range of attachments for these drills and we are enclosing a booklet giving full details and prices of these (paragraph) Should you decide to stock our (initial capital) Drills, we will be very pleased to supply you with advertising placards (sentence) I have asked our representative to call on you again in the near future (paragraph) Yours sincerely, Sales Manager. (Indicate that there is an enclosure)

Correction (point of insertion in dictated material to be indicated)

Closing paragraph . . . "decide to stock our"—insert the word (initial capital 'Power" before "Drills" . . .

R.S.A. Audio-typist's Certificate Examination
Stage II
Passage 3—text for Article—295 words.

Minutes
(*Paragraph*) Modern industries need a great many things in addition to
their raw materials. Machinery of different types, power and labour to work
½ them are necessary as well as transport to get | the finished products to
market. It may well happen that it pays to carry the raw materials over long
distances, in order to avoid transporting machinery or fuel. The business
1 man wants to produce his goods as economically as he || can, and get them
to the purchaser in the cheapest and most convenient way. It would certainly
be a very remarkable coincidence if he found a particular spot which was
½ most advantageous from every point of view. He has to | balance advantage
against disadvantage and make up his mind whether, for example, it is
better to have the expense of carrying his raw materials a long way in order
2 to be near his market for the finished goods, or save || the carriage on raw
materials but have to meet the extra cost of transporting his finished goods.
(*Paragraph*)
As circumstances change, so do the different factors become more or less
important. Until the (*Capital initials*) First World War the large majority of
½ manufacturing | industries relied on steam for their power, and this made
heavy demands on coal. As coal is a bulky article and expensive to carry, it
3 generally paid to settle the factory on or near the coalfields and bring all the ||
other necessary materials to it, rather than the other way round. When,
however, electricity began to replace steam as the chief form of power, this
concentration on the coalfields was no longer so essential. Industries could
½ then give greater weight | to other factors when deciding their location,
provided their power could be equally well supplied.

Passage 4—letter of 160 words to Mr. Perkins.

Minutes
Dear Sir,
We have recently set up business in Chesterfield and wish to appoint out-
side auditors as well as to have advice from expert accountants. We under-
½ stand from Messrs. Robert Jones & Co. Ltd. of this city that you are | both
auditors and consultants and as they have spoken highly of the service which
you have given them over the past years I should like to meet you to discuss
the possibility of your firm acting for us. (*Paragraph*)
1 Our turnover || at present is in the region of(*figures*) fifty thousand pounds
annually but it is expanding rapidly and we have already installed what
seems to be a satisfactory mechanized accounting system. However, we
½ should appreciate advice on the potentialities of the | system for expansion as
our business develops. (*Paragraph*)
If you are interested in the suggestion, I should be very pleased if you
would have lunch with me one day when I could give you fuller information
regarding our business.
2 Yours faithfully, ||

It will be noted that in the Scottish examination, Section One, the passage contains 167 words for transcription but 36 additional words of instruction, so that 203 words are to be dictated in 3½ minutes. In the R.S.A. examination the passages are dictated at an average speed of 80 words per minute and the number of additional words as instructions (in the letter of 160 words) is only three. There is bound to be a variation in the number of instructions from passage to passage, but it does seem that this is a point which teachers should investigate and discuss.

CHAPTER X

Teaching Transcription

HISTORY AND RESEARCH

HARM Harms,[1] writing in 1949, opens his chapter on transcription with the following paragraph—

Few articles about transcription appeared in the literature of business education prior to 1925. The reason is that transcription as a skill was not considered a separate subject until somewhere in the 'twenties. Stenographers struggled with the transcription hurdle without the aid of the teaching in the schools; they relied upon business experience to help them bridge this gap. Transcription involves so much that it seems strange that more attention was not given to it earlier. Many of the difficulties of the young office worker on his first job have been traced to the lack of proper transcription training. Today American schools and colleges treat transcription as a subject to which a fairly generous timetable allocation is made. One period daily for a semester is frequently given to this practical work. By contrast, in this country, little attention was given to typewritten transcription training until after the war and even today too many students have to struggle without the aid of teaching.

In 1950 and 1951 the following figures were obtained from inquiries by the author—

Extent to which Selected Techniques entered into the Training of Shorthand-typists

Selected Technique	A Lot		Fair Amount		Very Little		None	
	1950 %	1951 %	1950 %	1951 %	1950 %	1951 %	1950 %	1951 %
Typing from shorthand	14	32	32	29	36	25	18	12
Using carbons	8	19	34	32	34	32	24	16
Taking "office style" dictation	12	12	16	24	31	30	41	32

100 shorthand-typists were involved in the 1950 inquiry; 474 shorthand-typists were involved in the 1951 inquiry, though no answer was received from a small percentage of these.

Reports on the amount of time devoted to transcription work were

[1] *Methods in Vocational Business Education* (Cincinnati, South Western Publishing Co., 1949).

given for sixty-five courses and in almost 60 per cent of them it was only 16 per cent or less of the total course time for typewriting.

It is to be hoped that when any new inquiries are undertaken they will produce very much higher percentages, especially since the majority of employers test candidates for employment by dictation and typewritten transcription. Apart, however, from this latter fact, our understanding of general principles of learning as applied to the acquisition of skills will help us to understand the necessity for training students in this third skill. If there is a change in stimulus, then a previously acquired response may suffer interference or may need to be modified in order to take account of the new element in the situation. In typewritten transcription the habits of reading (eye span and speed) are bound to change from those used in reading longhand; the fact that punctuation signs have frequently to be supplied by the mind instead of being read by the eye constitutes another major change in the skill pattern in typing from shorthand as compared with typing from longhand. A third important change is in the layout of the copy. Shorthand notes are much more compact than longhand; one symbol may represent as many as four or five words and a very brief two-stroke symbol can represent a short word or a word of several syllables, e.g.  accommodation,  dish,  deficiency, while in the case of phrasing the difference between the length of the symbol and the number of words is even greater. The interference of previously acquired habits also comes into play in connexion with the speed of typing in the early attempts at typewritten transcription if this work is not started until the student has reached a certain standard in the separate skills, e.g. 40 words per minute in typewriting as is sometimes recommended. If this is the cruising speed of the student there is a tendency to begin typing from shorthand at that same speed—with, of course, very poor results. This means that there is a period of transition, which is also a period of frustration —trial and error, instead of trial and success.

The problem of when to start transcription training has been the subject of much discussion and study. Lauritsen[1] found there was no agreement on when to begin it. Although the author, as a result of her own experience, favours an early start, the more important factor is *how* it is started. A good transcription course should begin with

[1] Lauritsen, M., "Summary of Research in Shorthand Transcription," *American Shorthand Teacher* (May, 1933); quoted by Harm Harms, op. cit.

simple sentence and paragraph work from perfect copy (chalkboard or printed) and not with a dictated letter. More will be said on this later.

The two main schools of thought on when to begin transcription may be termed the "late" and the "early" starters. With the first approach typed transcription is delayed until the students can write shorthand at 70 to 80 words per minute and type from straight copy at 35 to 40 words per minute. The main argument in favour of this approach is that there is a danger of preventing the typewriting skill from developing as it should by introducing too many elements at once. But this point is not of fundamental importance if the transcription course is graded.

The second approach is to regard typewritten transcription as a skill which can be developed from small beginnings. Through carefully graded steps, which should be kept behind the separate skills, the material used can be selected from that which has been prepared in the English, shorthand and typewriting classes. In this way consolidation of the shorthand and typewriting knowledge takes place and it is possible to link the known to the unknown—the actual content being familiar, but the medium in which it is presented constituting the new element. In this method the *how* of training is of first importance. It would certainly be working against principles of skill acquisition to overload the early learning work.

All the studies which have been made of the transcription skill, both in this country and America, show that the majority of the errors made can be classified as English errors. Wanous[1] reported that 55·16 per cent of errors were in English mechanics, 27·37 were general content, 9·33 were typographical, and 8·14 were errors in letter mechanics. The following figures from the author's inquiry, referred to above, are interesting on this point—

Percentages of 193 Employers Reporting Weaknesses Met with "Very Often" and "Often" (Combined Figures)

Weakness	1951 %	1950 %
Poor punctuation	59	73
Slow in transcribing shorthand	49	51
Poor general knowledge	48	55

[1] Wanous, W. J., "Survey of Transcription Achievement in Secondary Schools," *Business Education Digest* (December, 1940).

Weakness	1951 %	1950 %
Inability to notice slips	48	70
Poor setting-out of letters	46	49
Poor knowledge of words	46	55
Poor spelling	44	55
Inaccurate typing	39	49
Inadequate shorthand speed	36	36
Lack of initiative	35	49
Submission of uncorrected work	30	55
Inability to read shorthand notes	28	42
Poor sense of responsibility	26	53
Poor general intelligence	19	38
Inability to remember instructions	18	33
Lack of interest in work	12	17
Resentful of correction	6	17

The examiners of the R.S.A. reporting on work done in the shorthand-typist's examinations in 1960–61 said "The majority of candidates appeared to be unable to concentrate on the reading of their notes and the typewriting of them at the same time. . . . Candidates who submitted poorly-typed transcriptions often showed that they were competent copy-typists by the manner in which they displayed the draft in another test. It would appear, therefore, that insufficient time had been devoted during training to the development of the skill of typing from shorthand notes, which is essential to anyone aspiring to become a successful shorthand-typist." From the 1964–65 report it is worth quoting the following passages: "Candidates who fail can be divided roughly into three groups—those who have not the necessary skill in shorthand writing, those whose knowledge of the English language is so poor that they are quite unfitted to be shorthand-typists, and those who are efficient but allocate their time incorrectly. . . . Candidates should also pay much more attention to punctuation when transcribing notes. Knowledge of the correct use of the comma and apostrophe was particularly weak." Such comments on the inadequacy of the typed-transcription skill are to be seen or heard frequently in all parts of the country and as long as we fail to give adequate planning and class time to helping students to develop the skill, the blame must go more to the teachers than to the students.

PROBLEMS AND OBJECTIVES OF TRANSCRIPTION

In order to plan transcription work it is first necessary to outline the problem and determine the objectives. As has been indicated, good transcription training needs the co-operation of English, shorthand and typewriting teachers. Transcription begins in the English class; the very first lesson in shorthand can prepare the way on one important point for typewritten transcription—the stressing of the importance of necessary punctuation. The first shorthand lesson will use the sentence as the learning unit. Insistence on the insertion of the shorthand symbol for the full stop (with explanation of the reason) will be a good first step. The important thing to remember is that no one subject teacher can fit in all the work which is necessary. Secondly, the training is far more effective if it comes from all sides and the students see that it is an integrated plan designed to help them along on a steady path of success.

Skills Required in Typewritten Transcription

If we now consider in more detail six of the seven sub-skills of the total transcription with which we opened Chapter IV (p. 39), this will lead on to what are desirable and achievable standards to set for different types of course, and also to the methods and materials which can be used during training.

1. *Fluent Reading of Shorthand Symbols.* The basis for this is, of course, good shorthand outlines with consistency of stroke length, clear curves, good position writing (in Pitman shorthand) and, above all, indication in the notes of any point which will help transcription, such as all full stops, paragraphing where it has been possible to determine this during the dictation, indication of capitals, etc.

Reading with understanding is the next technique to be developed. This does not mean that the shorthand-typist needs to read with the same degree of understanding as when one reads for knowledge, but that there should be a quick recognition that the outlines are conveying sense. It means reading in "sense groups" rather than individual outlines. The good typist reads further ahead than the poor typist and the better reader tends to be the better typist. Fluent transcription cannot be built upon single outline reading.

2. *Spontaneous Recognition of Sense.* In addition to the manner of shorthand reading as mentioned above, the ability to recognize the

sense of a passage quickly depends on the extent of one's English vocabulary, on general and other knowledge, according to the subject matter of the passage. Students whose shorthand reading and dictation matter is confined to narrow subject limits (e.g. simple business letters and company reports) will be good transcribers only within those narrow limits. A fairly broad selection of reading and dictation matter is necessary for all courses.

3. *Ability to Visualize Quickly the Necessary Punctuation.* This involves an understanding of sentence structure, and the ability to decide on necessary signs while reading ahead and to hold them in the mind until the fingers reach the point of that insertion. Punctuation work in the English class is most valuable, provided it is taken at a good pace. Transfer from the English class to the shorthand-typewriting situation will not take place unless there is some similarity of situation. The English teacher therefore needs to understand that situation and to create the right conditions for transfer, both by explanation and the methods of teaching. The shorthand teacher needs to give practice in oral punctuation when students read back their notes. In *every* reading the full stops should be indicated and in selected exercises the full punctuation should be given, together with capitals and any other point of importance for transcription. The typewriting teacher can help by giving longhand practice on the commonly used forms of sentence, e.g. those with restrictive clauses, parenthetical expressions, etc. It is often a weakness of the elementary exercises in shorthand and in typewriting that they consist of simple sentences or paragraphs with so little punctuation that by the time the students reach the stage of typewritten transcription, any punctuation skill which they had has almost disappeared.

4. *Mental Vision of Longhand Form, i.e. Spelling.* Shorthand-typists not only need to know how to spell words, but they must have the ability to spell them much more quickly and with greater confidence than many other workers. Here again the English teacher can help by speeding up the work on spelling in English lessons; if students are asked to give the spelling of a word orally, they must be expected to spell rapidly as well as correctly. Spelling bees may be out of fashion, but if they are used as a method of speeding up reaction to spelling, they are of great value. Practice can also be given, in the sentence unit, on homonyms; students can be presented with sentences in

longhand, with the one word written in shorthand, the exercise being to read the sentence rapidly and spell out the word which is given in shorthand. To get students to the stage of responding quickly and accurately to these words, regular practice is necessary, but if the sentences or passages are short and the speed of the work good, a great deal can be done in frequent short periods. The same method can be used in the shorthand and the typewriting classes.

5. *Division of Words at Line-ends.* Work on this topic all too frequently stops at the stage of "knowing the rules" and when an error is made it is assumed that there is a lack of knowledge, whereas more often than not it is a lack of skill. Practice in the English class in quick recognition of where a word may be divided is useful and can be linked with work on extension of vocabulary. In the typewriting class some intensive work should be included on this topic from time to time.

6. *Quick Decision on Display.* The ability needed here is to "register" points for transcription when the notes are being taken, and then to see ahead sufficiently in order to make the necessary machine adjustments in time, e.g. line spacing, capitalization, when to write words rather than figures, etc. A useful technique, especially for estimating the space which a passage in shorthand will take in typescript, is to let the students see shorthand notes and transcript side by side and discuss the various points. The Americans call this "pre-view" transcription (see p. 205) and the author has found it a very helpful method.

In addition to the above skills there are a number of other points on which students need guidance and practice and which are concerned more with the organization of the work. These matters can be listed as follows—

1. Handling and choosing material (size of paper, organizing paper, carbons, etc. on the table for quick handling).
2. Improving skill in erasing.
3. Skilful handling and annotating of carbon copies.
4. Taking information from other documents in completion of shorthand notes.
5. Rapid and accurate checking (especially for sense; the typing may be correct, but if words have been mistranscribed and the passage

does not make sense, the transcript will have to be rejected as unusable).

6. Dealing with alterations and additions to shorthand notes.

7. Deciding on order of priority for typing.

8. Assembling papers and presenting them for signature when production work—the typing of several letters or documents—is involved. Students should have a special "for signature" folder and should be penalized if the work submitted has finger marks, smudged carbon copies or badly creased papers.

STANDARDS OF ATTAINMENT

The next question to be decided is that of the standards to be set as goals. In this connexion there are really three levels to be considered. First, there is the training period; the student in training cannot be expected to reach the same standard of speed and accuracy as the student who is ready for the end-of-course tests. A second standard is that of the examination or final college test, when only perfection or very near perfection will obtain full marks and something lower (but how low?) is to be regarded as a pass. Thirdly, there is the office standard, where again perfection is the goal, but yet not the perfection of the examination test. For instance, in the examination an alternative rendering would not generally be acceptable, even though it makes sense, whereas it would be to many employers. Again, standards vary between employers—what should a college or school set as mailable? Many teachers have the experience of using actual business letters which they have received as examples of letters below the acceptable standard and Harm Harms[1] quotes the case of a teacher who asked each student to bring some sample letters for bulletin display—"It was found that fully a third of the letters brought in were not mailable according to the standard that had been set up in class." The following are three other estimates of what constitutes a good transcript, all quoted by Harms—

[Wanous and Whitmore] Letters should follow the dictation closely . . . should be centred, reasonably well . . . should contain no errors of spelling, punctuation, capitalization, or hyphenation. . . . There should be no uncorrected typographical errors in the letters and erasures should be made neatly.

[Faris and Curtis] Standards for a mailable letter must convey exact meaning of dictator; must not have more than three erasures or correctable errors; . . . must be arranged attractively; must be neat.

[1] Harms, Harm, op. cit.

[Sister Mary Ester Malone] A mailable letter is one which follows very closely the thought of the dictation . . . contains no uncorrected errors . . . looks reasonably neat . . . and contains no omissions.

One thing is certain: mailability does not mean adherence to one and only one style of layout. The main point of difference between examination mailability and office mailability is in the expression "a mailable letter is one which follows very closely the thought of the dictation." In some shorthand-typist's examinations, true office-style dictation is not given, for there is never any amendment during dictation. The practical aspect of the examination lies in the fact that a typewritten transcription of more than one letter or document is required and the dictation regulated to the minute, instead of being regulated to each quarter minute.

Another aspect of the standard to be required is in connexion with output standards. On this a number of authorities in America have given definite standards; in this country they are much more difficult to obtain. In the 1950 inquiry only six out of forty-five employers gave any indication; most of the answers stated that they did not assess the output of shorthand-typists. Those who answered positively made the following statements—

Forty letters a day (no indication of length or type of letter) were expected.

Twenty minutes were given for typing a quarto page.

120 letters a week were expected.

A record was kept of each girl's work.

In public examinations in this country transcription speeds of 15 to 20 words per minute are expected (maintained throughout the test and including the time for paper insertion, display, etc.).

American authorities seem to expect anything from 20 to 40 words per minute. Wanous and Whitmore[1] consider that—

A student who can type 60 words per minute from printed copy should be able to type 40 words per minute from shorthand notes, providing, of course, the material which is copied in both cases is similar in character and is equal in difficulty, and that writing periods are of equal length.

Wanous also gives a reduction of 15 words per minute for writing from letter copy compared with straight copy. This means that he

[1] Wanous, W. J., and Whitmore, J. L., *Effective Transcription Procedures*, Monograph No. 57 (Cincinnati, South Western Publishing Co., 1942).

expects shorthand transcribers to work at only five words a minute less than letter copy typists. It is doubtful whether many students in this country achieve such a standard.

Louis A. Leslie[1] gives the following standards—

> At the end of four semesters of shorthand and at least two semesters of typewriting, when dictation is given at 80 to 100 words per minute in a group of letters comprising a total dictation of 800 to 1,000 words, the learner should transcribe at the rate of 20 to 25 words per minute with 20 words as the minimum rate acceptable for credit. At least 75 per cent of the letters in any five consecutive daily transcription periods should be mailable.

Another authority quoted in *Methods of Teaching Business Subjects*[2] gives "seven letters containing eleven five-inch lines during an hour." This is the requirement of a business house. Assuming eight standard words to the line, this gives a total of 616 words, or roughly 10 words per minute. There is no indication, however, of whether this includes envelopes, names and addresses, carbon copies. In offices, and especially in international work where very experienced staff were recruited, the author has met many shorthand writers who could transcribe at speeds of 60 and 70 words per minute regularly and with a very high degree of accuracy; this represented only 5 to 10 words per minute less than their copying speed.

It is obvious from the foregoing standards that little uniformity and much uncertainty exist concerning a reasonable standard. Employers are no doubt influenced by what their employees actually do on an average; the colleges and schools in turn are influenced by what examining bodies require and by what they themselves think they can achieve in the short time available for transcription work. There is also the fact that no one has reached a decision on what constitutes a standard unit of work in this field. This is another topic on which teachers and employers could profitably co-operate.

Transcription Capacity of the Individual Student

For the purposes of training there is a very simple and sensible criterion and that is the capacity of the individual student, especially in relation to her copying speed. The author has found that by giving transcription work of a similar nature and standard to the copying work but always a little later, a transcription speed of between 10 and

[1] *Methods of Teaching Transcription* (New York, The Gregg Publishing Co., 1949).
[2] Tonne, H. A., Popham, E. L. and Freeman, M. H., *Methods of Teaching Business Subjects*, 2nd ed. (New York, McGraw-Hill Publishing Co. Inc., 1957).

5 words per minute less can be developed on straightforward material and from 20 down to 10 words per minute less on letters compared with copying from amended manuscript. During training it is a better policy to aim at mailable work at the speeds at which individual students can work, thus putting the emphasis on *success*, rather than set a speed criterion on which some students at any rate will experience *failure*. This is another reason for the author's preference for a fairly early start on typewritten transcription provided that it is in the form of progressive training, with guidance and achievable goals set for the different levels of capacity of the students.

The following is a summary of what the author feels to be a reasonable standard of time allocation and achievement—

Time Allocation and Achievement

During the first two-thirds of the course transcription training can take place in English, shorthand and typewriting lessons on a graduated scale from a few minutes regularly in some of the lessons to one lesson a week devoted entirely to transcription preparation or performance. In the last third of the course most of the work should be performed in the typewriting class with at least 25 per cent of class periods devoted to it. Some double periods are essential if reasonable training in production work is to be given.

1. *Achievement During Training.* In the early stages of transcription work in the typewriting class, accurate, neat work should form the criterion of success, not words per minute. When students have had some experience in simple, untimed work, timed writings can be introduced and any speed accepted at first provided the work reaches the accuracy standard of the student's copy work on similar matter. Speed of performance can then be given increasing importance until the students can work at 10 words *below their copying speed* on continuous matter. If the work is suitably graded this standard can be achieved by most students (provided the shorthand and English standards are adequate).

2. *Achievement at the End of the Course.* The *minimum* transcription speed for a pass (on continuous matter, as in copying) should be 15 words per minute behind the minimum copying speed allowed. Thus, if in a secretarial course the minimum copying speed is set at 35 words per minute for ten minutes, the transcription speed will be

20 words per minute for ten minutes. This is a fair standard and many students will surpass it. For more junior courses the transcription speed may be as low as 15 words per minute, but an employer would rather have this performance than an unusable first attempt at a higher speed.

3. *Achievement for Production Work.* The following minimum standards are suggested—

Copying Speed Minimum	*Minimum Production Standard*	*Typing Time*
35 w.p.m.	4 qto.-page letters of about 160 words each, with one carbon copy and envelope	55 min.
25 w.p.m.	3 qto.-page letters of about 160 words each, with one carbon copy and envelope	55 min.

This assumes that the letters are dictated "office style," with not more than two minor amendments during dictation, and at an average speed not exceeding the normal speed of the class.

The test should not, of course, always take the same form of, say, three or four letters; production work means variety, and very short memorandums, telegrams, telephone messages, etc., can take the place of one or more of the letters.

A second point to be considered in training and testing on production work is whether second and subsequent attempts shall be penalized. The author is strongly in favour of requiring good work at the first attempt on selected occasions during training and of penalizing false starts in the grading tests. Experience in the classroom and the office shows that typists develop an attitude of mind towards fresh starts; it requires confidence and discipline for any shorthand-typist to do good work without the necessity to retype and these are qualities which every teacher would wish students to develop. Another very important point, which is often neglected in typewriting classrooms, is the need to make students cost conscious. Since economy imposes restrictions on the quality and variety of stationery used in typewriting courses, students rarely have any idea of the cost to a firm of the correspondence and records which have to be typed. It is possible for typists to waste stationery to the tune of several pounds a week without realizing it. The teacher can, in a number of ways, help the students to be more knowledgeable about, and to take greater care of the materials which they use.

From the above very brief survey it is clear that today we have evidence from research workers, practising teachers, examiners and employers to show that planned, integrated transcription courses are a necessity, not a luxury, or something to be "put in at the end of the course if we have time." Whether transcription begins early or late, analysis of the task, teacher co-operation, graded practice material, adequate practice time and conditions should be the guiding principles on which any course is planned.

In the following pages suggestions are made on teaching methods, materials and aids based on the experience of the author and other practising teachers. Actual material quoted is given only as an indication of what may be used. Methods are offered as suggestions—they may or may not suit other teachers but they are worth trying. The aids may already be well known to most readers but are mentioned in order to make the account complete.

TEACHING MATERIAL

"Proceed from the simple to the complex" is admittedly a sound policy for the teacher to adopt once the students have a general impression of the goal which they are aiming to achieve. Shorthand students are familiar with the task of copying longhand words, phrases and sentences from the chalkboard; they are also used to reading shorthand outlines written by the teacher on the chalkboard. We can therefore assume (and it has been proved in practice) that students will be successful in typing from the chalkboard some of the simple matter *which they have already practised* in the shorthand and the typewriting classes.

The Plan of Presentation. This could be—

1. The shorthand teacher selects words or phrases which it would be useful for the students to practise as typewritten transcription, e.g. those which are valuable from the point of view of English (consolidation of spelling) and shorthand (short forms, important shorthand principles).

2. The English and typewriting teachers use this material in their classes (discussion of meanings, English, etc.; typewriting, keyboard practice).

3. The words (or phrases, or sentences) are written on the chal during the typewriting class and are read by the students (orally, silently). The typewriting teacher asks or reminds them about points spelling and meaning. The students then practise typing the matter from the chalkboard under the supervision of the teacher.

It is essential that this transcription work should be *consolidation* of previous work in typewriting, shorthand and English, and should include no new words or outlines. In this way there can be a systematic revision of some of the work done earlier in the course, the choice being determined by the needs of the students in English and typewritten transcription.

It is also important in the earliest exercises, if single words are used, that those with alternative spellings should *not* be included. Determination of the correct spelling must come from understanding the context.

Grading of Material. In this kind of plan, the grading of the teaching material given below follows almost naturally, and has proved to be most effective—

Medium of Presentation	*Form of Exercise*	*Content of Material*
Teacher's chalkboard shorthand.	Single words, phrases, sentences.	Easy
Printed textbook shorthand.	Sentences, short paragraphs.	Easy
Teacher's duplicated shorthand (copy for each student).	Sentences, short paragraphs, short articles, etc.	Easy to medium
Student's fair copy shorthand. Other students' fair copy shorthand.	Short paragraphs, short letters, short articles.	Easy to medium
Slow dictation (single items). Other students' notes.	Letters, memoranda, articles, messages, etc.	Easy to medium

Medium of Presentation	*Form of Exercise*	*Content of Material*
Dictation at student's normal speed—		
(*a*) single items, (*b*) more than one item.	Letters, reports, etc.	Graded
Office style dictation, with amendments—		
(*a*) single items, (*b*) more than one item.	Letters, reports, etc.	Graded

Selection of Material

The main aim of each exercise will be to give practice in typing from shorthand symbols, but the material chosen will be such that it consolidates the requisite basic knowledge in English and shorthand and develops thereby the skill to apply the knowledge quickly or, to put it another way, to respond intelligently when typing to the visual stimulus of the shorthand symbols. It is quite impossible to consolidate everything and once again it is a question of selection. The principles of selection on which the author has worked are—(*a*) to consolidate sections of the shorthand theory which are important or which need more practice by most students; (*b*) to enlarge and consolidate English and shorthand vocabulary; (*c*) to give practice on points of transcription which might give rise to hesitation and the consequent breaking of the typewriting fluency; and (*d*) in the later stages to increase general and business knowledge. The underlying aims are, of course, to prevent transcription errors and to bring the transcription skill as near as possible to the level of the copying skill. (In some cases it is the copying skill which remains at a slightly lower level.)

EXAMPLES OF EXERCISES TO CONSOLIDATE SHORTHAND THEORY

Form of Presentation and Method	*Matter*	*Aim*
1. *After study of Chapter V* New Course		
Chalkboard shorthand. Chorus or individual reading in class. Checking of spelling. Typing each line three times.	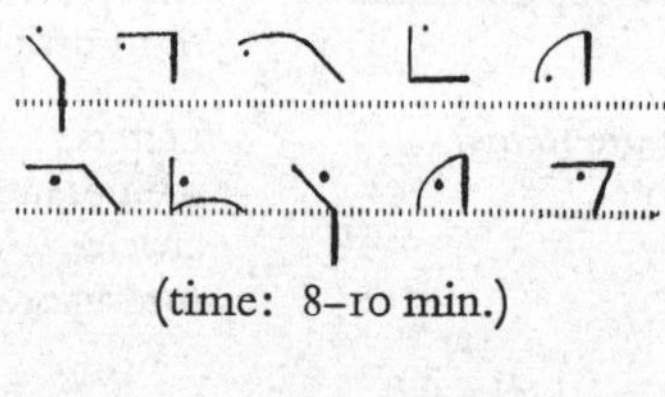 (time: 8–10 min.)	To consolidate vowel signs, outline position, spelling.

Form of Presentation and Method	*Matter*	*Aim*
2. *After Chapter VI*		
Similar exercise to above.	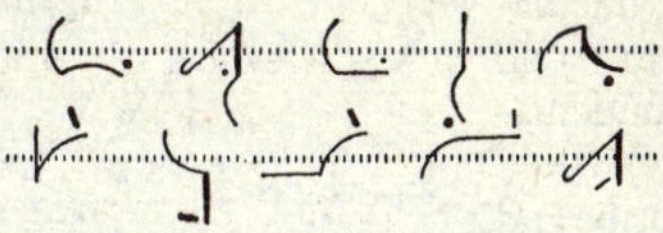	To consolidate vowel signs, outline position, spelling.

(Subsequent exercises used to complete vowel sequence.)

Form of Presentation and Method	*Matter*	*Aim*
3. *After Chapter XII*		
Chalkboard shorthand. Chorus or individual reading. Individuals are asked for missing word (and spelling) which teacher inserts in shorthand sentence. Students type each sentence twice.	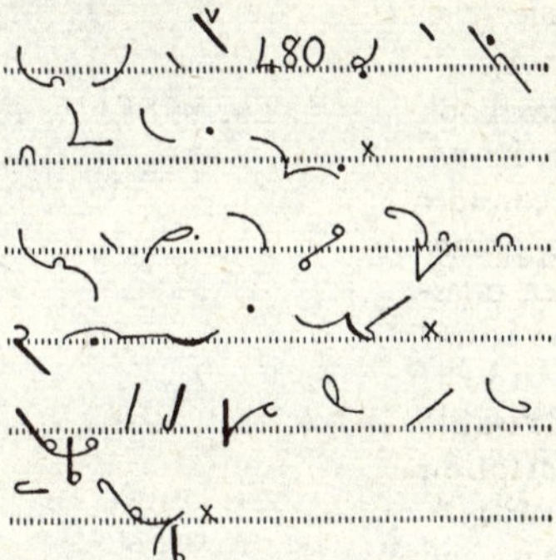 (time: 10 min.)	Vocabulary and short form consolidation.
4. *After Chapter XIV*		
Duplicated shorthand (one copy per student). Students read silently (3 min.). Teacher or selected student reads to class. Queries on spelling, use of apostrophe settled. Students type each sentence once.	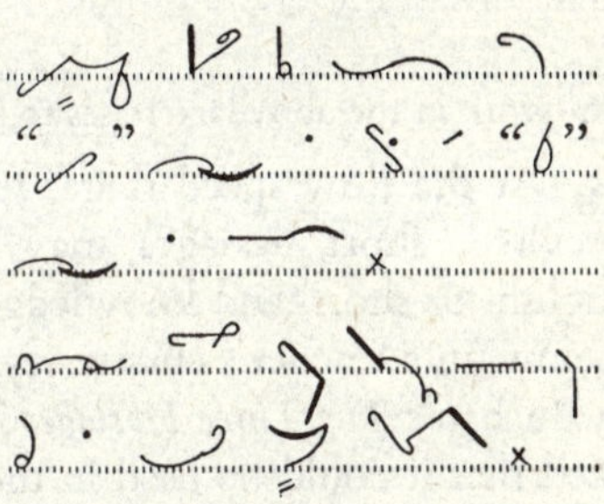 (time: 10–15 min.)	Vocabulary, use of apostrophe, short forms in phrases.
5. *After Chapter XVII*		
Duplicated shorthand (one copy per student). Teacher reads to class. Discussion on transcription points.	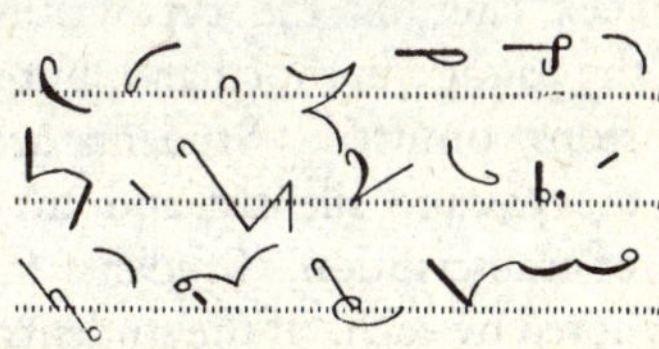	Background knowledge, punctuation, assessment of range of class attainment.

Form of Presentation and Method	*Matter*	*Aim*
Student reads to class (giving all punctuation—students do *not* insert punctuation on copy). Students transcribe and note time taken.	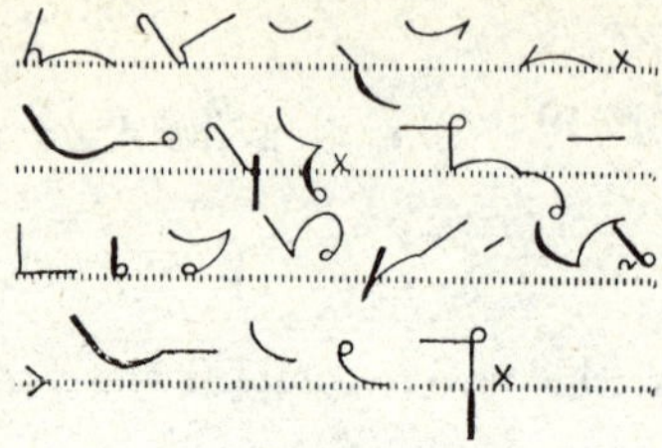	
6. *After any Chapter* (*e.g. after Chapter X*)		
Students read textbook exercise for homework and consider transcription points. In class teacher questions individual students and if thought advisable notes transcription points on board. Class transcribes, and notes time taken (if thought desirable by teacher).	Ex. 39 of *New Course*	Phrasing, spelling.

(All the students' work in the above exercises to be seen by the teacher.)

Prose Passages. At the slow speed stage, when the theory is being systematically revised, short passages may be chosen for interest, information, English, or shorthand knowledge.

The extract below (in a teacher's cursive style but with full punctuation) from John Buchan's *The Three Hostages* is an easy reading passage and it is suggested that it could be used in the following manner—

1. A copy of the shorthand, fully punctuated, is read in the shorthand class, brief comments are made on the book, and points of transcription, e.g. use of hyphens, punctuation, etc., are discussed.

2. About a week later, in the typewriting class, each student is given a copy of the passage in shorthand, but with punctuation marks, other than full stops, omitted. Students are given five minutes in which to read the passage silently and may ask questions on any doubtful points of transcription. Students then type the passage and the time taken is noted by each. If the students are sufficiently advanced

they may be asked to type the title of the book as a centred heading, and the author's name as a footnote to the passage.

The second extract is also taken from a modern work and is especially useful for shorthand vocabulary (circle *s*, final hooks combined with *s*, halving and phrasing). The passage could be used as follows—

1. The teacher reads the passage while the class follows the shorthand on individual copies.

2. The students fair copy the first paragraph, on every third line of their notebooks. The teacher walks round watching the manner of writing.

3. The teacher dictates the first paragraph twice, increasing the speed on the second dictation. The students complete the blank lines.

4. The students fair copy the next paragraph for homework, in a similar manner, in preparation for the next lesson.

5. At the next lesson a selected student reads from his own fair copy; the paragraph is then dictated twice.

6. The third paragraph is read by the class from the duplicated copies, and the spelling may be given of selected words (e.g. Fosse, spinney, draughtsmen, apparently).

7. The whole passage is dictated once at a fairly slow rate for good style of shorthand writing and the notes are given in for the teacher's inspection (and assessment, if this is appropriate).

The third and fourth passages are selected for their value in consolidating commercial knowledge. They can be dealt with in a similar manner. The fourth passage is not too difficult for a timed dictation (after reading), followed by a timed typed transcription.

EXTRACT FROM *The Three Hostages*

John Buchan (Thomas Nelson & Sons Ltd.)

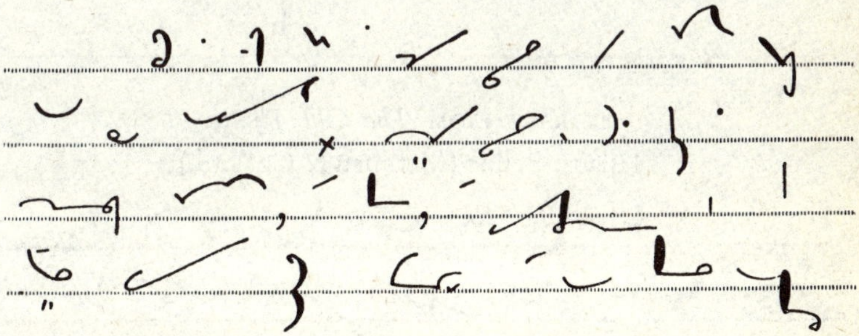

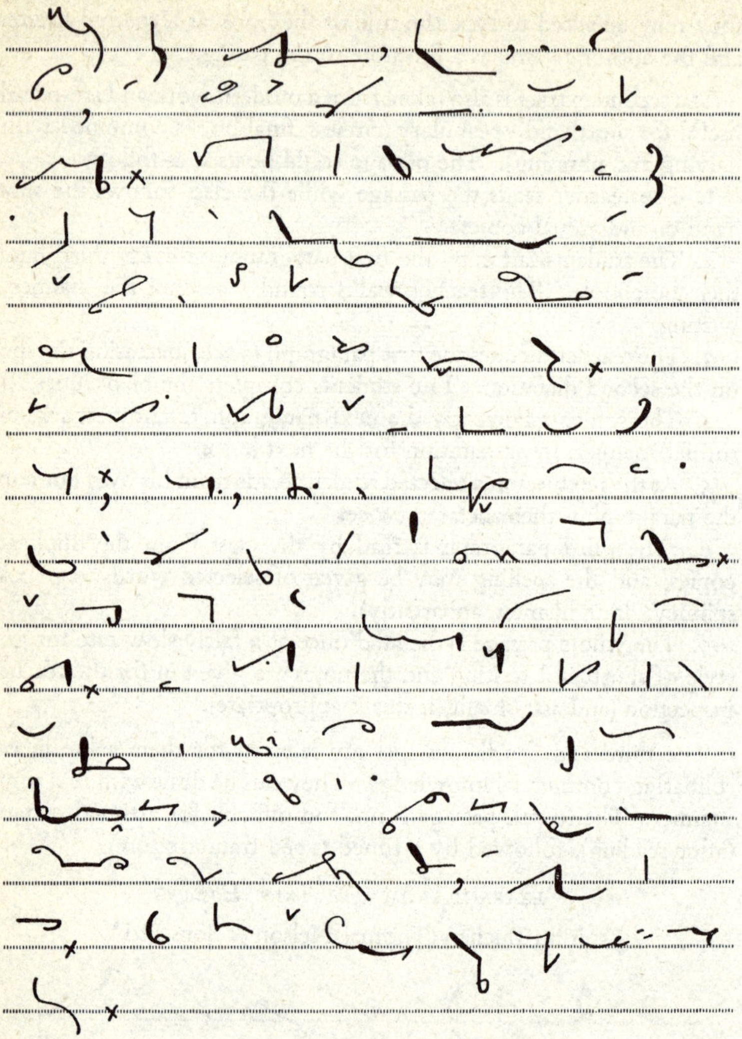

EXTRACT FROM *The Old Things*

Hilaire Belloc (Methuen & Co. Ltd.)

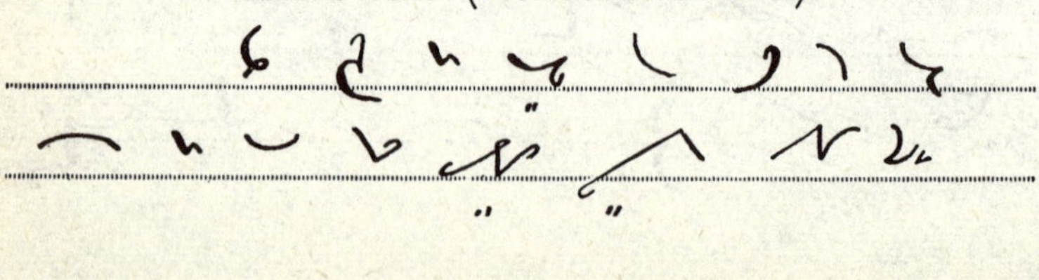

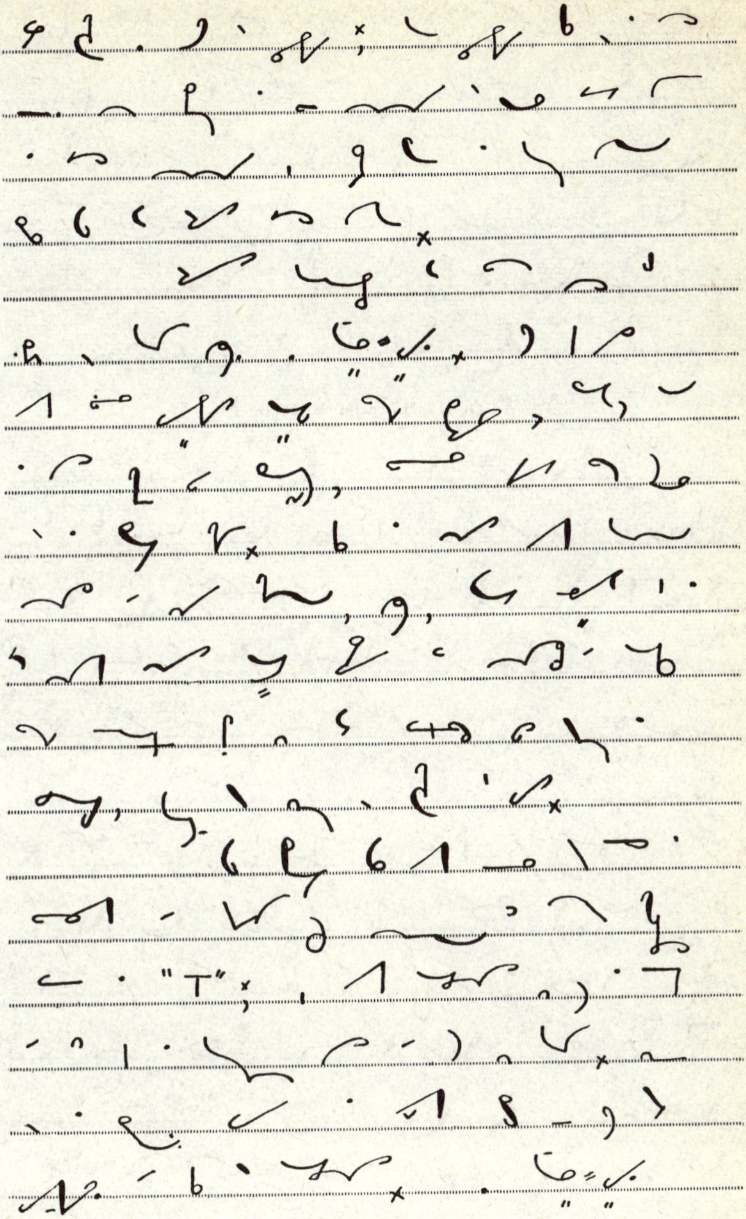

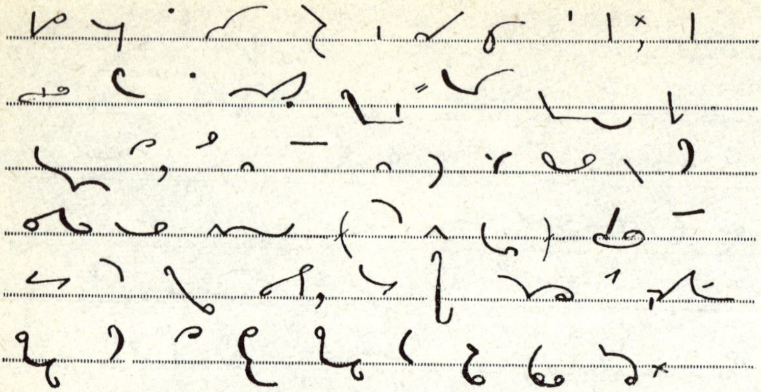

"GOODWILL" IN BUSINESS

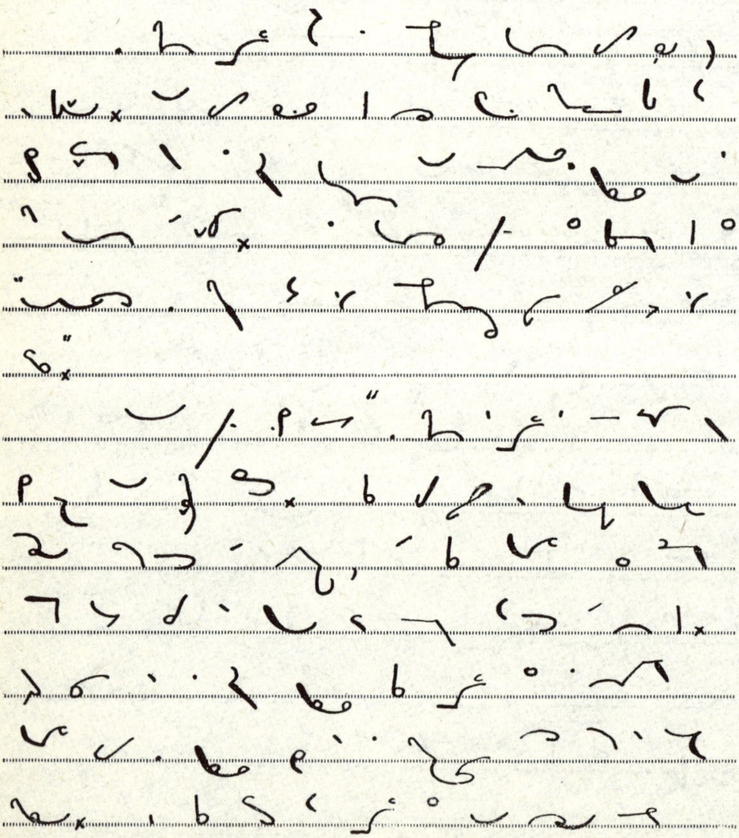

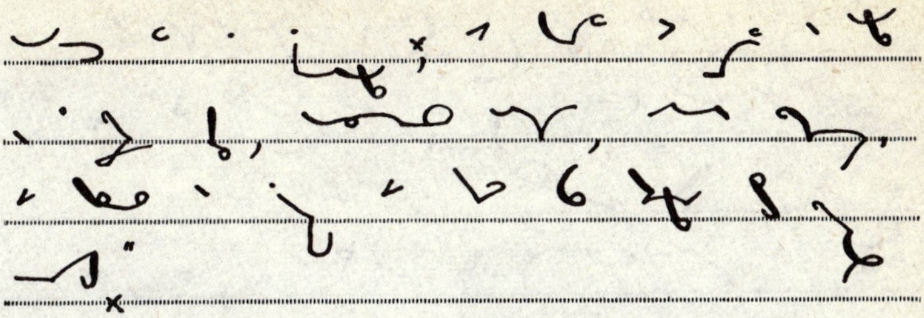

BONDED WAREHOUSES

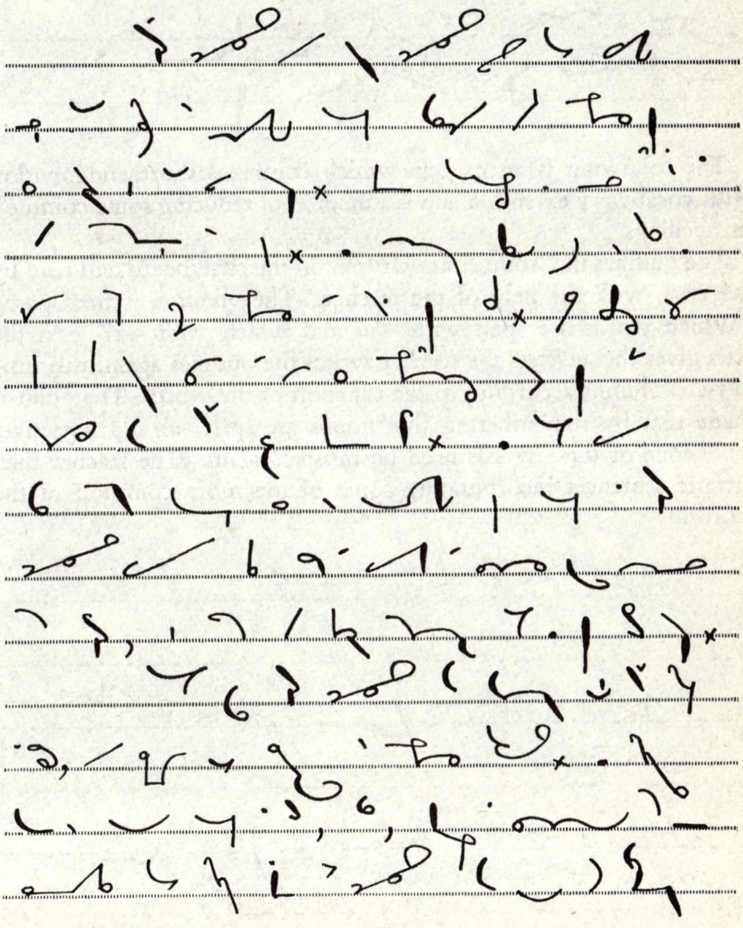

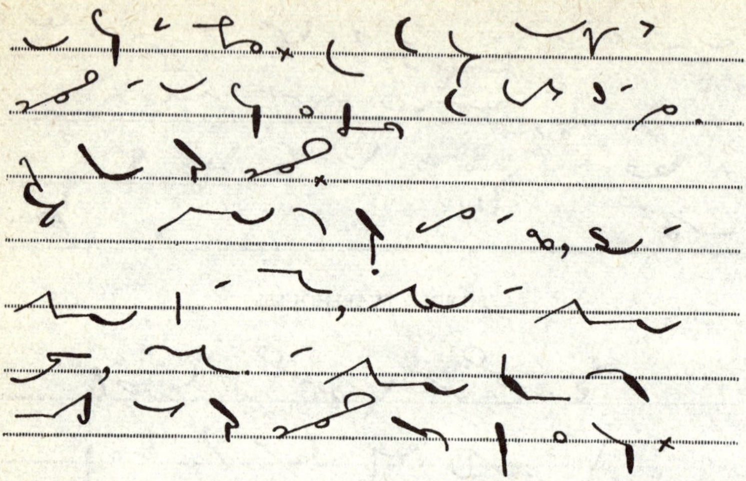

The following is an exercise which combines shorthand revision with vocabulary extension and is a method of reducing some common misspellings.

The outlines in Group A are written on the chalkboard and read by the class, with the help of the teacher. The question is then posed "Which words are spelt with *-ous* and which with *-us*?" As the class gives the answers the teacher writes the outlines again, this time in two columns according to the function of the word. The point is made that by remembering that nouns are spelt *-us* and adjectives *-ous*, none of these words need be misspelt again. The teacher then dictates sentences incorporating some of the more common of the words.

A.

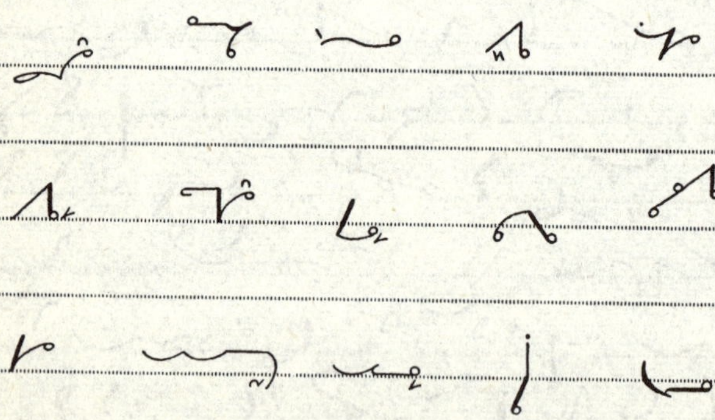

B. NOUNS C. ADJECTIVES

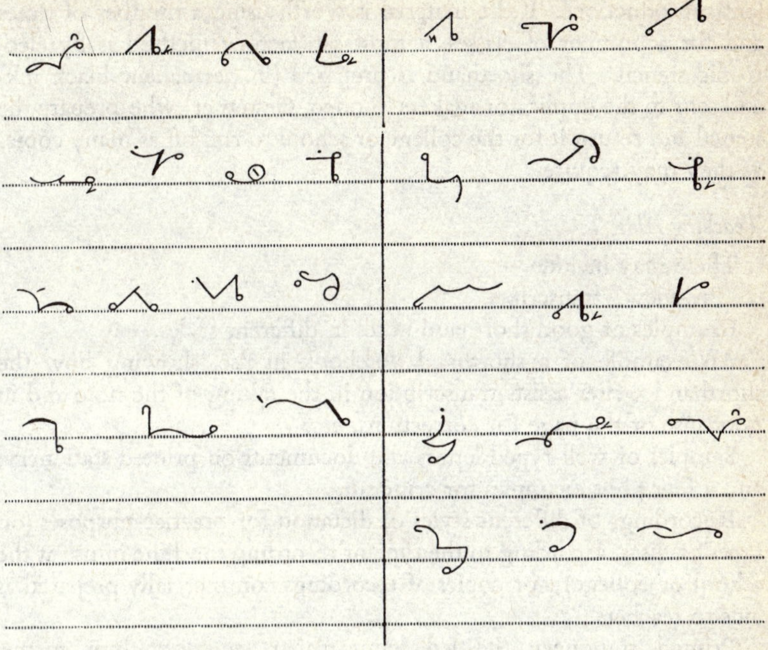

"Pre-view" Transcript

In order to train students to be mentally alert to other points of transcription, such as estimating the typing space required from the shorthand notes, points of display, use of words or figures, upper or lower case letters, etc., a most useful method is the "pre-view" transcript already mentioned. For this the teacher needs to prepare both the shorthand and the typed letter (or other document) in a sufficient number of copies so that the English or the shorthand class can have at least one between every two students. The points of transcription are indicated on the copies.

Duplication of Material

For the duplicating of the shorthand a choice of three methods is possible. The cheapest, but not the easiest, method is by spirit duplication. A master copy is prepared with a hectograph carbon and copies rolled off on a Banda (Ormigraph) machine. The next cheapest method is by one of the photocopying processes; these give excellent reproductions. If the material is worth using a number of times and for a number of classes, a most satisfactory method is by electronic stencil. The shorthand is prepared (in permanent black ink) and sent to the duplicator makers (Roneo, Gestetner) who prepare the stencil and return it for the college or school to run off as many copies as they may require.

Teaching Aids

These may include—

"Pre-view" transcripts.

Examples of good shorthand notes in different styles.

An example of a shorthand notebook in use, showing how the shorthand writer assists transcription in the taking of the note and in good use of the page for corrections, etc.

Samples of well-typed letters and documents on printed stationery, and a few poor examples for criticism.

Recordings of different styles of dictation for practice purposes (on tapes or discs, according to the type of recording machine in use at the school or college); or copies of recordings commercially prepared as aids to teachers.

Printed stationery (headed letter paper, memorandum forms, telegram forms, order forms, etc., for completion).

CHAPTER XI

Teachers' Examinations and Teacher-training Facilities

READERS of the foregoing pages will probably not need much persuading to be convinced that teaching shorthand and typewriting needs, no less than teaching any other subject, knowledge, imagination, reflection, planning and a twofold enthusiasm—enthusiasm for the subject and for teaching. Some fortunate few who become teachers do not need to be "taught" how to teach—they are naturally effective teachers with all the necessary qualities and abilities. For most people, however, training is at least an advantage, if not a necessity. Until 1946, when the Technical Teacher Training Colleges were established, there were but few facilities for the training of technical teachers, among whom teachers of commercial subjects are counted. Today there are various types of courses, some full time, some part time, some intended for new entrants to the profession, others for teachers already in service. The following summary is given so that readers may gain a general picture of the scope for training facilities offered today. Fuller details of any course or any qualifying examination can be obtained from the colleges or organizations concerned.

QUALIFICATIONS

The first point to be made is that the status of "qualified teacher" under the regulations of the Ministry of Education is granted only on certain conditions being fulfilled. All graduates of British universities are, by virtue of their degree, recognized as qualified teachers without further training. Non-graduate teachers must have successfully completed a course of training approved by the Minister (as set out in Pamphlet No. 6/59). The second point of importance is that this recognition by the Ministry of Education is only *necessary* if a person wishes to teach full time in a primary or secondary school. For teachers in further education (whether full or part time) this status is a condition neither for recruitment nor for the payment, on appointment, of the current negotiated rates of pay for qualified teachers.

Those candidates who are accepted to one of the full-time courses are "recognized students," that is, they receive free tuition and are paid a grant for the duration of the course. Hostel accommodation is also provided free for those who desire to be resident students, but naturally, in such cases, the amount of the grant awarded will be less than that for a day student. The amount of the grant varies according to the individual circumstances of the student, but the grants for mature students are higher than for students under twenty-five years of age, as it is recognized that the former will have greater financial responsibilities. It is also possible for untrained serving teachers to be seconded, on full pay, for one of the recognized courses provided that the local education authority agrees.

FACILITIES FOR TRAINING

Full-time courses of instruction for prospective candidates for the shorthand and the typewriting teachers' examinations of the Royal Society of Arts are offered by a number of Colleges of Education in England, Scotland and Wales, including the Bolton College of Education; Garnett College, London; the Moray House College of Education, Edinburgh; and the Swansea College of Education. The courses vary in content, duration, cost and student-grant arrangements, and intending students are advised to write to the individual colleges for information.

Correspondence courses are also available. Pitmans Correspondence College offers courses for the Royal Society of Arts shorthand teachers' certificate examinations, and full details of these correspondence courses are available from Pitman House, Godalming, Surrey.

The main qualification required by part-time teachers of shorthand and typewriting is that of the Royal Society of Arts teachers' certificates. Part-time courses in preparation for these examinations are usually centred in one technical college in each of the L.E.A. areas. The courses are held on two or three evenings a week for a period of one or two evening sessions (September to May or June). The usual requirement for acceptance to the course is the same as for entry to the examination—General Certificate of Education in at least four subjects (including English), or an R.S.A. English Certificate (Stage II, first class, or Stage III, pass), together with a Shorthand Certificate at 80 words per minute or an Intermediate Typewriting Certificate (35 words per minute). Details of courses and examination syllabuses can be obtained from the individual colleges. The R.S.A. also issue a syllabus for each of their teacher's certificate examinations.

Information about grants for full-time courses should be sought from the local education authority of the area in which the candidate lives.

For those teachers living in countries outside Great Britain where the R.S.A. examinations for teachers are not held, the Joint Examining Board for Pitman Shorthand (or Typewriting) Teacher's Diploma holds examinations of a similar nature. These, again, are for part-time teachers and do not give qualified teacher status under the Ministry of Education Regulations. Details of the Joint Board examinations should be sought from the Secretary, Joint Examining Board, 39 Parker Street, Kingsway, London, W.C.2. Postal courses for these and the R.S.A. examinations are also available.

All teacher's courses include a study of general principles of education, of teaching methods, and of the application of such principles and methods to the particular subject to be taught. In the full-time courses there is always a period of teaching practice, when the students work under the supervision of a permanent member of staff and the guidance of the training college tutors. In the part-time evening courses teaching practice is not always possible, but it is arranged on a limited scale in many courses.

TEACHERS' CERTIFICATES IN SHORTHAND AND TYPEWRITING

Examples of the papers in General Principles and Practice of Teaching and of Principles and Practice of Teaching Applied to Shorthand and Typewriting are given below.

Royal Society of Arts

EXAMINATION FOR A TEACHER'S CERTIFICATE IN SHORTHAND

(*May*, 1966)

PART II (*a*)—PRINCIPLES AND PRACTICE OF TEACHING APPLIED TO SHORTHAND

(Time allowed—2 hours)

Candidates must answer Question 1 *and any* THREE *other questions.*

1. Write lesson notes, with appropriate blackboard outlines, for a 45-minute period in which "Ses Circle" (Pitman) or the principles of joining for circle vowels (Gregg) will be the new topic to be introduced.

2. Describe how you would vary the speed practice of a class of advanced shorthand students so as to stimulate and maintain their interest.

3. What are your views, in the teaching of shorthand, on the use of (*a*) reading shorthand from the blackboard, (*b*) drilling single outlines, (*c*) reading back by individual students, (*d*) fair copying from printed shorthand?

4. What kind of homework would you give to a shorthand class of:—
(*a*) beginners
(*b*) intermediate students who had worked through the theory
(*c*) advanced students?

5. Discuss the importance and use of regular testing and prompt marking in the teaching of shorthand.

6. Discuss in some detail (*a*) the importance, (*b*) the technique of effective demonstration in the teaching of shorthand.

EXAMINATION FOR A TEACHER'S CERTIFICATE IN TYPEWRITING

(*November*, 1966)

PART II (*a*)—PRINCIPLES AND PRACTICE OF TEACHING APPLIED TO TYPEWRITING

(Time allowed—2 hours)

Answer Question 1 *and any* THREE *other questions.*

Where relevant, state the type of class you have in mind.

All answers must be handwritten.

1. For a second lesson in tabulation to EITHER an adult evening class OR a full-time day class of students aged 15+, give the following:—
(*a*) Students' previous knowledge and skill in tabulation
(*b*) Your lesson aim
(*c*) Type of exercise(s) you would choose
(*d*) Your teaching method(s)
(*e*) Your teaching aids
Give reasons for choice for items (*c*), (*d*) and (*e*).

2. What do you consider to be the characteristics of a good typewriting lesson of an hour's duration for:—
EITHER (*a*) an elementary full-time day class of post-G.C.E. students
OR (*b*) an intermediate part-time day release class.

3. Discuss the question of error analysis and elimination in typewriting teaching and learning.

4. What methods would you use in teaching typewriting to help your students to become reliable and speedy in the checking of their work?

5. In choosing copying matter for typewriting students at the elementary stage, by what principles of teaching and learning would you be guided?

6. For a class of intermediate students who are also learning audio-typing give your plan of work for a one-hour lesson. Assume that your students have some competency in audio work and give reasons for your choice of activities.

EXAMINATION FOR TEACHERS' CERTIFICATES IN SHORTHAND AND TYPEWRITING

(*May*, 1966)

PART II (*b*)—GENERAL PRINCIPLES AND PRACTICE OF TEACHING

(Time allowed—1 hour 30 minutes)

THREE *questions, and no more, are to be attempted.*

Answers must be in longhand.

1. "Ability to recall depends to some extent on the way in which the learning was done." Comment.
2. Why is it harder to eliminate a bad skill movement than to establish a good one?
3. Discuss the relative importance of routine and variety in the regular work of a class.
4. Explain the significance of "plateau periods" while acquiring a skill and suggest methods for dealing with them.
5. Describe the main causes which compel differences of teaching technique for full and part-time students, even if subject matter is the same.

APPENDIX I

English-shorthand Word List Correlated with *Pitman Shorthand New Course*

THESE words have been classified into "A," "B" and "C" groups according to word frequency in the Horn and Peterson[1] count; lists "A" include mainly words falling within the first *five* thousand, plus a minority in the *six* thousand, lists "B" fall within *nine* thousand, and lists "C" comprise mainly words outside the *ten* thousand frequency.

All shorthand-typists should be expected to be so familiar with the spelling of Group "A" words that reference to a dictionary is unnecessary when transcribing from shorthand or typing from manuscript. Group "B" words *should* be known (both spelling and meaning) by most shorthand-typists, though reference to a dictionary may sometimes be necessary. Group "C" words are included for vocabulary extension work wherever and whenever appropriate.

The lists should not be used when the shorthand theory of the particular chapters is first introduced, but when revision and consolidation of the shorthand theory takes place. The words for Chapters I–IV would therefore be used when the class had reached, say, Chapter VI.

Chapters I-IV (inclusive)

Group A	*Group B*	*Group C*
affect	agenda	addenda
attach	annum	allay
check (cheque)	data	allege
damage	knack	alleged
effect	mail (male)	appal
envelope	manage	decade
laid	memo	loath
lay	weigh (way)	opaque
package		

[1] Horn, Ernest and Peterson, Thelma, *The Basic Vocabulary of Business Letters* (New York, The Gregg Publishing Co., 1943).

Chapters V–VI

Group A	*Group B*	*Group C*
apology	ageing	anomaly
assure	career	arrears
authority	colleague	autonomy
ensure (insure)	emerge	dilemma
guarantee	error	epidemic
ream	indemnity	erratum
relief	invalid	fallacy
relieve	nominate	fatigue
remedy	width	rhythm

Chapter VII

Group A	*Group B*	*Group C*
arrive	by-law	alloy
berth (birth)	copyright	annuity
bureau	dyeing (dying)	dialect
issuing	endow	dynamo
lie	hygienic	indemnify
mileage	ingenuity	penury
occupy	mahogany	pneumatic
revenue	pursue	tenure
review	royalty	
schedule	verify	
variety		

Chapter VIII

Group A	*Group B*	*Group C*
apologies	anonymous	accede
apologize	apparatus	auspicious
canvas (canvass)	assess	connoisseur
ceiling	cargoes	disburse
desirous	cease	disparity
disappear	ceremony	elicit
dispatch (despatch)	deficit	forestall
facilities	endorse	illicit
magazine	gazette	harass
receive	gazetteer	pasteurize
salaries	immense	pseudonym
scarcely	install	psychology
seize	licence (license)	recede
series	municipal	sinecure
succeed	solely	sporadic
		succinct
		veracity

Chapter IX

Group A	*Group B*	*Group C*
adjusts	access	accessible
all right	census	apposite
already	collapses	cauterized
chooses	decease	diagnosis
disease	decisive	diffused
emphasize	dismissal	excise
excessive	forecast	fiscal
exercise	indexes (indexed)	fortuitous
exhaust	investor	indices
gas (gases)	monopolize	possessor
opposite	statistics	pursuance
seized	statutory	staccato
solicitor	sterling	
	summarized	

Chapter X

Group A	*Group B*	*Group C*
absolute	accelerate	accentuate
accept	accumulate	antique
accurate	amateur	assimilate
actually	analysed	desultory
allot	ascertain	disservice
allotted	benefited	emancipate
analysis	exhibit	emulate
anticipate	exhilarate	epitome
assorted	expedite	excerpt
catalogue	fascinate	format
exaggerate	hazardous	imminent
guaranteed	horizontal	inapt
necessarily	intimated	inaugurate
omit	mitigate	inept
omitted	obsolete	maturity
percentage	rapidity	morale
permitted	remitted	obsolescence
sentence	warehouse	salutary
sincerely	worsted	simulate
		subordinate

Chapter XI (Double consonants to straight strokes only)

Group A	*Group B*	*Group C*
across	accordance	abrogate
applied	aggravate	aperture
approximately	aggregate	apropos

article
available
bicycle
book-keeper
calculate
clerical
clothing
collected
correct
criticism
criticize
feasible
label
labelled
noticeable
obliged
occurrence
political
practically
principle (-pal)
procedure
proceed
professor
programme
rateable
regrettable
secretary
separate
visible

attributed
chemical
clothes
college
courtesy
credible
creditable
deliberately
exchequer
guard
indelible
literature
neighbour
personnel
perturbed
physical
precede
premature
proprietary
receptacle
straight (strait)
supersede
supervisor
tolerable

attorney
audible
calibre
collaborate
collapsible
corroborate
credulous
deprecate
discriminate
eligible
implicit
inevitable
integral
jeopardize
laboratory
plausible
promulgate
reciprocal
retrograde
scrupulously
susceptible
symmetrical
tributary
victualler

Chapter XI (Double consonants—curves)

Group A

abnormal
approval
artificial
average
chauffeur
develop
differed
effectively
endeavour
engineer
enormously
freight
fulfil
honorary

Group B

anniversary
anthracite
authoritatively
flourishing
fluctuate
inflammable
inflexible
manoeuvre
originally
personally
plenary
potential
residential
segregate

Group C

alternatively
averse
cantonal
cavil
credentials
frugal
generate
mercenary
nullify
panelling
panorama
paraphrase
philanthropy
pioneer

nominal
normal
nourish
offered
official
overhau
overrate
privilege
relatively
specialize
superficial
superfluous
vertical

treasury
versatile
virtually

plethora
primeval

Chapter XII

Group A

achieve
alternative
apparently
appearance
assistance
balance
beginning
between
Britain
Briton
chiefly
deferred
definitely
disappearance
disappoint
exhaustive
exorbitant
expenses
forbidden
foreign
fulfilment
inventory
keenness
preferred
preferring
president
reference
referred
referring

Group B

abundance
achievement
adjourn
admittance
allotment
amend
amendment
appliance
assessment
benevolent
determine
discipline
discrepancy
economical
economics
fraudulent
incident
lieutenant
maintenance
paraffin
persistent
precedent
preservative
pronounce
remittance
remunerate
resistance
suburban
suddenness

Group C

antecedent
archive
cumulative
inference
irrelevant
latent
legislature
mechanism
monograph
penicillin
pertinent
remunerative
replenish
rudiment
sedative
virulent

sergeant	voluntarily
tariffs	volunteer
tendency	
woollen	

Chapter XIII

Group A	*Group B*	*Group C*
additional	absorption	abstention
cancellation	accumulation	allegation
commission	aggression	allusion
corporation	cessation	annihilation
decision	commissioner	cohesion
edition	exceptional	culmination
emigration	function	dilapidation
exaggeration	physician	diminution
immigration	provisional	discretion
installation	remuneration	erosion
jurisdiction	repercussion	illusion
occasionally	succession	inflationary
possession	superannuation	mensuration
regulation	transitional	ratification
renovation	tuition	revelation
repetition	vacation	
specification	vaccination	
stationery (-ary)	vocational	

Chapter XIV

Group A	*Group B*	*Group C*
accustomed	ambiguous	acquittal
acquaintance	apprehensive	adjunct
acquainted	councillor	ambidextrous
acquire	counsellor	apprehend
acquisition	embody	bilingual
adequate	emboss	extempore
adhere	enamel	imbue
adjustment	equitable	impassable
ambulance	impartial	impeccable
campaign	imposition	impediment
distinctly	impunity	imperceptible
embargo	liquor	impetuous
embarrass	potential	impetus
embarrassment	prestige	implacable
equalled	quandary	impregnable

equipment	quorum	improvident
equipped	requisition	peremptory
equivalent	requisitioned	quixotic
inquiry (enquiry)		sanguine
leasehold		
likelihood		
neighbourhood		
questionnaire		
temporarily		
temporary		
whether		
wholesale		

Chapter XV

Group A	*Group B*	*Group C*
appeal(-ed)	accelerator	arduous
appeared	barometer	colander
calendar	collaborator	counterfeit
cancelled	debenture	countermand
centre	diameter	engender
centred	indebtedness	excavator
credited	intermittent	gasometer
enamelled	medicine	indispensable
extraordinary	Mediterranean	interpreter
immediately	medium	intersperse
installed	refrigerator	malingerer
interference	resigned	medicinal
interruption	structure	ordinance
	surrender	ordnance
	thermometer	rescind
		temperament
		underwrite

Chapter XVI

Group A	*Group B*	*Group C*
accommodate	achievement	commemorate
accommodation	alignment	commentator
accompany	awkward	complacence
admitting	commitment	complaisance
announcement	commodity	component
attempting	comparable	compositor
commit	comparative	contagious
committee	compatible	recognizance
compelled	concisely	reconnoitre
confidence	consensus	

confident(-ant)
connexion(-ction
continuous
convenience
forwardness
hopefulness
illegal
recommend
recommendation
requisitioning

contradictory
contravene
convalescence
illegible
inconsistent
legibly
recompense

Chapter XVII (and contractions)

Group A

agreeable
appointment
appreciable
conscientious
convenience
co-operate
courteous
frequently
goodwill
guardian
immediately
periodically
practice(-se)
procedure
qualify
realize
seriously

Group B

accruing
appropriate
assignment
composure
concession
continuously
enthusiasm
hardware
indispensable
irrespective
preliminary
reimburse
reinforce
simultaneously
subsequent

Group C

abeyance
appropriation
contingency
exigency
expediency
legislature
unanimous

Chapter XVIII (and intersections)

Group A

county council
distinguished
efficiency
foreign department
government official
local authorities
medical society
necessary form
necessary arrange-
ments
necessary attention
qualification
railway officials

Group B

amalgamate
amalgamation
bankruptcy
merchandise
metropolitan
prejudicial
proficiency
qualifications
television

Group C

circumstantial
constabulary
contemporary
experimental
imperturbable
inhibit
stringency
unanimity

APPENDIX 2

Some Audio and Visual Aids

THE USE OF THE LINTOGRAPH OR FELT BOARD

MANY topics included in a typewriting syllabus can be more effectively illustrated by actual documents or large-scale diagrams used with a felt board than by chalkboard diagrams. The former have the following advantages—

1. They can be prepared before a lesson and can be of a higher standard than chalkboard diagrams, since the latter generally have to be drawn hurriedly during lesson time.
2. More lesson time is available for student practice as the lintograph diagrams take less time to present.
3. Lintograph diagrams can be more realistic and vivid in presentation than chalkboard diagrams—more realistic because they can be produced in black and white as in most typescript or printing, and more vivid because colour can be used to highlight teaching points more effectively on paper than on the chalkboard (coloured arrows, for example, or other symbols can be superimposed on a diagram by using drawing pins).
4. Once prepared, lintograph diagrams are available for repeated use at any time and in any room.

Materials

Diagrams are fixed to a backcloth of lint or felt. For typewriting classes this should preferably be black or coloured, but not white.

Diagrams can be prepared on flock paper, a commercial product made of stout paper backed with small circles of flock, which is sold in sheets measuring 20 in. by 28 in. in a range of colours. The current price is about 5s. per sheet. Cartridge or other stout paper backed with small strips or squares of lint or felt can also be used. Good-quality blotting paper can be used for small diagrams and needs no backing. *Econasign* stencils are very suitable for the lettering and lines.

Topics Suitable for Lintographs

1. Paper sizes (proportionally enlarged sheets), can be illustrated, the print dimensions given with *Econasign* stencils. The relationship

between the different sizes of paper and type dimensions can be demonstrated quickly and clearly by moving the sheets around on the felt board.

2. Methods of centring headings, using both pica and elite type, can be demonstrated quickly.

3. Types of letter-headings (actual or enlarged) can be illustrated. A quick method is thus provided of showing the relationship between letter-head display and layout of typescript below.

4. Line diagrams of document display (for example, letters, memorandums, invoices, specifications, and other commercial documents) can be shown.

5. An extension of point 4 is to show line diagrams to illustrate modern stream-lining of partially-printed documents (for example, order forms, application forms, invoices, stock record sheets, requisition forms, etc.) in order to save the typists' time.

6. Line diagrams of types of paragraphs can be set out with bold titles for easy recall of the technical typewriting terms (for example, indented, block, hanging).

7. Display of actual envelopes and large-scale line diagrams of different forms and display of addresses on envelopes can be illustrated.

8. Tabulation exercises can be prepared as line diagrams, in conjunction with chalkboard work for calculations if desired. This use enables the arithmetical work to be presented more clearly and neatly on the chalkboard.

9. Actual documents from different types of offices (for example, of a legal or engineering company) can be shown.

10. Display of different types of agenda can be shown.

11. Important points of typewriting theory may be presented to the class at appropriate times as reminders before they type an exercise in the early stages (for example, the number of typing lines to the page, information on the continuation page of a letter, etc.; and in later stages information in concise form on methods of duplication, roman numerals, proof correction signs, etc.).

The above list is not exhaustive and teachers will have their own ideas on what is suitable for demonstrating on the lintograph. If well prepared and competently used, such illustrations as those suggested above will undoubtedly help students to learn more quickly and enable the most economic use to be made of the lesson time during which diagrams are introduced.

DEMONSTRATION STAND

In most fields of learning, demonstration is accepted as an essential teaching technique because students are expected to learn by imitation. Nevertheless, students frequently have little or no opportunity to imitate a good performance in typewriting, as a stand enabling the teacher to give a demonstration effectively, with economy of movement, time and effort, is still not found in all typewriting classrooms. An illustration of an appropriate demonstration stand is given below.

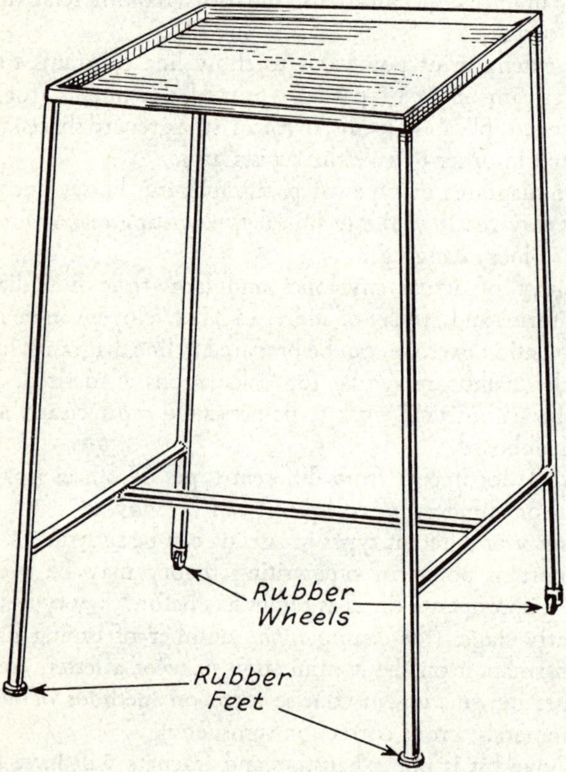

STAND		TRAY	
Height (back)	$38\frac{1}{2}$ in.	Length	15 in.
" (front)	38 in.	Width	21 in.
Width (top)	20 in. x 14 in.	Depth	$\frac{1}{2}$ in.
" (bottom)	21 in. x 19 in.		

LIST OF TYPEWRITING FILMS

Advanced Typewriting Short Cuts, 35 minutes (New York, Castle Films).
At Your Finger-tips (16 mm. and 35 mm.), 31 minutes (Imperial Typewriter Co. Ltd.).
Basic Typewriting Machine Operation, 29 minutes (New York, Castle Films).
Basic Typewriting Methods, 31 minutes (New York, Castle Films).
Better Typing at Your Finger-tips (Technicolor), 25–30 minutes (Smith-Corona Ltd.).
Building Typing Skill, 11 minutes (Chicago, Coronet Instructional Films).
Care for Qwerty (16 mm.), 16 minutes (Imperial Typewriter Co. Ltd.).
Electric Typing Time, 20 minutes (International Business Machines Co.).
Keys to Efficiency (16 mm.), 31 minutes (Imperial Typewriter Co. Ltd.).
Right at the Start (16 mm.), 15 minutes (Royal Typewriters Ltd.).
The Pool of Contentment (16 mm.), 19 minutes (H.M. Treasury).
Typing Technique (16 mm.), 22 minutes (H.M. Treasury).
Typing Tips (16 mm.), 21 minutes (Underwood Business Machines Ltd.).

AUDIO AIDS

Shorthand Instruction by Sound Tape

30 tapes, 5 in. spools, twin-track, 3¾ i.p.s. £90 a set, £3·25 a reel plus VAT.

These tapes are designed for use in conjunction with the *New Course Intensive Workbook*, and contain all the exercises in this series.

Shorthand Speed Development, Nos. 1, 2 & 3, Pitman—Pre-recorded Tapes

5 tapes, 5 in. spools, twin-track, 3¾ i.p.s. £3·25 a reel plus VAT.

These tapes support the students' book. The material is based on the Royal Society of Arts Shorthand Examination Papers.

Audio-copy Typewriting—Pre-recorded Tapes

4 tapes, 5 in. spools, twin-track, 3¾ i.p.s. £13 a set plus VAT.

8 tapes, 3 in. spools, plus one empty take-up reel; suitable for use only on Philips Audio Typing Trainer Model ET 1931 and Model EL 3581/54 (81R). £16 a set plus VAT.

These tapes contain all the exercises in the students' textbook.

Speedon Records—Series 2 Red Label

Four 7-inch extended play discs (33 r.p.m.) 40p plus VAT each.

Speeds 50/60, 70/80, 90/100, 110/120 w.p.m. Shorthand leaflet is inserted with each record.

APPENDIX 3

Questions on Teaching Shorthand and Typewriting

THE following are questions on topics related to general principles of teaching and are applicable to the teaching of shorthand and typewriting.

GENERAL QUESTIONS

1. Mention any two general principles underlying the acquisition of skills and say what teaching methods and type of material you would use in order that these principles could be applied in your teaching.

2. Distinguish between an examination syllabus and a scheme of work.

3. Explain the general principles to be borne in mind in demonstration.

4. What general principles of teaching and learning should be observed in order that a lesson may be an effective learning period?

5. Define and discuss fully (*a*) "whole" and (*b*) "part" learning.

6. Define and discuss "habit formation" in relation to skill acquisition.

7. From your own experience of acquiring knowledge or a particular skill give one or more instances of unwitting learning and assess the value of such learning.

8. Discuss the problem of establishing good class-relationships in evening classes.

9. What principles would guide you in planning a lesson period with a class of students of mixed ability?

10. Discuss the advantages and disadvantages of group and individual teaching in an evening class of adults learning a skill.

11. Drawing on your own experience as a learner, distinguish between "interest" and "having things made interesting."

12. Write a short essay on the value of imagination in teaching.

QUESTIONS ON SHORTHAND

1. Give concise notes of a first lesson in shorthand. Indicate the type of class concerned and give reasons for your methods.

2. "Competent writing of shorthand from dictation needs both mental and manual dexterity." Indicate the types of exercises you would use to develop these skills in your students. Give examples where possible.

3. Give a concise plan of a shorthand lesson to second-year students. Assume that most of them can take dictation at 70 words per minute.

4. From your own experience as a shorthand writer explain—

(*a*) Those aspects of reading and writing shorthand which you found most difficult to master.

(*b*) Those which you found easiest.

5. Discuss the relative importance of mental and manual skills in shorthand writing.

6. Make a study of how you read longhand and shorthand and try to draw some conclusions of value for the teaching of shorthand.

7. One of the handicaps in the learning of shorthand at evening classes is the period of time between succeeding lessons. What methods would you adopt in order to minimize the disadvantages which arise from this?

8. Discuss, in relation to shorthand, the statement that a quick movement is not a slow movement speeded up.

9. Draw up a scheme of work for ten lessons during which the main aims will be the revision of shorthand theory and the development of writing at speed. Assume that the average ability of the class is 50 words per minute.

10. Explain clearly some of the methods you would use in your teaching of shorthand to prepare your students for fluent typewritten transcription.

QUESTIONS ON TYPEWRITING

1. What do you understand by good work habits in typewriting? Give your ideas on how a teacher of typewriting can help students to develop good attitudes to and skilful habits in their work.

2. What steps would you take to ensure that a typewriting practice period would be an effective learning period for your students?

3. Discuss the relative merits of the vertical and horizontal methods of introducing keyboard work.

4. Give, with reasons, the main factors which would guide you in selecting a typewriting textbook.

5. In choosing copying matter for typewriting students at the intermediate stage, by what principles of teaching would you be guided?

6. "Early and graduated training in typewritten transcription of shorthand should be included in all typewriting courses for shorthand-typists." Discuss this statement and give some definite ways in which you would give such training.

7. As a teacher of typewriting, how would you help your students to develop a sense of responsibility in their work?

8. Suggest ways in which the typewriting teacher in a day school or college can overcome the difficulties involved in teaching students the use of a rotary duplicator and in giving sufficient practice in its use.

9. Choose a sequence of topics for *eight* lessons for a class of evening students (girls aged sixteen to eighteen years), assuming that they have had about twenty hours' instruction in typewriting. Give reasons for your choice and for the order in which you place the topics.

10. Draw up a scheme of work for the first ten lessons of a second-year class of evening students meeting twice a week. In the first year they have reached R.S.A. Stage I examination standard, or the elementary standard of a similar examining body.

Bibliography

GENERAL

Bugelski, B. R., *The Psychology of Learning* (New York, Henry Holt & Co. Inc.; London, Methuen & Co. Ltd.; 1936).

Dewey, John, "Interest as Related to Will," Second Supplement to *The Herbart Yearbook* (1903).

Downes, W. J., *Spelling and Vocabulary Studies* (Toronto, Sir Isaac Pitman (Canada) Ltd., 1950).

Ellis, Robert S., *Educational Psychology* (Princeton, D. Van Nostrand Co. Inc., 1951).

Gilbreth, F. B. and Gilbreth, Lilian M., *Applied Motion Study* (New York, Macmillan Co., 1919).

Harms, Harm, *Methods in Vocational Business Education* (Cincinnati, South Western Publishing Co., 1949).

Horn, Ernest and Peterson, Thelma, *The Basic Vocabulary of Business Letters* (New York, The Gregg Publishing Co., 1943).

Kellaway, F. W., *Part-time Teaching* (London, G. Bell & Sons Ltd., 1952).

Lester Smith, W. O., *Education in Great Britain*, 4th ed. (London, Oxford University Press, 1964).

Mace, C. A., "Incentives: Some Experimental Studies," *Report No.* 72 (Industrial Health Research Board (Gt. Britain), 1935).

de Madariaga, Salvador, *Englishmen, Frenchmen and Spaniards* (London, Oxford University Press, 1928).

Marrou, H. I., *A History of Education in Antiquity* (London, Sheed & Ward Ltd., 1956).

Panton, J. H., *Modern Teaching Practice and Technique* (London, Longmans, Green & Co. Ltd., 1948).

Peel, E. A., *The Psychological Basis of Education* (London, Oliver & Boyd Ltd., 1948).

Pickard, O. G., "Education for Office Work," *The Vocational Aspect of Secondary and Further Education*, Vol. I, No. 2 (May, 1949).

Pickard, O. G., "Office Work and Education, 1848–1948," *The Vocational Aspect of Secondary and Further Education*, Vol. I, No. 3 (November, 1949).

Pinsent, A., *The Principles of Teaching-method* (London, George G. Harrap & Co. Ltd., 1952).

Powell, L. S., *A Guide to the Use of Visual Aids* (London, B.A.C.I.E., 1961).

Price, Ray G. (Editor), "Auditory and Visual Aids in Business Education," *Proceedings of* 1946 *Business Education Institute* (Teachers' College, University of Cincinnati).

Sidney, Elizabeth, "The Theory of Learning and Management Training," *Education and Commerce*, No. 18 (January, 1957).

Sorenson, Herbert, *Psychology in Education* (New York, McGraw-Hill Publishing Co. Inc., 1948).

Sturt, Mary, "A Comparison of Speed with Accuracy in the Learning Process," *The British Journal of Psychology*, No. 12 (1921–2).

Tonne, H. A., Popham, E. L. and Freeman, M. H., *Methods of Teaching Business Subjects*, 2nd ed. (New York, McGraw-Hill Publishing Co. Inc., 1957).

Underwood, Benton, J., *Experimental Psychology* (New York, Appleton-Century-Crofts, 1949).

Valentine, C. W., *Psychology and its Bearing on Education* (London, Methuen & Co. Ltd., 1960 ed.).

Whitehead, A. N., *The Aims of Education* (London, Ernest Benn Ltd., 1959 ed.).

Yorkshire Council for Further Education, "Typewriting, Shorthand and Office Practice in Further Education," *Pamphlet No.* 62 (1961).

TYPEWRITING

Adams, H. L., "The Comparative Effectiveness of Electric and Manual Typewriters in the Acquisition of Skill," *U.S. Naval Personnel Research Activity*, (January, 1956). (See also *American Psychologist*, No. 11, 1956.)

Banner, Mary Ruth, *A Study of the Relationship Between Letter-production Test Rates and Straight-copy Test Rates in High School Typewriting (Virginia)*, (Knoxville, University of Tennessee, 1953).

Barrett, Dorothy M., "Prediction of Achievement in Typewriting and Stenography in a Liberal Arts College," *Journal of Applied Psychology*, (December, 1946).

Bell, Mary La Verne, *Some Factors of Typewriting Difficulty* (University of Oklahoma, 1949). (See also *The National Business Education Quarterly*, October, 1950.)

Blackstone, E. G., "Summary of Research in Typewriting," *The National Business Education Quarterly* (Washington, D.C., Spring, 1940).

Book, W. F., *Learning to Typewrite* (London, The Gregg Publishing Co., 1925).

Butsch, Russell L. C., "Eye Movements and the Eye—Hand span in Typewriting," *The Journal of Psychology*, No. 4 (1937).

Crooks, Maxwell, *Graded Lessons in Typewriting Theory* (London, Sir Isaac Pitman & Sons Ltd., 1962).

Davidson, P. S. and Tilley, K. W., "The Reading Span of Typists," *Education and Commerce*, No. 28 (July, 1959).

Dvorak, A., Merrick, N. L., Dealey, W. L. and Ford, G. C., *Typewriting Behaviour* (New York, American Book Co., 1936).

Fendrick, P., "Hierarchical Skills in Typewriting," *Journal of Educational Psychology*, No. 28 (1937).

Fries, A. C., "Developing Speed and Accuracy in Typewriting," *Proceedings of* 1945 *Business Education Institute* (Teachers' College, University of Cincinnati).

Fuller, D. C., "How to Read for Typewriting," *The National Business Education Quarterly* (Washington, D.C., December, 1943).

Genest, M., "An Analysis of Typing Speed," translated from the French by M. A. Le Cudenee and reported in *Education and Commerce*, No. 27 (April, 1959).

Gould, Rupert T., "The Story of the Typewriter," *Office Control and Management* (1950).

Hoke, R. E., "The Improvement of Speed and Accuracy in Typewriting," *Studies in Education*, No. 7 (Baltimore, The Johns Hopkins Press, 1922).

Lahy, J. M., "Motion Study in Typewriting: A Record of Experiments," *I.L.O. Studies and Reports, Series J. (Educational)*, No. 3 (1924).

Long, N. C., "An Experiment with the Relative Efficiency of Various Methods of Teaching the Typewriting Keyboard," Monograph No. 11, *Research Studies in Commercial Education* (University of Iowa, 1929).

Mattock, G. and Tilley, K. W., "Factors Involved in the Teaching of Typewriting," *Education and Commerce*, No. 16 (July, 1956).

Robinson, Mary T., *Theory Work for Intermediate and Advanced Typewriting Examinations* (London, Cassell & Co. Ltd., 1960).

Russon, A. R. and Wanous, S. J., *Philosophy and Psychology of Teaching Typewriting*.

Shawcross, A. J., *Audio-copy Typewriting* (London, Sir Isaac Pitman & Sons Ltd., 1963).

West, L. J., "An Experimental Comparison of Nonsense, Word and Sentence Materials in Early Typing Training," *Journal of Educational Psychology*, No. 47 (1956).

West, L. J., *Review of Research in Typewriting Learning with Recommendations for Training* (Texas, U.S.A.F. Personnel Training Research Center, 1957).

Whittle, Elma, *High-powered Typewriting Drills* (London, Sir Isaac Pitman & Sons Ltd., 1965).

AUDIO-TYPING

Campbell, J., Flockton, D. L. and Lyall, J. R. K., articles in *Shorthand Teachers' Supplement*, June and Nov. 1964, and Feb. 1965 (London, Sir Isaac Pitman & Sons Ltd.).

Canning, B. W., "A Survey of Audio-typing," *Shorthand Teachers' Supplement*, Issues February–June, 1966 (London, Sir Isaac Pitman & Sons Ltd.).

SHORTHAND AND TRANSCRIPTION

Brewington, Ann, "Classroom Techniques in Teaching Shorthand," *Proceedings of* 1945 *Business Education Institute* (Teachers' College, University of Cincinnati).

Butler, E. H., *The Story of British Shorthand* (London, Sir Isaac Pitman & Sons Ltd., 1951).

Canning, B. W., *Shorthand Teaching Technique* (London, Sir Isaac Pitman & Sons Ltd., 1964).

Davis, B. J., "A Study of Shorthand Teaching," *Contributions to Education*, No. 693 (Teachers' College, Columbia University, 1936).

Dewey, Godfrey, "Teaching Shorthand," *Proceedings of* 1945 *Business Education Institute* (Teachers' College, University of Cincinnati).

Friedlaender, Erna and Silverman, M. R., *The Audio-transcriber* (London, Edward Arnold (Publishers) Ltd., 1961).

Holland, Robert W., *Principles of Teaching Applied to Pitman Shorthand* (London, Sir Isaac Pitman & Sons Ltd., 1952).

James, T. L., *Shorthand Speed Tests*, 80 (90) *Standard Words a Minute* (New Zealand, Wellington Technical College, 1944).

Lauritsen, M., "Summary of Research in Shorthand Transcription," *American Shorthand Teacher* (May, 1933).

Leslie, A. L., *Methods of Teaching Transcription* (New York, The Gregg Publishing Co., 1949).

McNicol, Grace, "The Training and Work of Junior Shorthand-typists," *The Vocational Aspect of Secondary and Further Education*, Vol. III, No. 7 (November, 1951).

Smith, Emily D. (Editor), *High-speed Shorthand Round the World* (London, Sir Isaac Pitman & Sons Ltd., 1961).

Swem, Charles L., *The Technique of Shorthand Reporting* (New York, The Gregg Publishing Co., 1941).

Wanous, W. J., "Survey of Transcription Achievement in Secondary Schools," *Business Education Digest* (December, 1940).

Wanous, W. J. and Whitmore, J. L., *Effective Transcription Procedures*, Monograph No. 57 (Cincinnati, South Western Publishing Co., 1942).

REPORTS AND PERIODICALS

B.A.C.I.E. Journal.

Education for Business (National Association for Business Education).

Office Magazine (Current Affairs Ltd.).

Report of the Advisory Committee on Further Education for Commerce (H.M.S.O., 1959).

Shorthand Teachers' Supplement to Pitman's Office Training (Sir Isaac Pitman & Sons Ltd.) (before 1968).

The National Business Education Quarterly (Educational Press Association of America).

The United Business Education Forum.

The Vocational Aspect of Secondary and Further Education (published by editors from technical teachers' training colleges at Bolton, Huddersfield, London (Garnett), and Wolverhampton).

Memo Weekly magazine. (Pitman Publishing)

Memo Key (now) *Office Skills.* Monthly magazine for teachers. (Pitman Publishing)

Index

ACCURACY test, 164–6
Atmosphere, social, 54
Attainment standards—
  in audio-typing, 176
  in shorthand, 87–8
  in transcription, 189–94
Audio aids, 148, 223
Audio-typing—
  aims of, 174–5
  dictated instructions in, 178–81
  equipment for, 175–6
  standards of attainment in, 176
  teaching methods for, 176–8

BLACKSTONE, E. G., 35, 138, 139, 143
Blank keys, 139
Book, W. F., 8–9
Brewington, Ann, 103
Bugelski, B. R., 56, 61–2, 71
Butler, E. H., 3

CAMPBELL, J., 175
Canning, B. W., 174
Carlton Collection, 3
Carlton, W. J., 3
Chalkboard as teaching aid, 20
Charts, 21
Class and classroom organization, 14–15
  shorthand, 79–81
  typewriting, 129–30
Class teaching, 64
Classroom conditions, 54–5, 79–80, 129
Clem, J. E., 145–6
Continuous matter, typing of, 131
Copy holders, 128
  position of, 136
Correlation of subjects with typewriting, 160–1
Course planning, 15–18, 66–8, 69, 70
Course syllabus, 16
Curve—
  of normal distribution, 51–2
  skewed, 51–2
Cycles of work, repeated, 65

DAVIS, B. J., 83
Davison, P. S., 35
Dealey, W. L., 9, 141
Demonstration stand, 56, 128, 222
Dewey, Godfrey, 3
Dewey, John, 44
Diagrams, projected, 21
Dictation of shorthand, 121–4
Display, 188
  assessment of, 171
  in typewriting, 154–7
  of documents, 157
Duplication, 205–6
  equipment for, 128
  teaching of, 158–60
Dvorak, A., 9, 32–3, 141

ELECTRIC typewriter, 136
Eliot, T. S., 66, 116
Ellis, R. S., 50, 72–3
English—
  correlated with typewriting, 160–1
  in shorthand teaching, 5–6, 108–11
Equipment—
  duplicating, 128
  in the audio-typing room, 175–6
  in the shorthand room, 80–1
  in the typewriting room, 128–9
Erasing, teaching of, 158
Errors, typewriting, 143–5
Essay-type test, 74–5
Examination—
  syllabus of, 16
  teachers' certificates of, 207–11

FELT board, 20, 220–1
Figure-character keys, teaching of, 145
Files, students' typewriting, 161–2
Films and filmstrips, 21
  list of typewriting, 223
Flock paper, 220
Flockton, D. L., 175
Ford, G. C., 9, 141
Freeman, M. H., 145, 191
Fries, A. C., 168
Fuller, D. C., 35, 36

GATES, A. J., 120
Genest, M., 37–8
Gilbreth, F. B. and L. M., 9–10, 141
Gould, Rupert T., 6
Gross and net speeds, 165
Group teaching, 64
Guthrie, E. R., 56

HARMS, Harm, 103, 120, 145, 182, 189
Holland, R. W., 82
Homework—
  for shorthand, 91–2
  for typewriting, 135
Horn, E., 87, 212

IMITATION, learning by, 56–7
Incentives, 46–7
Individual differences, 49–54, 70
  in transcription, 191–2
Individual teaching, 65
Inductive method of teaching shorthand, 84–5
Interest, 43–7, 70–1
Interest value of material—
  for shorthand, 114–20
  for typewriting, 148, 151, 153, 162–4

KEYBOARD—
  order of presentation of typewriter, 137–8
  rate of introduction of, 138
  shields for, 139
Keys, blank, 139
Knowing the student, 13–14

LAHY, J. M., 31–2
Lauritsen, M., 183
Layout of typewriting practice material, 139–40
Learning—
  by doing, 58
  by imitation, 56–7
  ideal conditions of, 55–6
  likelihood of, 43–7, 55
  of speed and accuracy, 62, 140–2
  size of unit of, 61
  whole or part, 61–3
Leslie, L. A., 191
Lesson planning, 15–18, 45–6, 66–8
  shorthand, 90–6
  typewriting, 134–5
Lintograph, 20, 220–1
Literary matter as practice material—
  in shorthand, 110–16
  in transcription, 198–204
  in typewriting, 152–3
Long, N. C., 10
Lyall, J. R. K., 175

McGURRIN, F., 31
Machine manipulation, teaching of, 135–45
McNair Report, 71
McNicol, Grace, 42
Madariaga, S. de, 43
Marking—
  of accuracy tests, 164–6
  of shorthand, 124–7
  of transcription, 189–91
  of typewriting, 164–73
  records of, 18–19
Marrou, H. I., 3
Material, *see* Practice Material
Mattock, G., 37
Mental set, 43
Merrick, N. L., 9, 141
Motivation, 43–4
Music and typewriting, 145–8

New Course, Pitman Shorthand, and correlated word list, 87, 212–19
Net and gross speeds, 165

OBJECTIVE test, 75–8
Oral question and answer, 73–4

PANTON, G. H., 12, 13, 14–15, 74
Paper, flock, 220
Part or whole learning, 61–3
Peterson, Thelma, 87, 212
Photographs, 20
Phrasing in shorthand, 106–7
Pickard, O. G., 7, 48
Pictures, projected, 21
Pinsent, A., 12, 50, 55, 58, 61, 63, 67–8
Pitman shorthand—
  characteristics of, 98–100
  omission of vowel signs in, 85
Planning—
  course and lesson, 15–18, 66–8, 69, 70
  shorthand lesson, 90–6
  transcription lesson, 194–9
  typewriting lesson, 134–5
Plastigraph, 20
Plateaux of learning, 120–1
Popham, E. L., 145, 191
Posters, 21
Postman, L., 71
Powell, L. S., 20, 21
Practice—
  conditions for effective, 59
  and theory in shorthand, 83
  knowledge of results of, 62
  principles for effective, 60–1
  size of unit of, 61–2
  supervised, in typewriting, 142
Practice material—
  artificial, 149
  continuous matter for, 131, 151–3
  displayed matter as, 153
  extracts from books as, 152–3
  for shorthand, 97, 110–21
  for transcription, 194–205
  for typewriting, 131, 132, 148–54
  layout of, 139–40
  literary matter as, 111–16
  meaningful, 149
  pre-view transcript as, 205
  production work as, 153–4
  word and sentence, 148–51
Pre-view transcript, 188, 205
Production work, 153–4, 193–4
  arrangements for meetings as, 154
  assessment of, 171–2

Production work (*Contd.*)
business transaction sequence as, 153–4
committee work sequence as, 154
Progress chart, typewriting, 172–3
Progress records, typewriting, 168–9
Project work in typewriting, 162–4
Projected pictures and diagrams, 21
Punctuation (for audio-typing), 178

QUESTIONS on teaching—
general, 224
on shorthand, 224–5
on typewriting, 225–6

RECORD—
of shorthand progress, 126–7
of the teacher's work, 18–20
of typewriting progress, 168, 169, 172–3
Results, knowledge of, 62
Revision and recapitulation, 67–8
Rhythm, typewriting, 145–8
Routine (in lessons), 45–6
Royal Society of Arts, 42, 185, 208, 209
examination paper for audio-typist's certificate given by, 180
examination papers for teachers' certificates given by, 209–11
Russon, A. R., 54

SCHEME of work, 16
in shorthand, 89–90
in typewriting, 132–4
Scottish Council for Commercial Education, examination paper for audio-typewriting given by, 178–80
Senders, J. L., 71
Sequence work in typewriting, 153–4
Shields, keyboard, 139
Shorthand—
and class activities, 92–6
and English, 108–11
and plateaux of learning, 120–1
characteristics of Pitman, 98–100
dictation of, 121–4
history of, 2–4
homework for, 91–2
lesson plans for, 90–6
organization of classroom for, 79–81
phrasing in, 106–7
position for writing, 80
practice material for, 97, 110–21
problems of, and the learner, 100–2
reading of, 23–5, 186
records of progress in, 126–7
scheme of work for, 89–90
sources of teaching material for, 97
speed and style in writing of, 107–8
speed development, audio in, 124
standards of attainment in, 87–8

Shorthand (*Contd.*)
sub-skills of, 6, 23–30
syllabus for, 88–9
teaching aids for, 96
teaching of, 81–5
and the teaching unit, 102–7
combination of copying and dictation in, 83–4
functional method of, 81–2
inductive method of, 84–5
rate of introduction of theory in, 82–3
theory plus practice in, 83
traditional method of, 81
using intensive work plans, 116–20
testing and marking of, 124–7
writing of, 25–30, 107–8
Shorthand classroom—
equipment of, 80–1
organization of, 79–81
Sidney, E., 141
Smith, Emily D., 4
Social atmosphere, 54
Sorenson, H., 46–7, 53, 77
Speed and accuracy in typewriting, 62, 140–2
Student—
activity of, 47–9
file and folder of, in typewriting, 161–2
knowing the, 13–14
Swem, C. L., 26–7
Syllabus—
course, 16
examination, 16
shorthand, 88–9
typewriting, 130–5

TANGORA, Albert, 31
Teachers—
facilities for training of, 208–9
personal qualities of, 11–12
qualifications of, 207–8
Teaching—
class, 64
group, 64
individual, 65
selection in, 68–71
skill in, 11–15
techniques in, 12–13
testing and, 71–8
Teaching aids, 20–1
for shorthand, 96
for transcription, 206
for typewriting, 122
Teaching material—
shorthand, 114–20
transcription, 194–206
typewriting, 148–54, 160–1
Testing—
and marking shorthand, 124–7

Testing (*Contd.*)
 and teaching, 71–8
 of transcription, 189
 of typewriting in class, 150–1, 166–9
Tests—
 accuracy, 164–6
 types of, 73–8
Theory, shorthand, 83
Tilley, K. W., 35, 37
Tonne, H. A., 145, 191
Transcript, pre-view, 188, 205
Transcription—
 capacity of individual students in, 191–2
 component skills of, 39–40
 factors affecting skill of, 40–2
 history of and research into, 182–5
 problems and objectives of, 186–9
 standards of attainment in, 189–94
 teaching material for, 194–206
  grading of, 195–6
  prose passages as, 198–204
  selection of, 196
 time allocation of, 192–4
Transfer of training, 53–4
Typewriters—
 electric, 136
 with simplified keyboard, 32–3
Typewriting—
 accuracy in, 170
 and the accuracy test, 164–6
 correlation of English with, 160–1
 display in, 154–7
 equipment for, 128–9
 erasing in, 158
 errors in, 143–5
 examinations in, 164–73
 history of, 6–7
 homework for, 135
 layout of copy for, 139–40
 lesson plans for, 134–5
 machines, electric, 136
 marking of, 164–73
 organization of classroom for, 129–30
Typewriting (*Contd.*)
 position of copy for, 136
 practice material for, 131, 132, 148–54
 progress chart for, 172–3
 progress record for, 168, 169
 project work in, 162–4
 reading for, 35–6
 rhythm in, 145–8
 scheme of work for, 132–4
 short answer test in, 150–1
 speed and accuracy in, 140–2
 student's file and folder in, 161–2
 sub-skills of, 34–8
 supervised practice in, 142
 syllabus for, 130–5
 tabular work in, 156–7
 teaching of—
  and figure-character keys, 145
  and machine manipulation, 135–45
  keyboard presentation in, 137–8
  music and, 145–8
  rate of keyboard introduction in, 138
 testing of, 164–73

UNITS of work, 102–7
 size of, 61

VALENTINE, C. W., 51–2
Variety (in lessons), 45–6
Visual teaching aids, 20–1, 220
Vocabulary, active and passive, 22–3
Vowel signs, omission of, in Pitman Shorthand, 85

WANOUS, S. J., 54
Wanous, W. J., 184, 189, 190
West, L. J., 10–11, 137, 144, 146, 166, 167
White, E., 146
Whitehead, A. N., 67
Whitmore, J. L., 189, 190
Whole or part learning, 61–3
Word frequency, 85–7
Word list, correlated, 87, 212–9